# THE
# SHAKESPEARE
## TRAIL

# THE
# SHAKESPEARE
# TRAIL

## A JOURNEY INTO
## SHAKESPEARE'S ENGLAND

ZOE BRAMLEY

AMBERLEY

Dedicated to Mum, Dad, Carrie, Chris, Lily, Rowan and
William

Amberley Publishing
The Hill, Stroud
Gloucestershire, GL5 4EP

www.amberley-books.com

British Library Cataloguing in Publication Data.
A catalogue record for this book is available from the British
Library.

ISBN 978 1 4456 4684 8 (hardback)
ISBN 978 1 4456 4685 5 (ebook)

Typeset in 11pt on 17pt Sabon.
Typesetting and Origination by Amberley Publishing.
Printed in the UK.

# Contents

• Warwick

• Wilmcote

Shottery

• Charlecote

Temple Grafton

Stratford-upon-Avon

• Bidford-on-Avon

Map of Warwickshire

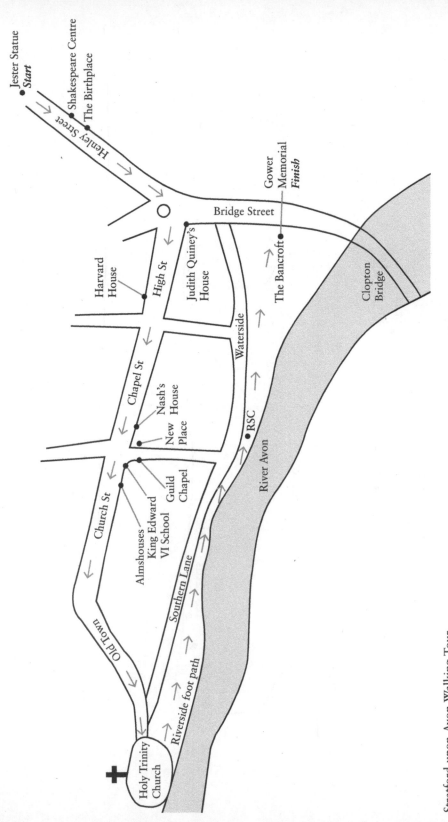

Jester Statue
**Start**

Shakespeare Centre

The Birthplace

Henley Street

Bridge Street

Gower
Memorial
**Finish**

Harvard
House

High St

Judith Quiney's
House

Clopton
Bridge

The Bancroft

Waterside

Chapel St

Nash's House

New Place

RSC

River Avon

Church St

Almshouses

King Edward
VI School

Guild
Chapel

Southern Lane

Old Town

Riverside foot path

Holy Trinity
Church

Stratford-upon-Avon Walking Tour

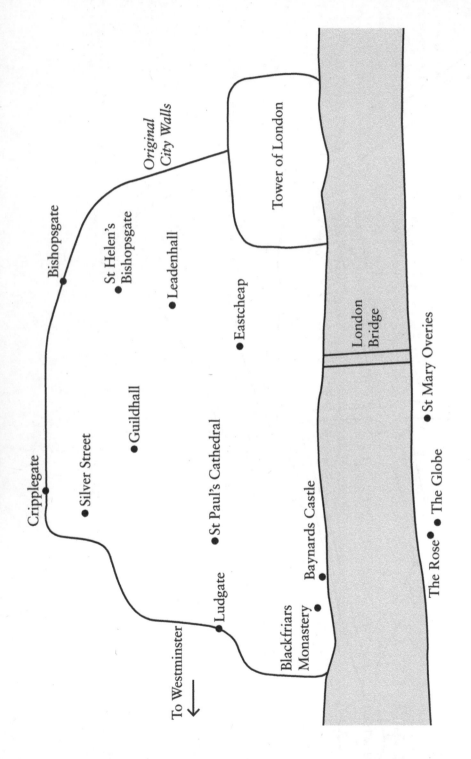

Map of Shakespeare's London

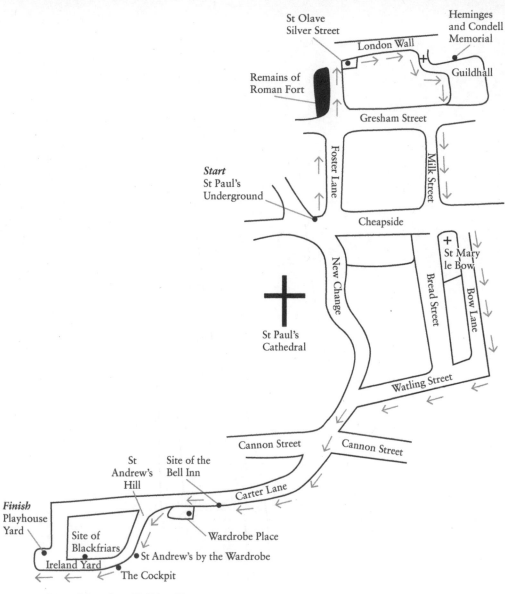

St Olave
Silver Street

Heminges
and Condell
Memorial

London Wall

Guildhall

Remains of
Roman Fort

Gresham Street

Foster Lane

Milk Street

*Start*
St Paul's
Underground

Cheapside

New Change

St Mary
le Bow

Bread Street

Bow Lane

St Paul's
Cathedral

Watling Street

Cannon Street

Cannon Street

St
Andrew's
Hill

Site of the
Bell Inn

Carter Lane

*Finish*
Playhouse
Yard

Site of
Blackfriars

Wardrobe Place

St Andrew's by the Wardrobe

Ireland Yard

The Cockpit

City of London Walking Tour

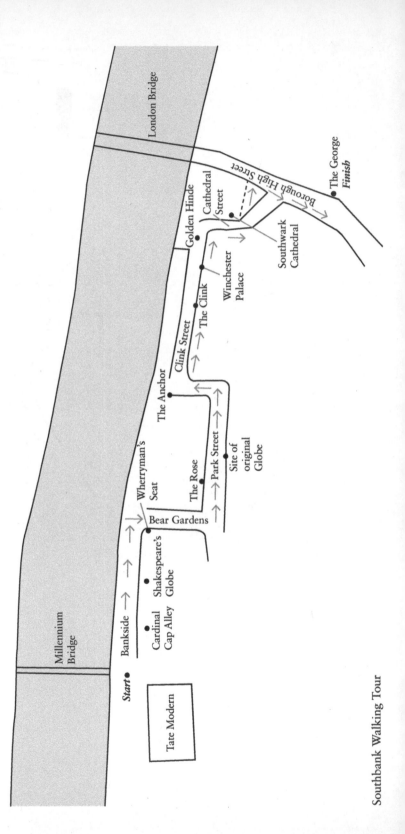

St Paul's

Millennium
Bridge

Tate Modern

**Start** •

Bankside →   →   ↑

Cardinal
Cap Alley •

Shakespeare's
Globe •

Wherryman's
Seat

Bear Gardens

The Anchor •

The Rose

Park Street →   →

Site of
original
Globe

Clink Street

The Clink →

Winchester
Palace •

Golden Hinde •

Cathedral
Street ↓

Southwark
Cathedral

London Bridge

Borough High Street

The George
**Finish** •

Southbank Walking Tour

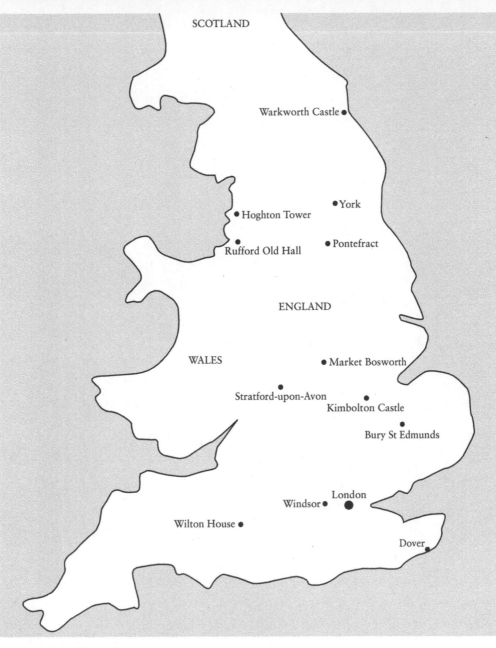

SCOTLAND

Warkworth Castle •

• York

• Hoghton Tower

• Pontefract

• Rufford Old Hall

ENGLAND

WALES

• Market Bosworth

• Stratford-upon-Avon

• Kimbolton Castle

• Bury St Edmunds

London
Windsor •  •

Wilton House •

Dover •

Map of Britain

# Preface

Weary with toil, I haste me to my bed,
The dear repose for limbs with travel tired;
But then begins a journey in my head,
To work my mind, when body's work's expired ...

From Sonnet 27

On 26 April 1616, William Shakespeare's journey ended forever as he breathed his last breath at home in Stratford-upon-Avon. He was fifty-two years old, a respectable age for a man raised in the age of plague outbreaks and fatal influenza. When we bear in mind the lack of antibiotics and the primitive knowledge of human anatomy it is a wonder that he survived as long as he did. Well-meaning doctors prescribed treatments that may as well have been devised by the witches in *Macbeth* for all the good they did; the Elizabethan physician John Hollybushe recommended drinking foxes' lungs mixed with wine and herbs as a cure for asthma. A patient with a headache should 'set a dish of tin on the bare head, put an ounce and a half, or two ounces of molten lead therein while he has it on the head.' If only they had known about the wonders of two aspirins and a cold flannel.

The details of Shakespeare's final illness are unknown but if we are to believe John Ward, a Stratford vicar, it may have come when 'Shakespeare, Drayton and Ben Jonson, had a merry meeting, and it seems drank too much, for Shakespeare died of a fever there contracted.'

Ward was born thirteen years after Shakespeare's death so it would be interesting to know where he got this gossip. It is, however, a strangely satisfying story. Perhaps the three playwrights had spent the evening in the warm glow of a local tavern, downing cups of sack and slurring their words as they reminisced about the old days. There are surely worse ways to bow out.

Such is the mark Shakespeare has left on our national consciousness, some might say his spirit never really went away. He is in the restless skies and in the gently rolling hills of Warwickshire. His shadow stalks the narrow streets of the City of London and haunts the river walks of Bankside. His words ring out in theatres across the globe. Structures from Shakespeare's Globe to the Royal Shakespeare Theatre have been erected in his honour. How strange and thrilling that people still want to see plays dating from the years after the Spanish Armada and the discovery of tobacco. Even those who despise the archaic language are familiar with lines such as 'To be or not to be'.

The characters in his plays come from all walks of life and must surely have been informed by the colourful cast of people who inhabited his world. The fishmonger shouting his wares on Friday Street, the doxies in the Southwark stews, the preening coxcomb in his feathered cap, the simple farmhand idling his Sunday away by a bubbling stream in Warwickshire. He is as ingrained in our imagination as we, the ordinary folk, were ingrained in his.

After a lifetime spent acting and writing for the fast-paced world of London theatre Shakespeare may have been relieved to return to Stratford. There must have come a moment when he knew his life's work was done and that it was time to exit the stage and disappear back to the country, to the clean, sharp air of Warwickshire. It would have been a natural desire. His friends and family were there. So were all the memories of youth. It was familiar, provincial and safe. As he crossed the Clopton Bridge into town it may have been with a sense of homecoming, of finality.

His journey ended in a quiet midlands market town in 1616, but ours has just begun.

# Introduction

As we mark the 400th anniversary of Shakespeare's death this book aims to follow in his footsteps and travel to the England that Shakespeare knew, whether personally or in his imagination. From taverns to churches, theatres to country houses, *The Shakespeare Trail* aims to be your torchbearer as you set off on the journey of our greatest playwright. This is a visitors' guide for both intrepid pilgrims and armchair travellers alike.

Get ready for a journey from Warwickshire to London, taking in Lancashire, Leicestershire and various battlefields along the way. Most of the sites are still standing and are open to visitors. Occasionally – especially in the fire and bomb-blasted city of London – there will be locations where the original building no longer exists. In these cases I appeal to your imagination as nothing lasts forever.

The book is structured into three acts, an interlude, and an epilogue which I will briefly outline here.

*Act One: Warwickshire*

Shakespeare's life began and ended in Stratford-upon-Avon where we will be exploring the locations that bore witness to the big events in his life, from the house on Henley Street where he was born, to the church where he was baptised and buried. At the start of this section is a walking tour of Stratford town centre which I had enormous fun planning. The High Street is blessed with an almost unbroken line of half-timbered houses, most of which were there in Shakespeare's day. From Stratford we venture out into the surrounding villages to seek out his family connections and the stories surrounding his youth. I have included one or two places where his presence is based on legend rather than certainty. At Charlecote for example he is said to have infuriated Sir Thomas Lucy by poaching for deer. There is no evidence to say that Shakespeare was a poacher but Charlecote House is mentioned enough times in the biographies to warrant its inclusion. It is also a very fine house and well worth a visit. Likewise the little village of Bidford-on-Avon whose connection with Shakespeare is based on nothing more than delicious gossip handed down over generations. We all love a good story so I have included Bidford on this whimsical yet irresistible basis; what if it is true?

*Interlude: The Lost Years*

There are two houses in Lancashire which claim a connection to Shakespeare in the short period between his leaving school and marrying Anne Hathaway. It cannot be proven that he ever set foot in Hoghton Tower or Rufford Old Hall but these locations have earned their places in this book because it is fun to imagine the different routes his life may have taken; to envisage him in places other than Warwickshire and London.

## Act Two: London

London is packed with Shakespeare locations, admittedly not all of them still standing. He bought property there, drank in the taverns, took up lodgings with French Huguenots and helped operate an indoor playhouse. On the City of London walking tour I guide you through the modern streets and attempt to paint a picture of their Elizabethan past. Each location is chosen to represent an aspect of Shakespeare's life in London, and the walk delves into some surprising corners of the city. To complement the walk there is also a self guided walking tour of Bankside with sites including the famous Globe, the Rose playhouse and an original wherryman's seat. Along with the walking tours we cover other locations such as the medieval great hall where his kinsman stood trial and the site of the first purpose-built playhouse.

## Act Three: Shakespeare's Imagination

At this point we move away from Shakespeare's own life and continue our journey by visiting locations mentioned in the plays themselves. I invite the reader to think of this section as a literary tour as we visit settings such as Windsor, the Tower of London, Bosworth Field and York. I have tried to give historical background to the plays and the locations, but have also allowed the characters to speak for themselves as much as possible and remind us why we are there.

## Epilogue: Further Ideas and Miscellanea

To finish I have collected together a mixed handful of locations which did not fit anywhere else in the book. The unproven legend that Shakespeare visited Wilton House in Wiltshire was an irresistible opportunity to explore the source of the rumour and to visit another country house. The glut of television adaptations of the plays such as *Hollow Crown* and films like *Shakespeare in Love* mean there are also film locations to explore.

At the end of each section I detail visitor information such as opening hours, entry fees and ideas for places to eat or further exploring. All this information is given in good faith and is accurate at the time of writing. I have included website addresses where possible and telephone numbers for the venues so it is always a good idea to check before travelling.

## Inspiration for the Book

In some ways it is a surprise that I should write about Shakespeare. I remember dismissively misnaming him Shakingbeard at the age of nine. He was nothing to me. Who needed some crusty old poet when you had the Famous Five? Who really needed Macbeth, or Romeo, or Puck, or Titania, or that tedious old fool Polonius? Years later, I had my answer. Something tapped me on the shoulder, spun me around and whispered in my ear, 'You do.' It was after attending a performance of *The Winter's Tale* at Shakespeare's Globe on Bankside. How thrilling it had been to spend the afternoon as a groundling, standing in that cathedral of drama just as people had done all those years ago. As the play unfolded, the rhythms of Shakespeare's language began to feel completely natural; it was as if some distant folk memory had been awakened within me.

It was exciting to realise that Shakespeare lived and worked not far from where we stood. He had breathed the same air and walked the same streets. As I exited the theatre that day, with music and poetry ringing in my ears, I realised that contrary to what my nine-year-old self may have thought, I did need Shakespeare. I also needed to know everything about him.

I became a volunteer steward at the Globe and spent many happy hours enjoying the shows whilst pretending to keep an eye on the patrons. (Sorry Jean!) On days when I was stationed outside on the piazza, I gave a thousand directions to the toilets and checked tickets. The heat, the crowds and the gory action on stage sometimes became too much for the groundlings and I would often watch helplessly as some poor soul staggered outside after fainting. My first aid trained colleagues were always on the scene quickly, gently guiding them to a seat in the shade, dispensing cold water and soothing words. Sometimes people would stop to chat and I spent some happy moments in the shadow of that theatre discussing Shakespeare with people from all around the world.

In the back of my mind I started to form an idea for a guided Shakespeare walk. I applied to join the City of London Tour Guiding course at the Guildhall and after a terrifying group interview which felt like the *X Factor* auditions I found myself accepted. It was without doubt the most challenging and rigorous course of training I had ever attended. The course tutor was the Blue Badge guide Trevor Jeanes, a brilliant, exacting taskmaster who skilfully moulded us into capable guides. He showed us how to structure a presentation and to avoid banging people over the head with lists of facts. We learnt how to weave stories that both educated and entertained. I have tried to apply some of that guidance in the writing of this book, allowing each location to tell its own story.

The London section of this book is the result of the research I conducted when I was planning my guided Shakespeare walks. The rest of the research is the result of charging around the country on day trips and the odd week's holiday, grilling local tour guides, taking pictures, spending hours in various libraries and cross-referencing facts. This is primarily a visitors' guide so I chose to include a select bibliography in place of footnotes and references.

Since qualifying as a guide in 2010 I have spent many hours talking to visitors about Shakespeare's life whilst standing at the very spots where certain episodes in his life played out. What a privilege it has been to walk in his footsteps and meet so many people who share my passion. It is my hope that this book will inspire you to grab a coffee and go for a walk around the city, or to take a day trip to the country and stand in the shadow of an ancient country house, struck by the knowledge that 400 years ago, a man named William Shakespeare stood there too.

# Shakespeare Timeline

There are famously few known facts about Shakespeare but it is possible to place his whereabouts at certain points in his career. In order to help you get the most out of this visitor's guide I have included an approximate timeline to the important events in his life. Here are the bare bones of what we know:

## 1564–1585

Shakespeare was born in 1564 in Stratford-upon-Avon and was baptised at Holy Trinity Church on 26 April. His mother was Mary Arden and his father John was a glove maker who held a string of powerful positions in local affairs. In his eclectic career he had been an ale taster, a constable, burgess, chamberlain, alderman and finally high bailiff. As son of a high-ranking town official, Shakespeare almost certainly attended the local grammar school, King's New School, from the age of seven to the age of fifteen where he would have had a good grounding in Latin.

In November 1582, he applied for a license to marry. The

bride is named as Anne Whately – probably a clerk's mistake as his actual bride was of course Anne Hathaway.

In May 1583 Anne was delivered of a baby girl, Susanna. Twins, Judith and Hamnet, followed in February 1585. The twins would only enjoy a few short years together – Hamnet died at the age of eleven whilst Judith lived until the good age of seventy-seven.

At this point the so-called 'lost years' begin.

## 1585–1592

The lost years are exactly that – lost! We know nothing about this period in Shakespeare's life, although some colourful theories have been suggested. Was he a private tutor in a wealthy Lancashire house? Did he travel to Italy and gain his knowledge of the country? Was he sailing on board the *Golden Hinde* with Sir Francis Drake? Or could he have been, more prosaically, living in London and steadily learning his craft? Unless some long-forgotten documents are one day discovered in an old attic somewhere, the guessing game will continue.

## 1592–1616

The year 1592 yielded the first certain mention we have of Shakespeare in London, and it was not complimentary. Rival playwright Robert Greene described him in a pamphlet as, among other things, an 'upstart crow', a 'johannes fac totem' (jack of all trades), and a 'shake-scene'. Greene is griping about the competition from this hot new playwright. It usually takes time and effort to annoy people so much. Perhaps by this point Shakespeare had been living in London for some years, slowly but surely winding up Robert Greene.

In 1594 he became a shareholder of the Chamberlain's Men. The company's patron was Henry Carey, Lord Hunsden, a cousin of Queen Elizabeth I. Between the years of 1587 and 1592 Hunsden kept Emilia Lanier, thought by some writers to be the Dark Lady of Shakespeare's sonnets, as his mistress.

In 1596, Shakespeare's son Hamnet died.

In 1597, Shakespeare bought New Place, an imposing house in Stratford-upon-Avon. Built by local mercer Hugh Clopton in the fifteenth century, it was remarkable for being one of the only local houses made from brick instead of timber. Shakespeare died here in 1616.

In 1598, the only surviving letter written to Shakespeare was composed in a coaching inn on Carter Lane in the City of London. Richard Quiney was asking his fellow Stratfordian for a loan of £30.

In 1599, the Globe was built on rented land in Southwark. Its location, in what was then still the county of Surrey, gave Shakespeare's company some protection from the puritanical impulses of the London Aldermen whose dislike of the playhouses made it impossible to perform in the city.

In 1601, the play *Richard II* was performed by special request of the Earl of Essex and his followers as a prelude to their planned insurrection against the queen. Previous performances of the play had omitted the 'deposition scene' in which the king loses his throne but Essex requested the company to reinsert it. He hoped to illustrate to the play goers how easily monarchs could be replaced. With their rebellious passions roused, they would turn out in their thousands to march on London in support of Essex's cause. Perhaps unsurprisingly, the steady, loyal and wise merchant class of London showed no willingness to risk their lives and the rebellion failed. Essex was beheaded the day after Shrove Tuesday. It was also in this year that Shakespeare's father John died.

In 1603, following the death of Elizabeth I and the accession of James I of England, Shakespeare's company became known as the King's Men. In April the following year Shakespeare and the other principal actors were summoned to the King's Wardrobe to be fitted with scarlet livery for His Majesty's coronation procession.

In 1608, Shakespeare's mother Mary died. The King's Men began playing at the Blackfriars Theatre in what was once part of the old Dominican monastery that had stood there until 1538. The later plays were performed here, such as *The Tempest, The Winter's Tale* and *Cymbeline*.

In 1613 the Globe burned down during a performance of *Henry VIII*. It was rebuilt in 1614 but did not survive the animosity of the Puritans who demolished it in the middle of the century.

In 1616, Shakespeare died at home in Stratford-upon-Avon. His will states, 'I give unto my wife my second-best bed with the furniture.' He also left £10 to the poor of Stratford and money to his colleagues John Heminges, Henry Condell and Richard Burbage to buy themselves memorial rings. He was buried in the church of Holy Trinity, Stratford.

# Warwickshire

## Non Sanz Droict

Even if fate had intervened to ensure that a certain Stratford lad had stayed at home and made gloves, instead of venturing to London and joining a company of players, the West Midlands county of Warwickshire would still be a cracking holiday destination for anyone willing to venture there. The countryside is a perfect blend of riverside walks, weeping willows and gently rolling hills. Thatched cottages and half timbered townhouses beautify nearly every settlement. The sense of history is overwhelming; from the haunting ruins at Kenilworth Castle to the bustling High Street of Stratford-upon-Avon and all the splendid villages in between.

Of course, despite this rich multitude of treasures, we all know why people really come.

Arriving by road, visitors are greeted by the plain white *Welcome to Warwickshire* signs, underneath which is the proud reminder: *Shakespeare's County.* At the right-hand side of the sign there is a picture of a bear laying its great paw upon what looks like a branch. This is the 'bear and ragged staff,' the emblem of Warwickshire which appears on the county coat of arms alongside Shakespeare's motto *Non Sanz Droict*, or, Not Without Right. As well as the county adopting his motto, he has also had whole streets named after him. There is a Shakespeare Avenue in Warwick, a Shakespeare Street in Stratford-upon-Avon, a Falstaff Close in Nuneaton and a Juliet Drive in Rugby. This is indeed Shakespeare's county.

His story begins in the southern part of Warwickshire on the edge of the Cotswolds. Although he would later conquer London, his boyhood universe was a constellation of villages and country houses dotted about the prosperous market town of Stratford-upon-Avon where he was born.

### The Tale of a Town

The church of Holy Trinity, where William Shakespeare was baptised and buried, stands in isolation upon the banks of the River Avon in Stratford. Its tall spire soars high above the weeping willows, pricking the sky with an iconic beauty seen on countless postcards and tourist snaps. Unusually for a parish church it lies at some distance from the town centre; this is due to Stratford's somewhat disjointed development as an urban settlement. Until 1196, Stratford was a small village located in the immediate vicinity of the church. That year, the Bishop of Worcester upgraded the village into a town and asked Richard I for permission to operate a market. The charter was duly granted and the town planners got to work expanding their settlement northwards with a grid of streets which still forms the skeleton of Stratford town centre today. The historic spine leads from the top of High Street all the way down to Holy Trinity and the Old Town, a picturesque route lined with Tudor and Georgian architecture.

The name Stratford describes the town's position by the River

Avon. *Strat* comes from the Old English word for street, and *ford* indicates a river crossing. *Avon* literally means river in Welsh. At the end of Bridge Street the River Avon is spanned by the fine Clopton Bridge, a stone crossing with fourteen arches built in 1480 by Hugh Clopton, a wealthy mercer. It was a much needed gift to the town; prior to its construction the townsfolk had had to brave a perilous timber construction which flooded when the river rose. Clopton Bridge is still one of the main routes in and out of town today.

In the Tudor era most households were clustered in the streets at the top end of town towards Henley Street where the Shakespeare family lived. Henley Street itself was a wide thoroughfare cut through by a brook which ran into town from the countryside beyond and into the nearby Meer Pool Lane, now Meer Street. Unlike today's pedestrianised Henley Street with its modern paving and pleasant cafés, the Tudor street would have been rustic and muddy. The pungent stench of horse urine was unavoidable for the townspeople, and a muck heap attracted flies and maggots. Residents were asked to use designated sites rather than dumping manure wherever it was convenient; in 1552 John Shakespeare, the poet's father, allowed a muck heap to develop outside his house and was fined 12*d* for antisocial behaviour.

The house on Henley Street was located a few steps from the market. Every Thursday, at the high cross – actually a hut standing upon wooden stilts – on the corner of Bridge Street and High Street, the traders would gather to sell their wares. Wool, leather, iron, cheese and gloves were some of the commodities on sale in the vicinity. As one of the handful of glove makers in town, John Shakespeare would have been there on those Thursdays, perhaps with his son William as assistant. John's gloves were made using the skin of sheep, an animal upon which Stratford's wealth was largely dependent. The valuable wool they yielded was an important source of tax revenue for the crown, and the wool trade was jealously protected. In order to boost sales, a statute of 1571 obliged English men below the rank of gentleman to wear woollen caps to church on Sundays and holy days. This deeply unpopular law was a source of concern for Stratford farmers who were losing land to sheep enclosures. John Shakespeare, however, must have been one of those who approved of the requirement. He had been quietly profiting as an illegal 'brogger', an unlicensed dealer of wool, until he was reported to the authorities. A few years later in 1583 his brother Henry, a tenant farmer, was fined for refusing to wear one of the hated caps. Here we have two Shakespeare brothers, both brought down by sheep.

It was in Sheep Street that the plague of 1564 started. An apprentice, Oliver Gunne, died on 11 July followed by his master's wife, Joanna Degge, who succumbed nine days later. As the pestilence spread, it is likely that Mary Shakespeare whisked her newborn son William away to her family home at Wilmcote, thus ensuring his survival of an outbreak which went on to kill over 200 local people.

The 1590s were difficult years for Stratford. At the beginning of the decade the Stratford Corporation noted in a petition that the town's cloth trade had declined to such an extent that the town had 'now fallen much into decay for want of such trade as hereto they had by clothinge and makeinge of yarn ymploying and maynteyninge a number of poore people by the same, which now live in great penury and misery.' Successive harvest failures caused serious famine among the poor and two fires ravaged the town in 1594 and 1595, devastating much of High Street, Henley Street and Sheep Street. The houses were made of timber so fire was a serious risk and for that reason many of the buildings lining the High Street today date from 1595 or later. Despite this, there is a surprising wealth of Tudor and medieval architecture left to enjoy, and Stratford's architectural heritage is certainly an asset to the tourism industry.

It is probably the eighteenth-century actor David Garrick who can be credited with turning Stratford-upon-Avon into a tourist hotspot. Garrick was the theatre impresario who had made his name in the role of Richard III in 1741. His style of acting was pioneering for his age; in contrast to the bombastic speech and stilted movements that his predecessors employed, he produced a more human, naturalistic effect. In later years he went on to become manager of the Theatre Royal in Drury Lane, where his staging of Shakespeare was often creative. In 1755 he adapted *A Midsummer Night's Dream* as an opera, dispensing completely with the Rude Mechanicals. Nevertheless, Garrick was a devoted admirer of the Bard. In 1769 he threw Stratford into the limelight with the Jubilee, a three-day celebration of Shakespeare's life intended to mark the 200th anniversary of his birth. The fact that Shakespeare was born in 1564 meant that Garrick was five years too late, but that was a mere detail. In an approximation of what he imagined the Globe playhouse may have looked like, Garrick erected a large wooden rotunda on the Bancroft, an area of greenery by the river. Here, he declaimed his *Ode to Shakespeare*. These lines give a taste of his high blown style:

> Tho' bards with envy-aching eyes,
> Behold a tow'ring eagle rise,
> And would his flight retard;
> Yet each to Shakespeare's genius bows,
> Each weaves a garland for his brows,
> To crown th' heaven distinguish'd Bard.

The Jubilee's programme of events was hampered by the weather; after two days of heavy downpours the banks of the River Avon burst and flooded the rotunda. The highlight of the third day was to have been a procession showcasing Shakespeare's characters but that had to be cancelled. Garrick decided not to make it a yearly event, and went home to London where he staged a version of the pageant on stage at Drury Lane to great success.

The modern town has a happy, positive feel to it. The presence of the Royal Shakespeare Company, as well as fringe theatre venues such as the Attic at the Lazy Cow pub, lends it a buzz of creative energy. The shopping centre has a good mix of independent boutiques as well as the usual chain stores. For eating and drinking there are riverside pubs such as the Dirty Duck where thirsty actors have been spotted imbibing a drink or two.

In this chapter we shall be exploring Stratford in more depth on the self-guided walking tour before heading out into the country. Warwickshire highlights include the imposing grandeur of Charlecote and the stunning ruins of Kenilworth. We will also be exploring the homes of Mary Arden, Anne Hathaway and other members of the Shakespeare family, not forgetting the pretty village of Bidford-on-Avon where a young Shakespeare is alleged to have enjoyed a boozy night out. The close proximity of many of these locations to Stratford makes it easy to explore them in a series of day trips making use of Stratford's excellent, if pricey, bus service. Other locations make an easy morning's walk. However you choose to do it, you will find Warwickshire a warm and welcoming place to begin the Shakespeare Trail.

## Stratford Walking Tour

It is now time to explore the town of Shakespeare's birth in more detail. Stratford-upon-Avon is compact enough to manage in a day or two depending on how long you wish to linger in each of the various houses managed by the Shakespeare Birthplace Trust. The self-guided walking tour outlined here is a semi circular walk beginning at the far end of Henley Street and ending at the Bancroft and the Gower Memorial. There are plenty of places to stop for a coffee or a bite to eat along the way and public conveniences are located in the Shakespeare houses as well as the gardens near Holy Trinity.

Start at the top of Henley Street by the Jester Statue.

### The Jester Statue

You are standing in front of a bronze statue which has quickly become an iconic Stratford landmark since it was unveiled in 1994. The Jester was commissioned by local businessman Anthony Bird, and sculptor James Butler has created a grinning Touchstone from *As You Like It*, kicking his leg in the air as if in the middle of a jig. In his right hand he holds aloft a comedy mask. He cuts a delightful figure. From the front, all is joyful, fun and innocent. Walk behind him, however, and you will see that in his left hand he hides a mask of tragedy, perhaps representing the sadness behind the smile. The inscriptions at the base of the statue come from Shakespeare's quotes about fools, '*Foolery sir, does walk about the orb like the sun; it shines everywhere*' (Twelfth Night), and '*the fool doth think he is wise but the wise man knows himself to be a fool*' (As You Like It).

After contemplating the wisdom, or otherwise, of fools, turn around and walk down Henley Street.

### Shakespeare Centre

On your left-hand side is the modern red brick Shakespeare Centre which houses a revolving exhibition of items related to his life and times. Highlights include rare books such as a copy of

*Holinshead's Chronicle*, which was published in 1586, a copy of the First Folio of 1623, and the letter written by Richard Quiney asking Shakespeare for a loan. These are just a few examples of the many treasures in the care of the Shakespeare Birthplace Trust. The exhibition changes every six months so it is worth checking the website ahead of your visit. For anyone wishing to conduct their own research into the Shakespeare archives, the Reading Room at the Centre is open Wednesday to Friday from 10:00–16:30 and Saturdays from 9:30–12:30.

Tickets to all the properties managed by the Shakespeare Birthplace Trust – Shakespeare's Birthplace, Anne Hathaway's Cottage, Mary Arden's Farm, Hall's Croft and Harvard House (until April 2016 when Nash's House reopens) – can be bought here either as single tickets or as a Five House Pass which, at £23.90 for adults, represents a worthwhile saving. Tickets can also be bought online at www.shakespeare.org.uk where you will also find a wealth of information about the exhibition collections. For general enquiries call 01789 204016.

Entry to Shakespeare's Birthplace is through the Shakespeare Centre Exhibition.

Before entering the Shakespeare Centre to buy your ticket, walk a few paces next door to view the Birthplace from outside.

### Shakespeare's Birthplace

This attractive honey-coloured house with its gables and timber framing is where Mary Arden gave birth to her eight children, five of whom survived to adulthood. Shakespeare was born on 23 April 1564 in an upstairs chamber. Standing in front of the house, the left-hand side of the building is roughly where the family lived, and the right-hand side comprised John Shakespeare's workshop. At this point you may wish to enter the house and explore further, or save it for later and continue on the walk. A full history of the Birthplace is outlined in the section entitled 'The Birthplace'.

Now walk to the end of Henley Street, noting the branch of Barclays which stands on the site of the market hall where John Shakespeare sold his gloves. Straight ahead is Bridge Street which leads to Clopton Bridge. In Shakespeare's day Bridge Street had a row of houses in the middle, splitting the street into two. Cross over the roundabout to the white, two-storey building on the corner of High Street and Bridge Street. At the time of writing this building houses a branch of Crabtree & Evelyn.

### The Cage

A brass plaque on the corner of the house states that this was the home of Shakespeare's daughter Judith, who lived here after an ill-starred marriage to Thomas Quiney. The couple wed in February 1616 during the Lenten period, a time in which it was forbidden to marry except with a special licence. For whatever reason, Quiney did not have such a thing so the church excommunicated the couple for a brief period. Perhaps even worse, Judith then suffered the humiliation of discovering that she was not the only woman in her new husband's life. In March, Margaret Wheeler died giving birth to Quiney's illegitimate baby. In an age dominated by the church, Elizabethans who indulged in fornication and adultery could find themselves publicly shamed. In this manner Quiney was hauled before the ecclesiastical Bawdy Court where he was sentenced to do public penance dressed in a white sheet. Fortunately for him, the degrading sentence was commuted and he was let off with a five-shilling fine.

As a vintner and tobacconist Quiney set up a tavern in the upper floor of the house. It was known as the Cage after the prison which had formerly been located in the cellar. His troubles continued when he was accused of selling contaminated wine and indulging in rowdy drinking sessions with his friends. His despairing father-in-law was probably in ill health by this time and Shakespeare erased Quiney's name from his will, altering it to make provision for Judith's future. Shakespeare died two months after his daughter's wedding, no doubt lamenting the unreliable match she had made.

Thomas Quiney's house is now occupied by a cosmetics company and, by coincidence, so is that of his father. Carefully cross over the High Street and look for Number 31, another white-painted building, this time run by Lush.

*High Street*

Richard Quiney, father to Thomas, lived in this house. Shakespeare and Richard were good friends, a fact substantiated by the letter Richard would send him in 1598 asking for a loan of £30. Continue down High Street until you reach Harvard House on the right. The Stars and Stripes hang proudly outside, giving a clue to its ownership.

Harvard House is one of the oldest houses in Stratford and is strikingly beautiful with its ornately carved timbers and friezes. Built in 1596, this was the home of a puritan butcher named Thomas Rogers whose name can be seen carved on the front of the house along with that of his wife Alice and the date of construction. As well as his butchering activities Rogers also served as an alderman at the Stratford Corporation alongside John Shakespeare. His grandson John Harvard emigrated to Massachusetts in 1637 and went on to found the college that bears his name.

In 1909 the local novelist and heritage campaigner Marie Corelli purchased what was by now a crumbling property, known as the Ancient House, and restored it with help from a wealthy American named Edward Morris. Harvard College now owns the building, but unfortunately it will only remain open to the public until April 2016 when Nash's House and New Place reopen in time for Shakespeare's birthday celebrations.

Cross the road and continue straight ahead passing Sheep Street on your left. The High Street now merges into Chapel Street, and at the end is Nash's House, a half-timbered building with two gables and an overhanging top storey. Its exact age is uncertain but it is thought to date from the Elizabethan era. Be aware that although the façade looks original it was added after restoration in 1912.

## Nash's House and New Place

Nash's House was the home of Shakespeare's granddaughter Elizabeth. She was the daughter of Susanna and John Hall and lived in this house with her first husband Thomas Nash, a local landowner whom she married in 1626. Run by the Shakespeare Birthplace Trust it functions as a museum but at the time of writing is closed to the public as it is undergoing structural repairs. The Shakespeare Birthplace Trust hopes to add an extension to display artefacts found during recent archaeological excavations at New Place.

Shakespeare's grand mansion of brick and timber was located next door. He purchased New Place in 1597 from William Underhill, paying the princely sum of £60. Built by Hugh Clopton in 1483, it had extensive grounds and a five gabled façade which wrapped itself around Chapel Street and Chapel Lane. This is where Anne Hathaway and the children lived during Shakespeare's long absences in London. It was much larger than the house in Henley Street and would have required a significant team of servants to help run the household. The ostentatiousness of his new abode was a sign that Shakespeare had truly arrived. He retired here in 1614 and after his death two years later the house passed to his daughter Susanna who moved in with her husband John Hall and their daughter Elizabeth. After Susanna's death the house passed to Elizabeth. When Elizabeth died in 1670 the direct Shakespeare line died with her. At this point the house reverted to Clopton ownership before finally falling into the hands of the Reverend Francis Gastrell. He demolished it in 1759 in irritation at the number of visitors and tourists his famous house attracted. It seems that a fledgling Shakespeare Trail had already begun.

The Birthplace Trust has ambitious plans to develop the site. When it reopens in April 2016 they hope that visitors will be able to enter via a door sited upon the footprint of the original gatehouse. Once inside the grounds the outline of the house will be easy to find, as it will be prominently highlighted in bronze. Somewhere in the centre will be a tranquil circle of trees and stone benches surrounding a deep pool of water. Quotations from Shakespeare's works will be etched upon the ground, the contemplative atmosphere broken only by the occasional performance. It sounds idyllic and by April 2016 may be a reality.

Cross Chapel Lane and enter the Gothic silence of the Guild Chapel, taking a moment to enjoy its sense of calm and quiet order.

### Guild Chapel and King Edward VI School

Despite the chapel's small size, the daylight streaming in through the high arched windows gives the interior a light and airy feel. It was not always thus. The eye is drawn from the plain whitewashed walls to the chancel arch where the faded ghost of the medieval Doom painting can still be seen. At one time the walls were decorated with vivid religious imagery to help medieval minds focus on the afterlife. This was still an age of mystery and sensory worship. The chapel was founded by the Guild of the Holy Cross, a religious brotherhood of local businessmen and dignitaries which, like other religious orders, was suppressed during the Reformation. It was on this site in 1269 that the guild founded a hospital but the present building dates mostly from the late fifteenth century when former guild member Hugh Clopton left money in his will to pay for the restoration work to be carried out.

After its suppression all of the guild's buildings and assets were transferred to the secular Corporation of Stratford-upon-Avon. By 1563, most visible traces of the old religion were in the process of being eradicated. That year John Shakespeare, as bailiff of the town, was paid two shillings to cover the Doom painting beneath a layer of white wash. It would have been hidden from view forever had it not been for restoration work in 1804 during which workmen stripped the plaster from the walls and uncovered the ancient art work.

The chapel today is very much part of the community and holds regular events and concerts. The pupils of the King Edward VI School next door attend the daily services, continuing their centuries old connection with the chapel. The school was founded by the Guild of the Holy Cross in a room above the Guildhall. Shakespeare attended the school from the age of seven and was subject to an intense curriculum of Latin, rhetoric and Greek. With the school day beginning at six o'clock and a teaching methodology based on the rote learning of facts, facts, facts, it is easy to imagine the fanciful young William 'creeping snail like to school' like the 'whining school boy' described by Jaques in *As You Like It*.

Shakespeare's old school room still exists and the King Edward VI School hopes to raise funds to open it to visitors from April 2016.

Exit the chapel and look up at the sandstone clock tower where Hugh Clopton's coat of arms can be seen, before walking down Church Street past the King Edward VI School and the charming row of medieval alms houses. These were built by the Guild of the Holy Cross in 1427 to house retired priests and guild members. The residents lived by a strict set of rules and were obliged to attend the chapel every day. Drunk and debauched behaviour was punished with the docking of the miscreant's pension. The building still functions as an alms house and provides shelter for eleven residents, each with a local connection.

Continue to the end of Church Street and turn left onto Old Town. Halfway down is Hall's Croft.

### Hall's Croft

We saw earlier how Shakespeare's daughter Judith made an unfortunate marriage to the womaniser Thomas Quiney and went on to live in a tavern called the Cage. His eldest daughter Susanna was much more fortunate. In 1607 she married Stratford-upon-Avon's only practicing doctor, the educated and upstanding Dr John Hall, a man of puritan persuasions whose book of medical case studies and herbal remedies went on to become a widely consulted reference book in the seventeenth century. His cure for scurvy included plants rich in vitamin C and he successfully treated Susanna when she contracted the disease. Despite their standing in the community the Halls were not popular with everyone. In 1613 one John Lane maliciously accused Susanna of having adulterous liaisons with a local haberdasher called Ralph Smith and catching venereal disease. A furious John Hall took Lane to court for defamation but the accuser failed to show up and was excommunicated.

Hall's Croft dates from the early sixteenth century and the

Halls extended it in 1613. Today it is run as a museum by the Shakespeare Birthplace Trust and showcases contemporary furniture and paintings as well as an exhibition dedicated to John Hall's profession. Visitors can stroll about the pretty garden which is planted with examples of the herbs used by Hall to treat his patients.

*Visitor Information*

Hall's Croft is located at Old Town, Stratford-upon-Avon, Warwickshire CV37 6BG. Tel: 01789 338533.

From March to the beginning of November the house is open from 10:00–17:00 and from November to March it is open from 11:00–16:00.

A Birthplace Pass which includes entry to Hall's Croft, Harvard House (until April 2016), Shakespeare's Birthplace and Shakespeare's grave costs £15.90 for adults, £9.50 for children, £14.90 for concessions and £41.50 for a family pass. Hall's Croft is also included in the Five House Pass which gives access to all of the above including Anne Hathaway's Cottage and Mary Arden's Farm. Tickets for the Five House Pass are £23.90 for adults, £14.00 for children, £21.90 for concessions and £61.90 for families.

Turn left out of Hall's Croft and continue down Old Town, past the Cenotaph in the garden on the right and into the churchyard of Holy Trinity Church.

*Holy Trinity*

The next stop on our tour is Holy Trinity, a church whose significance in the life of William Shakespeare generates interest from around the world. He was baptised in the church font – which still exists – on 26 April 1564. As a grown man he worshipped here during his visits to Stratford. He would also be buried here. The church's soaring steeple is an iconic sight in Stratford and can be seen from various vantage points, especially along the River Avon. There has been a church on this site since at least Saxon times, but the present building was started in the thirteenth century and is a stunning example of medieval Gothic architecture.

Entering the churchyard from Old Town, the visitor is drawn down a little pathway flanked by lime trees towards the impressive porch. As you approach the fifteenth-century door, look out for the sanctuary knocker. It hangs upon an iron effigy of a grim-looking man who perhaps represents the medieval outlaws who used to seek sanctuary within. The nave is suitably atmospheric with its stained-glass windows, pillars and arches. At the end of the nave is the crossing which stands directly below the tower and spire. It leads to the chancel where Shakespeare is buried and at this point visitors are asked for a contribution towards the astronomical costs of running the church. The Five House Pass which can be bought at any of the Shakespeare properties will allow you free entry.

Despite the number of visitors, a contemplative silence usually falls at the site of Shakespeare's grave. After his death, members of his family were buried next to him and he lies in company with his wife Anne Hathaway, their daughter Susanna, her husband Dr John Hall, and Thomas Nash, the first husband of Shakespeare's granddaughter Elizabeth. The famous curse warns future generations not to disturb him

> Good frend, for Jesus sake forbeare
> To dig the dust encloased here.
> Bleste be the man that spares thes stones
> And curst be he that moves my bones.

So far, nobody has attempted to move his bones, but with the discovery of Richard III's skeleton and the international excitement that caused, it is perhaps only a matter of time before someone makes the request. A memorial bust made in 1623 can be seen in a niche just to the side. Anne Hathaway is said to have approved of its likeness to her late husband to the evident disappointment of his biographer Anthony Burgess, who thought it made Shakespeare look like a 'self satisfied pork butcher'.

Items within the chancel that Shakespeare would surely have been familiar with include a bible dating from 1611 and his baptismal font. Nearby is a set of twenty-six wooden misericords, upon which the congregation could sit during services. Dating from around 1500, the person who carved them clearly had a bawdy sense of humour, as they are quite frankly hilarious. Among the usual images of angels, unicorns and St George, there is the irreverent vision of a husband groping his wife.

The friendly and helpful staff members are happy to assist with questions about the church. Before you exit, don't forget to visit the bookshop where you will find a good range of interesting titles.

Public toilets are located in the gardens outside.

Step back out of the porch and turn right, following the footpath round towards the pleasant riverside walk which leads you back into town. On the left-hand side you will pass a blue gabled building which housed the Royal Shakespeare Company's Courtyard Theatre, its temporary base during the redevelopment of the Royal Shakespeare and Swan Theatres. Close by is the Dirty Duck. This famous riverside pub has an attractive outdoor patio and is often frequented by actors from the Royal Shakespeare Company. The pub has a two-sided sign – on one side is its original name, The Black Swan, and on the other side is the Dirty Duck, the nickname given to it by American GIs stationed nearby during the Second World War.

Just over the road is the world-class Royal Shakespeare Theatre, a venue at which some of our most celebrated actors have performed.

*Royal Shakespeare Company*

As you approach from the direction of the Dirty Duck, the extravagantly handsome home of the Royal Shakespeare Company comes into view. It stands near the site of its predecessor, the Memorial Theatre, which opened in 1879 and was consumed by fire in 1926. The oldest part of the present building was constructed in 1932 to the design of Elisabeth Scott who was great niece to George Gilbert Scott. The building underwent a major transformation in 2006 which included the addition of public spaces and an observation tower affording spectacular views of the river.

This is the home of the world-class Royal Shakespeare Company which was formed in 1961.

*Visitor Information*

Performances are held in both the Royal Shakespeare Theatre and the Swan Theatre all year round and the shows usually transfer to the West End. For tickets contact the Box Office on 0844 800 1110 or visit www.rsc.org.uk.

Tickets to the tower are £2.50 per person, £1.50 for under 18s and £1 for members of the RSC and the disabled.

Enter the building and walk through the lobby to the other end, noting the excellent bookshop and the display of costumes worn in past productions. Exiting the building at the other end you will find yourself in the beautiful Bancroft Gardens. In Shakespeare's day this was an area of common grazing land but is now a peaceful spot where people can stroll by the river. Boatmen ply their trade from rows of pretty vessels named after Shakespeare's female characters. At the far end of the Bancroft is the Gower Memorial where our walk ends.

*Gower Memorial*

Lord Ronald Gower was a sculptor and writer who at one time was trustee to the National Portrait Gallery. He created this flamboyant memorial to Shakespeare in 1888. It shows the cloaked playwright sitting high upon a plinth surrounded by four statues depicting some his best known characters in scenes from the plays. Prince Hal represents History, Lady Macbeth represents Tragedy, a deep-in-thought Hamlet represents Philosophy and Falstaff – who has a drunken twinkle in his eye – represents Comedy. The statue was originally sited outside the Memorial Theatre. Following the devastating fire of 1926, Elisabeth Scott commenced the rebuilding work and the statue was moved to its present spot. It is a cheering sight to end the walk and a reminder that Stratford is truly Shakespeare's town. At this point you may also wish to view the nearby Clopton Bridge whose fourteen arches have spanned the Avon since the fifteenth century. Despite the endless stream of vehicles roaring over the bridge on their way in and out of town it is easy to imagine an earlier time when Shakespeare might have made the crossing on foot and the only traffic was from horses and carts.

If all this walking has made you hungry, the Lazy Cow steakhouse is nearby as well as restaurants such as Carluccio's. At the bottom of nearby Bridge Street there are buses serving the whole of Warwickshire if you feel ready to venture further.

## Mary Arden's Farm

What, would you make me mad? Am I not Christopher Sly, old Sly's son of Burtonheath, by birth a pedlar, by education a cardmaker, by transmutation a bear-herd, and now by present profession a tinker? Ask Marian Hacket, the fat ale-wife of Wincot, if she know me not.

*The Taming of the Shrew*: Christopher Sly, Prologue, Scene II

### Country Beginnings

Shakespeare may have been a city boy in later life but he never lost touch with his country roots. We don't know whether or not he ever met a drunken tinker called Christopher Sly, but it is clear from the character's references to Warwickshire that he knew the type. Sly speaks of Burtonheath, probably Barton-on-the-Heath and appeals to Marian Hacket, the fat ale-wife of Wincot. This was Wilmcote, a pleasant village surrounded by farmland and limestone quarries which lay three miles north of Stratford. Wilmcote forms the prologue of Shakespeare's story for it was here, in 1537, that Mary Arden was born.

Mary was the youngest of eight sisters. Her father Robert was a well-to-do gentleman farmer who owned 150 acres of land, some of which was rented out to tenant farmers such as Richard Shakespeare of Snitterfield. Robert compiled a fascinating inventory of his belongings shortly before his death in 1556. We know for instance that he was in a position to own a team of eight oxen and a dovecote. He also listed mundane household items such as his cauldrons, candlesticks, pots and pillows. In an indication of how much he trusted his youngest daughter, he appointed Mary as the executor of his will. She was certainly literate and had her own letter seal, a galloping horse, which she used on official documents such as the deeds to her share of the farm, which she would eventually sell in 1579.

The farmhouse was built in 1514 in the reign of Henry VIII and by modern standards it was a crowded household. Mary and all her sisters had to share the space with their stepmother Agnes Webb and her four children. There would have been no room for privacy. The hall was the main living area and it was open to the rafters with a fireplace in the centre of the earthenware floor. The kitchen was to one side and was also used as a store room and workshop. Robert and Agnes slept in a private chamber at the other side of the hall. Upstairs was a small chamber reached by ladder and it is possible that Mary and her sisters slept here. It would have been warm and cosy from the heat of the fire below.

It has been suggested that Mary and her sisters did not enjoy a warm relationship with their stepmother Agnes. When Robert died he felt it necessary to warn Agnes that his daughter Alice should be left to enjoy her inheritance in peace

> I give and bequeath to Agnes my wife £6, 8 shillings and 4 pence upon this condition that she will suffer my daughter Alice to quietly to enjoy half my copyhold in Wilmcote during the time of her widowhood; and if she will not suffer my daughter Alice quietly to occupy half with her, then I will that my wife shall have but £3, 6 shillings, and 8 pence.

The wording hints at possible discord over who was entitled to what and why. To Mary he bequeathed 'all my land at Wilmcote called Asbies, and the crop upon the ground sown and tilled as it is.' She also inherited a sum of money, enough to attract the attention of Richard Shakespeare's son John, who was even now purchasing property in Henley Street, Stratford, in anticipation of welcoming home a wife. When Agnes Webb died she left her stepchildren nothing.

The farmhouse is part of a complex of buildings managed by the Shakespeare Birthplace Trust who run the site as a countryside museum. There are a number of farm buildings within the site meaning that the correct identification of Mary's home has been something of a comedy of errors over the years. It was John Jordan, an eighteenth-century tour guide, who first started telling people that the attractive half-timbered white house facing the road was Mary Arden's home. Whether it was through a storyteller's reluctance to admit that she had actually lived in Glebe Farm, the smaller, less flashy building round the corner, or whether it was through genuine ignorance, he helped perpetuate a myth which endured until 2000 when the Shakespeare Birthplace Trust commissioned some definitive research. Through dendrochronology – the science of tree-ring dating – it was discovered that the big white house, previously known as Mary Arden's House, dated only from the 1570s. By this time Mary was a Stratford housewife so it was much too late for her to have lived there. By contrast the wood used to construct Glebe Farm dated from 1514. The Arden residency at Glebe Farm was backed up by documentary evidence from contemporary deeds. By amazing fortune, or foresight, the Trust had already purchased the house in the 1960s. The big white house is now known to have been occupied by one Adam Palmer, a friend of the Ardens.

Visitors enter the complex via a door to the side of the car park. From there it is an easy stroll through the woodwork barn and out into the Rickyard, an outdoor space with a picnic area, café, barn and animal hovel. Around the corner is the farmyard and Palmer's House which is furnished in the Tudor style. Mary Arden's house with its separate farm buildings is accessed down a footpath to the right. Its red-brick façade dates from the nineteenth century and it has been steadily modified over the years but the Tudor shell remains an integral part of the building. As a visitor attraction Mary Arden's Farm is very family-oriented. It puts on falconry displays and animal-petting sessions as well as offering fascinating insights into ancient farming techniques. Costumed volunteers can be seen tending to the livestock which includes pigs, chickens and a beautiful grey horse. They also offer demonstrations of traditional cookery; the smells wafting from the kitchens are quite delicious. Countryside nature trails meander through the meadows and rare breed animals roam freely. This is as close as it gets to stepping back in time and experiencing the same sights and sounds as the Arden family did.

As a young man growing up in nearby Stratford-upon-Avon, William Shakespeare would undoubtedly have visited the farm, perhaps in company with his mother and siblings. Regardless of ancient family disputes about money and wills, Wilmcote was in his blood and was almost certainly in the back of his mind when he wrote Christopher Sly's confused protestations in *The Taming of the Shrew*.

## Visitor Information

It is easy to get to Wilmcote from Stratford-upon-Avon. On a summer's day it is nice to walk along the canal towpath, a journey which takes approximately an hour and a half. Simply start from the Swan Fountain located near the Royal Shakespeare Theatre and head northwards. The 'Hop-on, Hop-off' sightseeing bus includes Wilmcote on its circuit of the town. Alternatively there are regular trains to Wilmcote from Stratford and is a short journey of approximately seven minutes. Turn left out of Wilmcote Station and walk straight down the road for approximately ten minutes. Mary Arden's Farm is across the road on your right.

Once you have worked up a healthy thirst at the farm, The Mary Arden Inn is situated over the road and offers a good selection of pub food. Disappointingly for Shakespeare fans, the beer is no longer served by Marian Hacket, the 'fat ale-wife of Wincot.' Mary Arden's Farm is located on Station Road, Wilmcote, Stratford-upon-Avon CV37 9UN. Tel: 01789 338535.

Due to the outdoor nature of this site, opening hours are limited to the spring and summer. From 14 March through to 1 November it is open from 10:00–17:00.

Tickets are £12.50 for adults, £8.00 for children, £11.50 for concessions and £33.00 for a family pass. You may find it more economical to buy a Five House Pass which gives access to all the Shakespeare Birthplace Trust properties. Tickets for the Five House Pass are £23.90 for adults, £14.00 for children, £21.90 for concessions and £61.90 for families.

If Mary Arden had been raised on the gentle rhythms of a country farm, then so too was her husband. John Shakespeare was the son of Richard, one of Robert Arden's tenants. The Shakespeare family worked the land in the fields outside Snitterfield, a small hamlet situated between Stratford and Warwick. This large village still boasts several Tudor era houses and may be worth a visit for anyone who wants to follow in the footsteps of Shakespeare's father.

## The Birthplace

> But thou art fair, and at thy birth, dear boy,
> Nature and Fortune join'd to make thee great:
> Of nature's gifts thou mayst with lilies boast,
> And with the half-blown rose.
>
> *King John*: Constance, Act III, Scene I

*A Star is Born*

The house known today as the Birthplace is a handsome, honey-coloured building complete with gables, timber framing and mullioned windows. It is dreamily Tudor; a magnet for the tourists and devotees who flock here in their thousands. Nobody knows exactly when it was built and in some ways it hardly matters because it is not the architecture which attracts, but the people who lived within its walls. Even without the Shakespeare connection the house offers a fascinating glimpse into the workings of an early English home. The rooms are intimately furnished in sixteenth-century style; the dining hall table is laid out for a meal, children's toys are scattered in the birth room, leather gloves lie on John Shakespeare's worktop. As you wander from room to room it almost feels like an intrusion, as if the family had not died hundreds of years ago but had simply gone out for the day.

John Shakespeare had been living here since 1552, the year of the muck heap incident in which he was fined for keeping a huge pile of steaming manure outside the house. At this time the property was formed of two separate buildings side by side. He purchased them both and joined them together with a cross passageway running between the living quarters and his glove-making workshop. Until 1556 he had been a tenant but that year he purchased it from one Edward West, possibly in anticipation of his impending marriage to Mary Arden which would take place the following year.

Mary Arden, that capable young woman whose intelligence and character had so impressed her father, was finally mistress of her own household. It must have been a relief to leave the crowded farmhouse at Wilmcote and step over the threshold at Henley Street into a house she could call her own. She fell pregnant quickly but her first two children, Joan and Margaret, died in infancy. She gave birth to William in April 1564. When the plague arrived three months later the young Shakespeare couple would have been uncomfortably aware of the difficulties of keeping an infant alive. By some miracle William survived and Mary went on to give birth to Gilbert, Joan, Anne, Richard and Edmund.

Visitors enter the grounds via the Shakespeare Centre Exhibition from which you emerge into the pretty back garden with its delicate herbs and flowers. The atmosphere is heightened by costumed actors who roam the grounds performing scenes from Shakespeare's plays. During the Shakespeare residency the garden would have been an important source of food for the family. Mary would have tended herbs and vegetables for the kitchen. There would also have been outbuildings and sheds for the running of John's glove-making workshop. The entrance to the house itself is via a small room which was part of a little adjoining cottage where Shakespeare had lived with his new wife Anne Hathaway after their marriage. Next door is the parlour with its original limestone flagged floor. The centrepiece within the parlour is an example of a sixteenth-century four-poster bed of the type which would have been kept on display and reserved for the use of guests. Shakespeare famously left his second-best bed to Anne Hathaway in his will, although this was not the snub it might first appear since the second-best bed would have been a more personal item to the couple. What became of the best bed is unknown.

Walking through the parlour you pass the small dining hall on the left-hand side with its original fireplace. The table is laid with cutlery dating from the period. It would have been a warm and cosy room with the family gathering here for the main meal of the day at around 11:00 or 12:00. Next door is John Shakespeare's light and airy workshop. The room is adorned with sheepskins, tools and finished gloves. As a reminder of John's illicit dabbling in the unlicensed wool trade, there are also baskets of wool on display.

The room where Shakespeare was born is upstairs. The birth room is furnished much as it would have been when young William came into the world. Inside is a lying-in bed of the type that Mary would have recovered in after the dangerous and exhausting ordeal of childbirth. She would have remained in bed for a month afterwards before being churched and re-entering society. Her babies, in common with all newborns, were kept tightly swaddled for the first nine months of their lives in the belief that restricting their movement would help them to grow without deformity. They were placed in a cradle like the example on display in the room until they grew into toddlers at which point they would graduate to a little truckle bed to the side of their parent's four-poster.

For a period in the 1580s the house on Henley Street would have been alive with youthful energy. Shakespeare was only nineteen when Anne Hathaway gave birth to Susanna. At this time his brothers Richard and Edmund were still only seven and three years old respectively. Just two years later his twins Judith and Hamnet arrived. It would have been a crowded and boisterous environment, full of teasing and fun. Standing in the birth room today, surrounded by toys and clothes, you can almost hear the childish laughter; a distant echo through time.

John and Mary were just the first generation of Shakespeare folk in ownership of the property. Shakespeare inherited the house in 1601 when his father died. He rented it out to Lewis Hiccox who turned it into a tavern called the Maidenhead, a venue which survived into the first decades of the nineteenth century, albeit under the name Swan and Maidenhead. Shakespeare's sister Joan stayed on in the cottage with her husband William

Hart. When Shakespeare died the ownership of the property transferred to his daughter Susanna Hall. Joan was allowed to remain in the cottage for a peppercorn rent of one shilling a year and she stayed until her death in 1646. When Susanna died the property passed to her daughter Elizabeth and then on to Joan Hart's descendants who remained its custodians until the late eighteenth century.

The Shakespeare Birthplace Trust has owned the property since 1847. By this time it had fallen into a state of neglect and disrepair. It started to attract the interest of the American entertainer P. T. Barnum who wanted to buy the house and ship it off to the States. Charles Dickens was among those who sprung into action and organised fundraising events to save it for Britain. It was restored back to its former state and is now a good approximation of what it would have looked like when Shakespeare lived there. The Trust has achieved the impressive feat of interpreting the house with sensitivity and verve. For children there are tactile displays such as the gloves in John's workshop. For everyone, including the kids, there is a team of tour guides whose intelligent and knowledgeable commentary ensures that the house which nurtured Shakespeare's imagination continues to inspire ours.

*Visitor Information*

The Shakespeare Centre is located on Henley Street, Stratford-upon-Avon, Warwickshire CV37 6QW. Tel: 01789 204016.

Opening hours vary depending on the season but as a rough guide it is 9:00–17:00 in spring and autumn, 9:00–17:30 in summer and 10:00–16:00 in winter.

Tickets are £15.90 for adults, £9.50 for children, £14.90 for concessions and £41.50 for a family pass. You may find it more economical to buy a Five House Pass which gives access to all the Shakespeare Birthplace Trust properties. Tickets for the Five House Pass are £23.90 for adults, £14.00 for children, £21.90 for concessions and £61.90 for families.

## The Forest of Arden

> And this our life exempt from public hand
> Finds tongues in trees, books in the running brooks,
> Sermons in stones and good in everything.
> I would not change it.
> *As You Like It*: Duke Senior, Act II, Scene I

### Hobgoblins and Outlaws

Just beyond the boundaries of Shakespeare's neatly ordered town lie the wilds of Warwickshire. To the south of the River Avon were the flatlands of the Feldon, a gentle patchwork of sheep farms and agricultural land. To the north was the Arden, its clay soil making it unsuitable for crop farming. Oak trees had once grown in abundance; during the Middle Ages much of the Arden was a huge expanse of untamed forest. Dark and primeval, it was a place where the laws of man did not quite reach. As a medieval traveller, it would have been the little things that unnerved: a skeletal branch silhouetted against a darkening sky; the sudden sound of dead leaves crunching in the ground. In an age of superstition, hobgoblins lurked in the shadows of the trees. More realistically, so did bandits and robbers. Just outside the village of Coughton there is a medieval stone which formed the base of a cross where people would stop to pray for safe passage before venturing forth. The Romans had neglected to build any roads through the forest so it is probable that people had to make do with dirt tracks.

Arden had been the childhood home of Shakespeare's mother Mary, and as her family name suggests, the forest was in her blood. On dark nights, gathered around the fire at Wilmcote or at Henley Street, she may have fed her son's imagination by telling folk stories about Robin Hood and other mythical creatures of the greenwood. The play *As You Like It* is deeply rooted in the Forest of Arden and describes a community of romantic exiles who seem to find contentment by wandering about the forest playing courtship games and writing bad love poetry. Far from being scary, Shakespeare's forest is a place of safety and innocence.

Six years after he wrote this comedy, however, the forest was the scene of a much darker drama.

Not far from the remains of the medieval cross is Coughton Court. Started in the early sixteenth century on the site of an older house, it has been the ancestral home of the Throckmorton family since 1409. The oldest part of the building is the stunning gatehouse with its far-reaching views over the parkland. It was in the top chamber of the gatehouse that a dramatic vigil played out in the aftermath of the Gunpowder Plot of 1605. One of the conspirators, Sir Everard Digby, had rented the house from Thomas Throckmorton as a base for the planned uprising and it was here that the Jesuit priest Henry Garnet waited for news in company with Digby's wife. From the gatehouse it would have been easy to have seen any approaching riders; to quickly decide whether they were friendly or whether they were officials bearing arrest warrants. Garnet was taking a terrible risk. Even without consorting with traitors, to be a Catholic priest in the age of Shakespeare was illegal and carried the threat of torture and execution. For this reason the gatehouse at Coughton Court was equipped with a priest hole. After his arrest Garnet protested that he had done everything he could to prevent the plot from developing but the authorities were reluctant to believe him. Why should they? Perhaps they remembered his 1598 guidebook, *A Treatise of Equivocation*. He was executed in May 1606 and is recognised as a martyr by the Catholic Church. Shakespeare would go on to make a teasing reference to Garnet in *Macbeth*

> Faith, here's an equivocator, that could
> Swear in both the scales against either scale,
> Who committed treason enough for God's sake, yet could
> Not equivocate to heaven. O, come in, equivocator.
>
> *Macbeth*: The Porter, Act II, Scene III

The players in the Gunpowder Plot were mostly Warwickshire men and Shakespeare may have known some of them. He would certainly have known of Coughton Court and the medieval cross nearby. By this time deforestation had stripped the land of much of its density but patches of woodland still remained.

Today, much of the forest has been swallowed up by the sprawl of Birmingham and Coventry but the Warwickshire countryside still bears the traces of it with several ancient oak trees still in existence such as the one at Ragley Park in nearby Alcester. The names of villages such as Henley-in-Arden and Tanworth-in-Arden evoke a time when the people of the Arden lived in the midst of a thick green wilderness.

The ghosts and outlaws may have long since left but Arden is still a place of magic and history and gives context to Shakespeare's world.

## Visitor Information
Coughton Cross is a Grade II listed monument located on the corner of Coughton Fields Lane. The Number 26 bus from Stratford-upon-Avon stops just over the road. To reach

Coughton Court after viewing the cross, you can either walk five minutes up Coughton Fields Lane and turn left into the driveway or cut diagonally across the field, following the footpath. Dogs are welcome in the extensive grounds but there are sheep in the field so they must be kept on leads. No dogs are allowed in the house or gardens.

The Coughton Court priest hole can still be seen in the gatehouse. On display is a gown purported to have been worn by Mary Queen of Scots at her execution.

The café is situated in the old Tudor kitchens and bookworms will love the second-hand book shop in the old stables.

Check the website for opening hours and prices, www. nationaltrust.org.uk/coughton-court or call 01789 400777 for up-to-date information.

# Kenilworth Castle

Oberon: My gentle Puck, come hither. Thou rememberest
Since once I sat upon a promontory
And heard a mermaid on a dolphin's back
Uttering such dulcet and harmonious breath
That the rude sea grew civil at her song
And certain stars shot madly from their spheres
To hear the seamaid's music?
Puck: I remember
*A Midsummer Night's Dream*: Act II, Scene I

*Fireworks and Dolphins*
In July 1575 Warwickshire witnessed a feast of such extravagance that it has become the stuff of legend. Elizabeth I had been on progress around the Midlands and on 9 July she stopped at

Kenilworth Castle to stay with Robert Dudley, the Earl of Leicester. She brought hundreds of courtiers and they stayed for nearly three weeks, eating and drinking at Dudley's expense. Not that he would have minded. During this time Dudley, who was hoping to marry the queen and needed to impress her, lavished the party with entertainments. There were pageants and dances, mystery plays and bear-baiting. On one spectacular evening a floating island was built upon the Great Mere, an expanse of water just outside the castle walls. Bobbing around on the mere was a boat decked out to look like a dolphin. An actor, dressed as the classical figure Arion, sat upon the dolphin's back and played music which drifted across the water accompanied by fireworks.

This was pure theatre. Shakespeare scholars have often suggested that a young William Shakespeare was among the audience members. As the son of a Stratford dignitary he may have attended with his father and watched the spectacle from the banks of the Great Mere, perhaps reflecting on the castle's long and bloody history which he would later write about.

Kenilworth Castle was started in 1120 by Geoffrey de Clinton, chamberlain to Henry I. He intended it as a fortress and indeed it was used by Simon de Montfort in the thirteenth century as his base in the campaign against Henry III. In 1266 it came under siege by the king's forces, turning the Great Mere into a defensive moat.

It was at Kenilworth in 1414 that Henry V received his unwanted gift of tennis balls from the French, a scene Shakespeare used for dramatic effect.

Henry V: What treasure, uncle?
Exeter: Tennis balls, my liege.
Henry V: We are glad the Dauphin is so pleasant with us;

His present and your pains we thank you for:
When we have march'd our rackets to these balls,
We will, in France, by God's grace, play a set
Shall strike his father's crown into the hazard.

*Henry V*: Act I, Scene II

The castle would also feature in the play *Henry VI, Part II* when the king muses on his wish to be a subject and not a ruler.

The remains of Kenilworth are interesting for the spectrum of historical eras they represent. The oldest ruin is Geoffrey de Clinton's Great Tower which dates from his arrival in the 1120s. Mortimer's Tower, located not far from the visitors' entrance, dates from the thirteenth century when King John improved the defences.

The castle first came into Dudley hands in the reign of Edward VI when John Dudley, Robert's father, acquired it. In the short period between his possession of the castle and losing his head for treason, he built the half-timbered stable block which can still be seen today and which now functions as the café. Elizabeth I granted the castle to Robert Dudley in 1563 and he proceeded to modernise it with a programme of building work designed to bring luxury and comfort to his new home. In 1572 he constructed Leicester's Building, a grand renaissance-style house with four storeys and breathtaking views over the countryside. This was to be Elizabeth's base during her visits. She stayed there shortly after its construction and again in 1575 after it had been improved. The building is now a shell but recently-constructed internal stairs and walkways allow the visitor to climb to the level of the queen's privy chamber and get a proper feel for its layout.

Behind the Great Tower is the privy garden, a fine recreation of the knot garden that a love-struck Dudley laid out for his queen. English Heritage, the custodian of Kenilworth Castle, has restored Elizabeth's garden based on a contemporary description by one of Dudley's servants, Robert Langham. He described 'redolent plants and fragrant herbs and flowers, in form, colour and quantity so deliciously variant.' Visitors access the garden via a raised open gallery from where you can look down over the geometric patterns of the hedge rows. As in Dudley's day, an aviary is located at the back of the garden.

The gatehouse, known as Leicester's Gatehouse, lies to the north of the complex and was built in 1571. Look out for the 1590s tester bed in the Elizabethan bedroom and Dudley's family motto, 'Droit en Loyal', on the fireplace in the Oak Room. Upstairs is an exhibition telling the story of his love for Elizabeth.

It seems that everything Dudley did here was in some way inspired by the queen and their pursuit of pleasure. Like all good things, however, the days of Elizabethan romance would soon come to an end; opposing sides in the Civil War tussled over the castle in the seventeenth century before the Parliamentarians partially destroyed it in 1649. The Great Mere was drained to prevent the possibility of it ever being used as a moat again.

The mere is now just a boggy field. From the adjoining footpath the red sandstone castle looks scarred and wounded; a victim to its martial history. Despite Robert Dudley's romantic vision of a palace fit for Gloriana, the castle's final tumbledown state is the unhandy work of soldiers. But we are here to celebrate a poet. Gazing across the field at the atmospheric ruins silhouetted against the sky, vivid images come to mind. Perhaps this is where an imaginative eleven year old boy from Stratford first saw magic dolphins, mermaids and fireworks, those *certain stars shot madly from their spheres.*

It is a lovely thought.

*Visitor Information*

Kenilworth Castle is located on Castle Green, Kenilworth, Warwickshire CV8 INE. Tel: 01926 852078.

Opening hours are variable so please call for up to date information or check www.english-heritage.org.uk/visit/places/kenilworth-castle.

Tickets are £9.60 for adults, £5.80 for children, £8.60 for concessions and £25.00 for a family pass. English Heritage also offers twelve month membership which gives free access to all their properties.

The Number 28 bus from Stratford-upon-Avon will take you to the town of Kenilworth. Ask the driver to stop at the Clock Tower near the Holiday Inn. It is then a short walk to the castle. On bank holidays the castle runs a free shuttle bus from outside the Holiday Inn. Drivers can make use of the free car park at the castle, but bear in mind that you will need to keep some change handy as a £2 deposit is payable upon arrival. You get this back when you purchase your entry tickets.

Around the same time that Geoffrey de Clinton was building his castle he also constructed an Augustinian abbey in the fields nearby. The remains can still be seen in the Abbey Fields, a large open space adjacent to the castle.

# Bidford-on-Avon

> We'll teach you to drink deep ere you depart.
>
> *Hamlet*: Hamlet, Act I, Scene II

*Drinking with the Bidford Sippers*

One morning, after a night of heavy drinking, William Shakespeare is said to have woken up in the open air beneath a crab tree. His head must have been clanging, or maybe he was still drunk, for that can be the only excuse for the bizarre lines of poetry that he is said to have uttered to his companions. Legend has it that the previous morning he had walked from Stratford to Bidford-on-Avon in search of the amiable local men who were renowned for their drinking competitions. On the way he had asked a shepherd where he could find the Bidford drinkers. The shepherd replied that they were absent – but would the Bidford sippers do instead? Shakespeare readily agreed that they would and went off to find them. After a night of carousing he collapsed underneath the crab tree to recover, only to be awoken the next morning by thirsty Bidford men imploring him to continue the session. Shakespeare declined but instead recited some strangely robotic lines about the local villages:

> Piping Pebworth, Dancing Marston,
> Haunted Hillboro, Hungry Grafton,
> Dodging Exhall, Papist Wixford,
> Beggarly Broom and Drunken Bidford.

He clearly needed some painkillers.

'Drunken' Bidford lies on the Stratford to Evesham road with 'beggarly' Broom just to the north. 'Hungry Grafton' may refer to Temple Grafton to the north east, and 'Dancing Marston' is probably Long Marston to the south west.

The story originated in 1762 when an anonymous letter was published in the *British Magazine* purporting to be from someone who had got the tale from a Stratford landlord acquainted with Shakespeare's descendants. It is a nice story and like most folk legends, may be rooted in some truth even if the details have been embellished along the way. The exact location of Shakespeare's crab tree has been forgotten as the tree was uprooted in 1824. Perhaps it stood somewhere along the banks of the River Avon. If the legend is true then Shakespeare may have followed the course of the river on the seven-mile-long walk from Stratford. Arriving into the village he would have seen the medieval packhorse bridge which dates from the early fifteenth century. Tradition has it that he met the Bidford sippers in the Old Falcon Inn, a huge gabled house on the corner of Church Street which dates from the mid-sixteenth century. Its stone façade hides a timber-framed section around the corner. The building has an interesting and varied history. As well as its time as an inn it has also functioned as a Victorian warehouse, an antiques centre and more recently, private apartments. At the time of writing it is on the market with a price tag of £750,000.

Across the road is the beautiful church of St Laurence which was founded in the thirteenth century. The tower and the chancel are medieval but the rest of the building dates from 1835. Walking through the peaceful churchyard you may see pheasants pecking around in the grass. The churchyard backs onto the river and there are some great views of the Big Meadow on the other side, a vast open space of twenty-six acres where the local residents enjoy picnics, dog walking and other activities.

On high days and holidays look out for the Shakespeare Morris Men who have performed in the local area since 1959 when they were formed by some alumni of King Edward VI School, Shakespeare's old school. They proudly wear the playwright's coat of arms upon their livery. Bidford is a charming little stop on the Shakespeare Trail and makes for a great day out.

*Visitor Information*

With several tempting pubs idyllically situated on the banks of the Avon, 'Drunken' Bidford still lives up to its name. Overlooking the bridge is the aptly named pub, the Bridge, which has an outdoor terrace on the river front and serves locally sourced food. For details call 01789 773700. Bidford High Street is quaint yet functional and offers the usual array of shops, including a French bakery, a post office and a supermarket.

The Number 28 bus from Stratford stops outside St Laurence. Catch the return bus from over the road outside the post office. Walkers may wish to follow in Shakespeare's footsteps and take the pleasant Avon Valley Footpath from Stratford which follows the bank of River Avon past the village of Welford on Avon with its pretty thatched cottages.

# Charlecote House

A parliament member, a justice of peace,
At home a poor scarecrow, at London an ass,
If lousy is Lucy as some folk miscall it,
Then Lucy is lousy whatever befall it.

Anonymous local ballad

### *Poaching for deer*
Like Bidford-on-Avon, Shakespeare's connection with our next destination is founded on a colourful legend. The unflattering lines above refer to Sir Thomas Lucy, a wealthy local landowner who built Charlecote Park in 1558. As the ballad says, he was the Member of Parliament for Warwickshire from 1571 and also Justice of the Peace. He had puritan leanings and in his role as Justice of the Peace took part in raids upon the homes of local Catholics in the 1580s after an alleged plot to kill the queen. Among those arrested were Edward Arden, kinsman to Shakespeare, and Arden's son in law John Somerville.

Lucy gets a bad press in Shakespeare mythology. The character of Justice Shallow in *The Merry Wives of Windsor* is often said to be based upon him. Another legend which originated in the late seventeenth century has the clergyman Richard Davies claiming that:

> Shakespeare was much given to all unluckiness in stealing venison and rabbits, particularly from Sir Lucy who oft had him whipped and sometimes imprisoned and at last made him fly his native country to his great advancement.

The fact that there is no contemporary evidence to support the poaching theory does not make the story any less appealing. Indeed, along with Lucy's persecution of the Ardens, it may explain any animosity the playwright bore him.

Whatever the truth, there is ample reason to visit Charlecote and enjoy the surrounding countryside. As you enter the grounds the first thing you notice is the grand gatehouse dating from 1600 which straddles the Main Drive. Above the arched doorway is an upper floor where members of the family and their guests would retire after dinner to eat sweetmeats. The drive continues through the gatehouse and up to the front door of the house itself. Charlecote House is a stunning red-bricked mansion with two wings on either side forming a small courtyard with pretty lawns leading to the front door. The building work started in 1558 but the Victorian residents did much to restore and improve it. Sir Thomas Lucy built the porch to mark the occasion of the queen's visit in 1572.

The first room you enter is the Great Hall with its fine collection of family portraits. This leads into the billiards room. The bedchamber where Elizabeth I slept during her visit is now displayed as it was when it served as a Victorian drawing room. Although the site is managed by the National Trust, the current

Lucy family still lives in one of the wings and items of their furniture can be seen roped off.

A pretty parterre garden at the back of the house leads down to the River Avon with perfect views of the rolling parkland beyond. Charlecote has 185 acres of grounds for visitors to wander so walkers may wish to bring suitable footwear and explore. Place's Meadow beyond the cricket pitch is a secluded spot by the river. In summer the wild flowers transform it into a sea of yellow. Across the lake from Place's Meadow is the Front Park where deer bucks roam. Unfortunately, there was no deer park in Sir Thomas Lucy's day so we must be content to imagine Shakespeare poaching rabbits instead. Or indeed, poaching nothing at all.

Younger visitors will enjoy seeing the Charlecote pigs and bees, as well as helping out in the Victorian kitchens where cooking displays take place. In the nearby Tack Room you can see the Lucy family's Victorian carriages and horse tack.

Not far from the park is the church of St Leonards where the Lucy family worshipped. The current church dates from 1851 when the young mistress of the house, Mary Elizabeth Lucy, demolished the medieval building and constructed something more cheerful and comfortable. Inside can be seen a twelfth-century font as well as the tomb chest of Sir Thomas Lucy. He lies there in alabaster stillness, his hands clasped in eternal prayer. Whether or not this man was William Shakespeare's nemesis, the dour puritan who inspired Justice Shallow, he left us an extraordinary cultural legacy and for that reason should be remembered kindly.

*Visitor Information*
Charlecote Park is located in Wellesbourne, Warwick, Warwickshire CV35 9ER. Tel: 01789 470277.

The Orangery tea room at Charlecote is a lovely place to stop off and recharge. Unsurprisingly for a deer park they produce their own venison which is used in some of the recipes. Alternatively you could take a picnic and find a pleasant spot somewhere in the grounds.

Opening hours are variable so please call for up to date information or see www.nationaltrust.org.uk/charlecote-park/ opening-times. Please note that although the grounds are open every day, the house itself is closed on Wednesdays.

Tickets for entrance to the whole property, including the house and grounds are £10.05 for adults, £5.00 for children and £25.00 for a family pass. The National Trust offers slightly lower prices for access to just the garden, park and outbuildings.

The Number X18 bus from Stratford-upon-Avon stops just around the corner from the entrance to the park. On my journey one kind passenger drew my attention to a huge herd of deer standing in a field by the roadside. There is free parking for drivers.


## Anne Hathaway's House

See how she leans her cheek upon her hand.
O that I were a glove upon that hand,
That I might touch that cheek.
*Romeo and Juliet*: Romeo, Act II, Scene II

*Shakespeare in Love*
The summer of 1582 marks William Shakespeare's transition from boy to man. In the August of that year Stratford enjoyed a bumper harvest and it seems that he had been paying visits to Newlands Farm, one mile away in the village of Shottery. Maybe

he had simply intended to help bring in the hay and the grain, perhaps even sew the rye. He would have been aware that the farmer, Richard Hathaway, had died the previous year leaving eight children behind who would have been grateful for the help. With his own father's finances in disarray, the extra money would have been useful to the family at Henley Street. Whatever his intentions had been, the outcome was clear enough. By the end of that month the farmer's eldest daughter, Anne Hathaway, was pregnant. It seems that Shakespeare had been sowing more than just rye.

It was not uncommon for women to say their vows with a rounded belly, but it meant the ceremony needed to be performed in haste. Between August and November when they eventually married, Anne would have stayed with her siblings at the farmhouse in Shottery, perhaps anxiously waiting for the first quickening of the child and hoping it would not be born a bastard. With no time for the banns to be read the customary three times, Shakespeare applied for a special licence from the Bishop of Worcester's court and attended in company with two local farmers, Fulke Sandells and John Richardson, who vouched for the legitimacy of the match. William was eighteen at the time and Anne was twenty-six. In his will, Richard Hathaway had left his daughter a legacy of £6, 13s and 4d so the young couple were comfortably well-off.

Richard left the cottage to Anne's brother Bartholomew and the house remained in Hathaway hands until 1746 when the line died out. The Shakespeare Birthplace Trust purchased the cottage in 1892 from Mary Baker, the wife of William Taylor, who was a distant Hathaway descendant. Mary continued to live in the cottage after its acquisition by the Trust and she acted as custodian, welcoming the first visitors. Items of her furniture and personal belongings remain on display inside.

The house that Anne Hathaway grew up in continues to be a popular visitor attraction today. Its peaceful location at the edge of rolling farmland, with the Shottery brook babbling away nearby, gives it a rural feel even though the bustle of Stratford-upon-Avon is only one mile away. Visitors come from all over the world to see her childhood home. It is a pretty half-timbered dwelling with whitewashed walls and chimneys. The most striking feature viewed from outside is the roof with its generous layers of thatch draped over it like a thick blanket. Altogether, the cottage has the soft, gentle appearance of a typical English country home. Like many ancient houses, this one is the result of generations of building and extension work with the result of having several layers of history. The oldest part of the house is the bottom floor which dates from the mid-fifteenth century.

Visitors enter via the original front door to be met by a tour guide who leads you into the hall. In Anne's day the upper floor had not yet been built so the house consisted of two rooms, one of which was the hall which would have had a high ceiling, open to the rafters. Owing to the high cost of glass, there were no windows on the north side and the room would have been very dark. Near the fireplace is an old wooden settle, or bench, which is believed to date back to Anne's residency here. Perhaps William and Anne sat here together during their courtship, discussing plans for the future. Or maybe they had used 'Shakespeare's Courting Chair', a wooden chair which dates from the early seventeenth century. The chair itself is displayed upstairs in one of the bedchambers. In the eighteenth century descendants of Joan Hart claimed that it belonged to the playwright and that he used to sit on it with Anne Hathaway upon his knee. The Shakespeare Birthplace Trust managed to buy this curiosity when it came up for auction in 2002.

Outside in the extensive grounds there is a pretty flower garden and a sculpture trail with statues representing Shakespeare's characters including Titania, Falstaff and King Lear. On a summer's day the grounds are idyllic; the blossom-scented air is abuzz with honey bees and the excited chatter of fellow tourists. In Anne's day this would have been a working farmyard with all hands on deck. A signpost points in the direction of a footpath which leads away from the cottage and into a secluded woodland walk. As you enter the woods, the chatter of visitors is suddenly replaced by birdsong and the quiet whispering of the leaves in the trees. It is a beautiful spot in which to contemplate that August of 1582 when the harvest was underway and the cider was flowing. It is likely that Anne would have been a visible presence around the farm, supervising, helping, cajoling. Amid all this frenzied activity, William Shakespeare conceived his first child and found a wife. Despite being eight years his elder, Anne Hathaway outlived her husband by seven years.

*Visitor Information*
Anne Hathaway's Cottage is located at 22 Cottage Lane, Shottery, Stratford-upon-Avon, Warwickshire CV37 9HH. Tel: 01789 338532.

Opening hours vary depending on the season but as a rough guide it is 9:00–17:00 between March and October and 10:00–16:00 in winter.

Tickets are £9.50 for adults, £5.50 for children, £8.50 for concessions and £24.50 for a family pass. You may find it more economical to buy a Five House Pass which gives access to all the Shakespeare Birthplace Trust properties. Tickets for the Five House Pass are £23.90 for adults, £14.00 for children, £21.90 for concessions and £61.90 for families.

To reach Anne Hathaway's cottage on foot, as Shakespeare

would have done, take the well-signposted footpath which leads from Evesham Place just outside the centre of Stratford-upon-Avon. It is a pleasant walk and takes approximately twenty minutes. Alternatively the cottage is included in the 'Hop-on, Hop-off' bus itinerary.

If you plan to have lunch at the site the Cottage Garden Café is open all year round from 10:00 and serves hot and cold food with extra seating outside. The village of Shottery itself has some fine old buildings and it is worth exploring. For refreshments in the village try the Bell pub which also has a children's menu.

## Temple Grafton

> Let me not to the marriage of true minds
> Admit impediments. Love is not love
> Which alters when it alteration finds,
> Or bends with the remover to remove:
> O no! It is an ever fixed mark
> That looks on tempests and is never shaken
>
> From Sonnet 116

*William and Anne Shakespeare*
William Shakespeare and Anne Hathaway were married for thirty-four years. For most of that time they lived apart, effectively leading separate lives. While Shakespeare based himself in London, living in rented accommodation and slowly writing his way to wealth and fame, Anne stayed in Stratford where she raised their children and ran the household. It would be easy to think of this arrangement in clichéd terms: a poetic soul fleeing from his shrewish wife and escaping to the bohemian theatre scene of London while she remained at home; the downtrodden

country housewife, struggling alone with a growing brood of brats. The truth is probably much more down to earth. Far from being an unloved drudge, we could also see Anne Hathaway as Shakespeare's rock. After all it was she who managed their household affairs in his absence, a role which would have taken skill as well as boundless energy.

We do not know for certain where they married but tradition says the ceremony took place in the village of Temple Grafton. In her book *Ungentle Shakespeare: Scenes From His Life*, the writer Katherine Duncan-Jones posits that when Anne got pregnant, her relatives moved her to the village until she could be married. This would help avoid any gossip and scandal arising from her situation and seems to be the most likely scenario.

For all the ambiguity surrounding the location of their marriage, Temple Grafton is certainly worth a visit if only to see one of the prettiest villages in Warwickshire. Set in the midst of some gorgeous countryside the village has a varied architectural style ranging from honey-pot thatched cottages to red-brick terraces.

Located approximately five miles to the west of Stratford-upon-Avon, Temple Grafton is one of the 'Shakespeare Villages' included in lines traditionally said to have been written by the playwright after a drinking binge in Bidford-upon-Avon. He calls the village 'Hungry Grafton'. It is sometimes suggested the 'hungry' tag was inspired by the poorness of the soil here and consequent harvest failures. It is a village of ancient roots. The Knights Hospitallers were granted land here in 1189 and ruled as lords of the manor until 1540 when the land was transferred to the Crown.

If William and Anne married here it would have been in the church of St Andrew. The present building dates only from 1875, however there has been a place of worship on this site since at least the thirteenth century when the Knights Hospitaller built a chapel here. The church today is Victorian Gothic with arched windows and a tall spire. Its grey façade is softened by brown stonework around the borders of the windows. According to Pevsner, the new church was modelled on the fourteenth-century style of architecture so the church building in which Shakespeare and Anne married may have looked similar. The ceremony would have taken place in the church porch in full view of the parishioners, after which the party would have moved inside for prayers.

It was the beginning of a marriage that continues to attract much speculation but it is unlikely that the truth about their relationship will ever be known. Until the unlikely event that historians unearth any correspondence between the two, Anne Shakespeare will remain a peripheral character in Shakespeare's story.

*Visitor Information*

The church of St Andrew's is open every day and invites visitors to take a look inside.

Nearby, the Shakespearean-sounding Blue Boar Inn offers food as well as accommodation. Serving the thirsty folk of Temple Grafton since 1600, the pub offers a menu of freshly cooked food. The patio garden enjoys views over the nearby countryside. Call 01789 750010 for details.

# The Lost Years

## Where's Willy?

> I would there were no age between ten and
> three-and-twenty, or that youth would sleep out
> the rest; for there is nothing in the between but
> getting wenches with child, wronging the
> ancientry, stealing, fighting...
> *The Winter's Tale*: Shepherd, Act III, Scene III

Between 1585 and 1592 there is no record of Shakespeare's whereabouts and he effectively goes missing. This period has been the subject of fevered speculation about what he could have been doing, and some of the theories are very plausible, if not exactly provable. In the eighteenth century Samuel Johnson helped to perpetuate an old story that Shakespeare had spent time holding horses outside the playhouse. He asserted that:

In the time of Elizabeth, coaches being yet uncommon, and hired coaches not at all in use, those who were too proud, too tender, or too idle to walk, went on horseback to any distant business or diversion. Many came on horseback to the play, and when Shakespear fled to London from the terrour of a criminal prosecution, his first expedient was to wait at the door of the play-house, and hold the horses of those that had no servants, that they might be ready again after the performance.

Johnson's tale was just one of several romantic explanations for Shakespeare's absence from the records.

Another theory suggests that he was travelling abroad, expanding his horizons and gaining firsthand knowledge of the exotic locations that would provide the settings in some of his plays – Rousillon, Paris, Navarre, Rome, Padua, Verona, Venice and Elsinore. The problem with this is the lack of local colour in the plays. He writes about people, not places. The settings are just incidental backdrops to the story. He also made an infamous blunder about the geography of Bohemia, giving the landlocked region a coastline.

Then there are those who support the theory Shakespeare was a secret Catholic and that he spent time on pilgrimage to Rome. Several mysterious signatures appear in the visitors' book at the English College, the seminary for English priests. In 1585 one 'Arthuris Stratfordus Wigomniensis' signed the book. The College says the name roughly translates as 'King Arthur's Compatriot from Stratford in the diocese of Worcester.' Four years later the signature of one 'Gulielmus Clerkue Stratfordiensis', or 'William the Clerk from Stratford' appears. Regardless of whether he was Catholic, Protestant, or neither, William Shakespeare was the father of small children at this time and money would have been tight. Is it likely that Anne Hathaway would have allowed him to go gallivanting off to Rome?

The more likely scenario is that he was in London. In 1592

the playwright Robert Greene wrote a scathing pamphlet, *The Groatsworth of Wit*, in which he complains about an

> upstart crow beautified with our feathers, that with his tiger's heart wrapped in a player's hide supposes he is as well able to bombast out a blank verse as the best of you: and being an absolute Johannes fac totum, is in his own conceit the only Shake-scene in a country.

Greene was furious. He saw players as mere puppets. They were not supposed to write plays, especially not if they lacked a university education. *'Johannes fac totum'* roughly translates as Jack-of-all-trades, a contemptuous slur on this multi talented rival. The 'tiger's heart wrapped in a player's hide' is a reference to a line in *Henry VI, Part III*. By 1592 Shakespeare may have written all three parts of the *Henry VI* trilogy.

The date of his arrival in the capital is another source of uncertainty but writers such as Anthony Holden suggest that he may have joined the Queen's Men in 1587 when they passed through Stratford-upon-Avon. The company was in the midst of a fractious tour of the provinces. They were short-staffed as a result of an argument in Thame, Oxfordshire, which resulted in John Towne stabbing William Knell to death. Towne pleaded self-defence and was pardoned by the company's patron, the queen herself. When they arrived in Stratford Shakespeare may have seized the opportunity to join them. This seems to be the most straightforward and plausible theory but does not account for all his absences from the records.

The timescale of the so called 'Lost Years' are rather fluid and some scholars suggest an earlier period starting in the late 1570s. In the short gap between 1578 when he left school and 1582 when he conceived his first child, he went off the radar. Thanks to some intriguing seventeenth-century gossip and the last will and testament of a dying man, Shakespeare's name has become linked to two of our most beautiful country houses. It is these locations that we shall be exploring now.

## Hoghton Tower

I rather would entreat thy company
To see the wonders of the world abroad,
Than, living dully sluggardized at home,
Wear out thy youth with shapeless idleness.
*The Two Gentlemen of Verona*: Valentine, Act I, Scene I

### Shakeshafte in Lancashire

Hoghton Tower in Lancashire stands high on a windswept hill roughly halfway between Preston and Blackburn. At 650 feet above sea level its sweeping views extend to the Lake District in the north and the Welsh mountains to the south-west. There has been a building on this site since 1109 when the de Walters family, who came over with the Normans, constructed a fortress here. In 1150 the de Walters changed their name to de Hoghton to reflect the name of the local area.

The present building dates from 1565 and was built by Thomas de Hoghton who was a recusant Catholic. Tired of the penal laws, he eventually left for France where he died in exile in 1580. He left the house to his brother Alexander. When the Jesuit priest Edmund Campion arrived on English soil that year with a mission to save his countrymen's souls, one of the houses he stayed at was Hoghton Tower. Alexander Hoghton hosted him over the Easter of 1581 just months before Campion's arrest. Alexander died that September but he left behind a will that intrigues and fascinates Shakespeare scholars. For it may give a clue as to what the teenage William Shakespeare was doing. The will states that he would like his half brother Thomas Hoghton to have his musical instruments and play clothes, if he sees fit to keep players. He continues:

And if he will not keep players, then it is my will that Sir Thomas Hesketh, knight, shall have the same instruments and play clothes. And I most heartily require the said Sir Thomas to be friendly unto Fulk Gillam and William Shakeshafte now dwelling with me, and either to take them into his service or else to help them to some good master, as my trust is he will.

Name spellings were not yet standardised so it cannot be ruled out that this player, William Shakeshafte, was a fifteen-year-old boy from Henley Street.

The theory of Shakespeare embedding himself in another household is backed up by John Aubrey who wrote in the seventeenth century that Shakespeare had spent time as a schoolmaster in the country. He got this gossip from the son of Kit Beeston, one of Shakespeare's fellow players in the King's Men, but does not say in which household, to the eternal frustration of researchers and biographers. If that household was indeed Hoghton then that gives us just one of many reasons to pay a visit.

As you travel up the long driveway towards Hoghton Tower, the imposing gatehouse looms into view. Its grey stonework and battlements give it a rugged, martial feel. Through the stone archway of the gatehouse is the Lower Courtyard which leads down two flights of steps into the Inner Courtyard. Straight ahead is the King's Hall through which James I is said to have ridden his horse during a three-day visit in 1617. He then rode upstairs in search of a suitable bedchamber in which to sleep before settling on a room which is now known as the King's Bedchamber. During his stay he dined in the Banqueting Hall and it was in here that he is said to have knighted a loin of beef, dubbing it 'Sir Loin.' If Shakespeare spent time here as one of Alexander Hoghton's players, this is likely to be the room in which he performed. The minstrels' gallery is at one end of the large wood-panelled hall. An open fireplace is set into the side of the wall, giving the impression that this would have been a cosy and inviting place in which to enjoy music and revels in the depths of a Lancashire winter.

On display in the King's Bedchamber is the gown worn by Lady Philomena de Hoghton at the coronation of Elizabeth II in 1953. Scenes from the film *Last Tango in Paris* were shot in the marble-floored King's Hall. The house has a wonderful doll's house collection dating from the nineteenth and twentieth centuries. Ghost fans will enjoy the dungeons which are reputed to be haunted.

High up on the ramparts there are views stretching for miles around, from the grounds of the house to neighbouring counties and beyond. The stretch of greenery in front of the house is known as the Tilting Green after the medieval jousts which took place here. To the east of the house is a walled garden known as the Wilderness with smaller gardens nearby. The Great Barn dates from 1692.

*Visitor Information*

Hoghton Tower is located in Hoghton, near Preston, Lancashire PR5 0SH. Tel: 01254 852986.

Opening times vary depending on the season so call ahead before visiting or check the website at www.hoghtontower.co.uk/explore/take-a-tour.

Tickets cost £8.00 for adults, £6.00 for concessions and children and £2.20 for admission to the grounds only.

## Rufford Old Hall

> Stay, illusion!
> If thou hast any sound, or use of voice,
> Speak to me:
> If there be any good thing to be done,
> That may to thee do ease and grace to me,
> Speak to me
>
> *Hamlet*: Horatio, Act I, Scene I

*Helped to a Good Master*

Our next destination is said to be one of the most haunted buildings in England. People have reported seeing the ghost of a man in Elizabethan costume loitering in the great hall near the site where a priest hole was uncovered in 1949. As well as the loitering priest, other restless spirits include that of Elizabeth I and a ubiquitous 'grey lady.' Considering his reputed connection with the house, maybe the ghost of William Shakespeare should also join the list.

Rufford Old Hall lies in the flat pastures of south west Lancashire, five miles from the town of Ormskirk. Started in 1530 by the Hesketh family, it was originally a three-winged manor house until the west wing burned down. The oldest part of the building is the original great hall, while the east wing dates from the seventeenth century. Until his death in 1588 this was the home of Sir Thomas Hesketh, a rich landowner who adhered to the Catholic faith albeit as a 'church papist', one who conformed outwardly to the state religion while continuing to hear illegal

Masses at home. He was arrested on several occasions for failing to bring his wife Alice to church with him. In 1581 he was arrested as a 'disaffected papist.' That year, his neighbour Alexander Hoghton died and recommended to Hesketh's care the players Fulk Gillam and William Shakeshafte. Local legend has it that Shakespeare moved here for a short while after his time at Hoghton Tower. He would not have stayed long, even if the legend is true, as the following year he was in Stratford with his new wife Anne Hathaway.

The focal point of Rufford Old Hall is its timber-framed Great Hall with its intricate wall carvings. The eye is drawn to the wooden hammer-beamed roof where a legion of carved angels stands guard, shields held aloft as if ready for combat. From the skylight, broad beams of sunlight bathe the hall in a celestial haze. Various suits of armour are displayed along the walls. At the eastern end of the flagstone floor is an original wooden screen. Might this have been used as the backdrop to performances in the Great Hall? Shakespeare may have entertained the Hesketh family in this space as they dined. The high table would have been located at the western end and the Heskeths would have entered the hall from the family apartments in the west wing, which is now missing, via a connecting passage.

In the adjoining Dining Room there is a table laden with food and candles, set out as if Sir Thomas Hesketh's descendants were about to sit down to dinner. Examples of sixteenth and seventeenth-century oak furniture are everywhere, as well as tapestries and family portraits.

Outside there are fourteen acres of grounds to explore including the gardens which are laid out to emulate the formal style of the late Victorian and early Edwardian eras. Two topiary squirrels add a charming, Alice in Wonderland-like feel. The nearby orchard has been around since the sixteenth century and still grows varieties such as the Scotch Bridget and the Keswick Codling. It is nice to think of the young Shakespeare going scrumping here, perhaps in company with his colleague Fulk Gillam. Visitors can also stroll along the section of the Leeds and Liverpool Canal which passes close to the grounds, watching the wild fowl and listening to the water lapping against the boats as they pass by.

*Visitor Information*

Ruffold Old Hall is located at 200 Liverpool Road, Rufford, near Ormskirk, Lancashire L40 1SG. Tel: 01704 821251.

Opening hours are variable so please call before travelling or check the website at www.nationaltrust.org.uk/rufford-old-hall/opening-times.

Access to the whole property including house and grounds costs £8.40 for adults and £4.30 for children, with a family ticket costing £21.00.

The village of Rufford itself is worth a look with its pretty tea shops and cafés. You may also wish to raise a glass to Sir Thomas Hesketh at the Hesketh Arms, an inn which dates from the late eighteenth century.

ACT TWO

# London

I hope to see London once ere I die

*Henry IV, Part II*: Davy, Act V, Scene III

We have now left the rural idylls of Warwickshire and Lancashire behind as we follow Shakespeare down to London and on to the next, dazzling stage of his career. Although he was born in Stratford and ultimately returned there to die, he spent most of his time living and working in the capital. Between the years 1592 and 1616 he lived variously in Bishopsgate, Southwark and Silver Street, near today's Barbican Centre, steadily working as an actor, playwright and poet. According to John Aubrey who heard it from the son of Kit Beeston, one of Shakespeare's fellow actors, 'he was not a company keeper; lived in Shoreditch; wouldn't be debauched.' Despite his lack of appetite for Falstaffian carousing, however, he would have been a familiar figure around town.

In this section we are going to visit some of London's quirky corners and hidden spaces in an attempt to seek him out. The journey will take us to the architectural remains of the

Shoreditch playhouses, as well as the bustling Bankside area with its theatres. We start our journey in the City, the oldest part of London and a place Shakespeare knew well.

Founded by the Romans in AD 50, the City boasts 2,000 years of history. Successive disasters such as the Great Fire of 1666 and the Blitz have led to centuries of regeneration and rebuilding. As you walk through its narrow streets, you will be struck by the eclectic jumble of architectural styles on show. Whilst it is true that most of the medieval and Tudor era buildings have gone, replaced with modern steel towers, or grand old Victorian designs, we still have ghostly remnants of an earlier age. Look out for ruined churchyards and crumbling monastery walls. The street plan, too, is essentially the same as it was before the Great Fire, so it is still possible to get a good feel for the Elizabethan layout and topography.

One of the joys of wandering around the city is noting the evocative names of the streets. Here we have Bread Street, Milk Street, Honey Lane, Ironmonger Lane, Friday Street and, simply, Poultry. All are reminders of the medieval trades which were conducted here. You also get a sense of how small Shakespeare's world was. London was still confined within the old Roman walls which encircled an area the size of just one square mile. In the year 1600, roughly the mid-way point of his career, the population was 200,000. Imagine all those people living cheek by jowl, crammed into such a small space. This was what Shakespeare understood as 'London.' The city's onward sprawl was a thing for the future. Hoxton was still a hamlet and there was no such thing as the West End.

It was a city of terrible contrast; both beauty and terror took prominent roles in everyday life. The people lived in the midst of glorious Gothic church architecture, amid a soundscape of bells and polyphonic singing. They could go to the playhouse and, for a penny, hear sublime poetry being spoken by famous actors such as Edward Alleyn and the knockabout clowning of Will Kempe. Conversely, if they turned into the cattle market at Smithfield, perhaps stepping over rivulets of blood and piles of dung from the terrified animals facing their slaughter, they might stumble upon a grisly execution. At London Bridge, the parboiled heads of traitors grinned down at the folk below.

The streets were narrow and noisome. Many of the houses Shakespeare knew had 'juttied' top floors which leaned into the narrow thoroughfares, crowding out the light and presumably giving the streets a feeling of darkness and claustrophobia. The widest street, Cheapside, was also its grandest, used for coronation processions and, by Shakespeare's day, inhabited by goldsmiths.

Today, the city is a booming centre of finance, perhaps a natural fate for a place built on international trade. The Romans chose this particular spot on the Thames to found their settlement because it was situated at the narrowest, shallowest place on the river and was therefore convenient to build a bridge, or crossing, to facilitate trade with the Roman Empire. Old London Bridge was completed in 1209 and spanned the Thames alone until 1750 when Westminster Bridge was built. In Shakespeare's day, theatregoers and revellers looking for fun on Bankside either crossed the river via the bridge or hailed a wherryman to row them over in a small passenger boat, known as a wherry. It is a strange thought that Bankside was not part of London at all but was located within the Clink and Paris Garden 'liberties' in the county of Surrey. We shall be exploring the delights of Bankside in this section, but for now, let us stay in London and explore the capital Shakespeare knew. The buildings may have changed but if you roam the streets on a quiet weekend, when all the office workers have gone home and the ghosts of the past return, there is still an eerie sense of what went before.

As with the Warwickshire chapter visitor information is given at the end of each section with contact details for the locations covered. Please double check opening times and admission prices before travelling.

# Guildhall

Treason is not inherited, my lord;
Or, if we did derive it from our friends,
What's that to me? My father was no traitor.

*As You Like It*: Rosalind, Act I, Scene III

*Show Trial*

This Gothic building is the hidden jewel of the Square Mile. Often over-looked by visitors due to its rather tucked-away location, it is well worth seeking out. The fact of its continued existence after six centuries of fire and bombs is a small miracle. Indeed it is the only secular building to have survived the Great Fire of London.

Started in 1430 in the reign of Henry VI by the master mason, John Croxton, the Guildhall is the centre of City of London governance. For six centuries, the Court of Common Council has held its meetings in the Great Hall to discuss the everyday business of running the City. The Lord Mayor, who oversees proceedings, is sworn in annually during the highly symbolic Silent Ceremony; so called because no words are spoken. Inside the hall, high above the ancient walls, are a series of chevron shaped windows; each etched with the name of one of the 800 plus Lord Mayors who have served since Henry Fitzailwyn was created the first in 1189. Other notable names include Geoffrey Boleyn, great grandfather to Anne, and a certain Richard Whittington, who was Lord Mayor in the fifteenth century.

Although this is a working building, the hall is open to the public so visitors are free to wander about and enjoy some truly awe-inspiring surroundings, often finding they have the place to themselves.

The eye is drawn to the West Gallery upon which sit the two monstrous figures of Gog and Magog, dressed in the garb of pre-Roman Britons. These particular sculptures date from the 1950s and replace an earlier set which was destroyed in 1940 when a bomb came through the roof and gutted the hall. Shakespeare would have been familiar with Gog and Magog, whose effigies were paraded about the city every November during the Lord Mayor's Show, a tradition which still continues today.

Another point of interest within the hall is a poignant list of names upon a white plaque. Lady Jane Grey, Thomas Cranmer, Roderigo Lopez and Henry Garnet are among those whose names appear. All have one thing in common – they were placed on trial in the Guildhall and then executed on charges of treason or heresy.

One name, however, is missing from this list of unfortunates; Edward Arden, kinsman to Shakespeare, was another victim of the religious squabbles which scarred Tudor England. On 16 December 1583 he stood inside the Guildhall and listened as the judges sentenced him to death by hanging, drawing and quartering. His alleged crime was to have conspired to kill Queen Elizabeth I in a dastardly plot which would see an end to Protestant rule in England and a return to the Catholic faith.

The Ardens were an ancient Catholic family from Park Hall in Warwickshire. It seems that Edward was unlucky enough to have made an enemy of the queen's favourite, Robert Dudley, the Earl of Leicester, who had entertained her majesty at his castle in Kenilworth in 1575. Edward attended the festivities but offended the Earl by declining to wear his livery and insulting him with accusations of adultery. Such a public snub would not be forgotten and Leicester soon saw his chance to destroy the Ardens.

One fateful day, Edward's son-in-law, John Somerville, set off for London telling everyone he was going to kill the queen. In the days of hanging, drawing and quartering this openness about his intentions – if they can be taken seriously, considering that he was widely considered to be mentally unstable – was unwise in the extreme. He was arrested at an inn and taken to the Tower of London. Under torture, he implicated Edward in his regicidal fantasy, leading to his father-in-law being dragged off to London and tortured at the Tower.

It is not clear why some important prisoners were tried at the Guildhall when others, such as the Gunpowder Plotters, Sir Thomas More and those accused of adultery with Anne Boleyn, were tried at Westminster. One theory is that the short journey from the Tower to the Guildhall gave prisoners less opportunity to escape, or indeed, be rescued. Nevertheless, Edward Arden was found guilty of treason and was executed at Smithfield on 20 December. His wife was sentenced to be hanged but she was reprieved.

Shakespeare's mother, Mary, was an Arden and the playwright was proud of his kinship with this illustrious, if tragic, family. In 1596 when he applied to the College of Arms for the right to be called a gentleman, he emphasised Mary's connection to the Ardens of Park Hall. Warwickshire was a small world and people were conscious of their ties of kinship. So when news of Edward's fate began to spread, the shockwaves would certainly have been felt in Henley Street. Shakespeare was nineteen at the time of Arden's downfall, newly-married and a father. It is unlikely that he attended the trial but when he later moved to London, the memory of what had happened to his kinsman here may have been fresh enough for the Guildhall to be a place of fascination and dread.

*Visitor information*

When it is not being used for council meetings or official functions, the Great Hall is open to visitors to wander around at will. As well as viewing Gog and Magog you may also wish to admire some of the flamboyant statues which celebrate statesmen and national heroes such as Horatio Nelson, the Duke of Wellington and William Pitt the Younger. The sculpture of Sir Winston Churchill has a cleverly designed face – on one side he looks very stern and on the other side he smiles benignly. Tradition has it that when new members of the Common Council are about to give their maiden speech, they rub Churchill's foot for luck. Most of the windows are post-war replacements after a bomb gutted the hall in 1940. The exception is a small window to the right of the main entrance. It dates from the construction of the hall in the fifteenth century and is made of cheap cow's horn rather than glass, which was more expensive and difficult to work. Incidentally the word *'lantern'* comes from *'lanthorn'*, from the days when the flame would be protected behind a film of boiled cow's horn. In Act V, Scene I of *A Midsummer Night's Dream*, Starveling uses a lanthorn to represent the moon, 'This lanthorn doth the horned moon present.'

Entrance to the hall is free but it is a working building so closes at short notice. Do call ahead on 0207 606 3030 to check if it is open on the day you wish to visit. The Guildhall complex also houses a fantastic library, founded by Dick Whittington in the fifteenth century, and the art gallery with its vast collection of works includes paintings by the Pre-Raphaelites. Downstairs lie the atmospheric remains of the Roman Amphitheatre.

See www.cityoflondon.gov.uk for an in-depth history of the City of London's governance, from Lord Mayors, Sheriffs and Aldermen to the Court of Common Council.

## The Theatre and The Curtain

> Now, my co-mates and brothers in exile,
> Hath not old custom made this life more sweet
> Than that of painted pomp?
> *As You Like It*: Duke Senior, Act II, Scene I

*Beyond the Pale*

Having had a taste of the brutality inflicted upon Elizabethan traitors, we are now going to step outside the old City walls and visit a pleasanter subject – the playhouses of Shoreditch.

What we know as a trendy district of East London was once a semi-rural beauty spot, dotted with cottages and parkland. With London becoming ever more crowded, the wealthy were starting to build second homes outside the City walls where the air was sweeter. In an age of plague it was a good idea to have a country bolthole.

For reasons of their own, the theatre companies were also considering the move. London was becoming positively hostile for those in the playmaking business. Successive mayors, in their puritanical zeal, hindered life to such an extent that in 1576 James Burbage, manager of the Chamberlain's Men company, decided that they too would head for the fields beyond the City walls. It was an effective exile, although not a harmful one. He settled upon the 'liberty' of Shoreditch which was outside the jurisdiction of the city. Having sourced a plot of land from landlord Giles Allen, he signed a lease of twenty-one years. There, within the grounds of the dissolved Holywell Priory, he raised The Theatre, and thus began a golden age of drama.

Despite some sniping from Puritan preachers such as John Stockwood, who stood at Paul's Cross in 1578 to rail against what he called that 'gorgeous playing place erected in the fields,' The Theatre thrived and was swiftly followed by another playhouse, The Curtain, which was erected nearby. Far from being seen as a threat, this interloper was accepted and the two ventures acted in a spirit of cooperation with each other. When Burbage dismantled The Theatre in 1598, his company moved into The Curtain on a temporary basis while the Globe was constructed on Bankside. It was at The Curtain that the Chamberlain's Men performed plays such as *Henry V* and *Romeo and Juliet*.

As you walk down Curtain Road today, the traffic roaring in your ears, it is difficult to sense any trace of Shakespeare's presence. The locals – office workers and hipsters – dash about their business as if this were just another street in London. The only tribute to the district's theatrical legacy is a small plaque outside a modern building which marks the approximate location of The Theatre. It seems, however, that Shoreditch may soon be firmly back on the Shakespeare map.

In 2008, the Museum of London Archaeology (MOLA) was investigating a site at New Inn Yard, just off Curtain Road, when they uncovered the remains of an intriguing structure. It was polygonal in shape, echoing The Rose, a playhouse on Bankside. Fragments of the outer walls remained and it had a gravelled yard. The fact that it was so close to the assumed location of The Theatre meant that this had to be Burbage's playhouse. A media frenzy ensued with actors such as Sir Ian McKellen and Paul McGann paying visits to the site. Four years later, MOLA completed the puzzle. During a dig at a site in Hewett Street they unearthed what they believe to be the remains of The Curtain although, unlike The Rose and The Theatre, this particular structure is square-shaped.

Developers hope to bring both sites back to their original use. The Hackney Planning committee has given planning permission for the site of The Theatre to be transformed into a six-storey building with café and theatre space. Visitors will be able to view the archaeological remains through a glass floor. There are similar plans for The Curtain where developers hope to build a 250 seat open air performance space. As with The Theatre, the archaeological remains will be underneath a glass floor.

Both projects are currently a work in progress but will be an exciting addition to the Shakespeare Trail once completed.

*Visitor information*

At the time of writing the rediscovered playhouses are subject to planning applications so are not yet open to the public but you may find it interesting to visit the area and enjoy the witty Shakespeare themed graffiti on the hoardings outside The Theatre.

The easiest way to get there is to take the tube to Liverpool Street Station (Central Line) and exit out onto Bishopsgate. Turn left and walk down the busy road until it becomes Norton Folgate, a rather shabby strip of boarded up shops and takeaways where Christopher Marlowe once lived. Turn left onto Worship Street then right onto Curtain Road. Continue for approximately 50 yards until you reach Hewitt Street on your left. The uninspiring warehouses mark the approximate site of The Curtain.

Retrace your steps back onto Curtain Road and turn right, continuing in the same direction. Note Holywell Lane to your right, a sign that we are now entering the precincts of the old priory and nearing the site of The Theatre. Carefully cross Great Eastern Street and take the first right onto New Inn Yard then turn left into New Inn Broadway. This is the site of The Theatre, or the original Globe, as the bright graffiti on the hoardings calls it.

It is also worth noting that Hoxton Square is a short walk away. It was somewhere in Hoxton that Shakespeare's friend and rival, Ben Jonson, killed his fellow actor Gabriel Spencer in a swordfight in 1598. To avoid the gallows Jonson successfully pleaded 'benefit of clergy', an antiquated custom which allowed the felon to prove he was literate by reading a passage from the Bible in return for mercy. A memorial plaque to Gabriel Spencer was erected in 1913 at the church of St Leonard's, Shoreditch nearby. Other members of the Early Modern theatre scene buried at St Leonards are James and Richard Burbage, and the comedian Richard Tarlton.

Hoxton and Shoreditch are replete with interesting bars and cafés where you can rest your feet and refuel for the next adventure.

## St Paul's Cathedral

> Lord Polonius: What do you read, my lord?
> Hamlet: Words, words, words.
> Lord Polonius: What is the matter, my lord?
> Hamlet: Between who?
> Lord Polonius: I mean, the matter that you read, my lord.
> *Hamlet*: Act II, Scene II

## The Book Trade

It is usually assumed that Shakespeare was not all that concerned about getting his plays into print. As the mere writer of the works he did not own the copyright and therefore did not profit from book sales in the way that modern writers do. His money came from the playhouse box office. There was nothing to stop anyone else from printing his plays however and indeed there is evidence to suggest that some of the actors in *Henry V* sold a bastardised version of the play to a publisher. The so-called 'bad quarto' of the play appeared in the year 1600, printed by Thomas Creede at his shop on Carter Lane. Some scholars think the text was derived from reported speech – someone remembering the lines and relaying them to the best of his memory. Unfortunately the mystery entrepreneurs seem to have suffered from faulty powers of recollection because this version bears little relation to the text in the First Folio. It is much shorter for a start. Lines are misattributed or jumbled up and the stage directions are all askew. The two characters in the play whose lines are perfect are those of Gower and Exeter, leading some writers to think that the text was sold by whoever it was that played those parts. Maybe they were penniless bit-players who needed to earn some cash. Whoever they were evidently acted against the wishes of the Chamberlain's Men for the Stationer's Company noted that any further copies should 'be staied.' Was this Shakespeare's attempt at protecting his literary reputation?

Thomas Creede's print shop was located on Carter Lane directly opposite the churchyard of St Paul's Cathedral. He was in good company as the whole churchyard was a colony of booksellers and printers. Their wooden stalls lined the walls of the cathedral and spilled out into the lanes beyond. The book trade had been centred here since the Dissolution when the outbuildings at St Paul's were sold off and put to secular use.

The whole area would have felt like a flea market or car boot sale with people browsing for the latest news pamphlet, religious tract or book of poetry. This would undoubtedly have been one of Shakespeare's regular haunts.

Today the churchyard of St Paul's Cathedral is one of those unexpected green oases in the City of London. As you enter through the gate on New Change you are drawn into a beautifully landscaped space dotted with old headstones, trees and monuments. Its tranquillity is in fabulous contrast to the manic street traffic outside. On fine days it is a popular place for tourists to while away an afternoon in the sun-dappled shade of the plane trees. An easily missed feature in the churchyard is a small paved octagon on the ground to the eastern end of the cathedral. It contains the words, 'Here Stood Paul's Cross' and marks the site of the medieval pulpit from where speakers would make public announcements such as royal births and military victories. If a royal child was born people would hear about it at Paul's Cross. It was here in 1588 that the defeat of the Spanish Armada was announced to a jubilant crowd. The oral dissemination of news was important in the days of low literacy rates, so much so that the Victorian writer Thomas Carlyle justifiably described Paul's Cross as the 'Times Newspaper of the Middle Ages'. It was also a place of spectacle and visual propaganda from where the ideas of the reformation communicated with great impact. The Catholic fight back was also conducted here; in 1521 Cardinal Wolsey conducted a book burning of the reformer Martin Luther's writings. Erected in the late fifteenth century, Paul's Cross survived until the Civil War when the Puritans tore it down.

The cathedral that towered over the booksellers – and the book burners – was a very different building to Sir Christopher Wren's baroque creation. Started in 1087 it was built in the medieval Romanesque style with arched windows and flying buttresses. A tall spire soared above the tower until 1561 when it was destroyed by fire. By Shakespeare's day the cathedral was a crumbling shadow of its former self, the aisles filled with hawkers and merchants. The central aisle, Paul's Walk, was a popular shortcut for those on their way to and from Cheapside. People used it as a meeting place, even bringing horses inside.

In 1666 the Great Fire of London razed it to the ground in a conflagration that endured over three days. The cathedral we see today is Sir Christopher Wren's masterpiece. The great dome stands 365 feet above ground level and affords dizzying views of the city. Inside, there is a feeling of lightness and space. The floor is laid with black and white marble tiles in a distinctive chequerboard design. In Wren's concession to the dawn of enlightenment the large windows are mostly absent of stained glass, allowing the clear light of day to stream in. Back out in the churchyard, a paved area to the south of the cathedral shows part of the outline of the medieval building giving a sense of its alignment.

The statue of Queen Anne at the front of the cathedral is a Victorian replacement of the original which was erected in 1712. Anne was the reigning monarch at the time of Wren's building work. To the left-hand side of the statue (as you face the cathedral) is Temple Bar which is the only surviving city gate. It was located on the Strand between 1672 and 1878 and formed the western entrance to the city. Made of Portland stone it is thought to have been designed by Sir Christopher Wren. Look up at the statues of Charles I, Charles II, James I and his wife, Anne of Denmark, which stand in niches above the arch. Through Temple Bar is Paternoster Square where you will find a supermarket, public toilets and plenty of cafés.

*Visitor Information*

St Paul's Cathedral is located at St Paul's Churchyard, London, EC4M 8AD. Tel: 0207 246 8350.

Opening hours to the cathedral are Monday to Saturday, 8:30–16:30. On Sundays it is not open to sightseers but visitors are welcome to join a service.

Admission costs £18.00 for adults, £16.00 for concession and £8.00 for children aged between six and seventeen. There is a family ticket available for two adults and two children, costing £44.00. Tickets bought online attract a slightly cheaper rate. See www.stpauls.co.uk/visits/sightseeing-times-prices for details.

The cathedral crypt is free to enter and contains a café and gift shop.

# College of Arms

> Take but degree away, untune that string,
> And, hark, what discord follows!
>> *Troilus and Cressida*: Ulysses, Act I, Scene III

*Non Sanz Droict*

On the corner of Peter's Hill and Queen Victoria Street in the City of London is an ancient red-bricked building. It is in a slightly set back position, standing behind a row of ornate black railings and is often over looked by people hurrying to cross over onto the Millennium Bridge. This is the College of Arms and this particular incarnation of the building has stood here since 1671. Its function is to process applications for coats of arms for both individuals and corporations and also to help organise state events such as coronations. The College has a long and fascinating history. It was founded in 1484 in the reign of Richard III and is made up of a colourful cast of officers with titles evoking the age of chivalry: Clarenceux King of Arms, Windsor Herald, Rouge Dragon Pursuivant and Portcullis Pursuivant are among the officers still working there today. These names are a reminder of the College's medieval roots when the heralds acted as stage managers at jousting tournaments, marshalling the contestants and announcing them as they rode into the lists. The knights taking part were identified by their coats of arms which were worn over their armour so the heralds needed to be familiar with each one. In time their role expanded to cover genealogy and the research of family pedigrees as well as allowing applications for coats of arms.

Like Ulysses in *Troilus and Cressida*, the Tudors were serious about upholding the divisions in rank that helped keep an ordered society. The sense of honour that came with the award of a coat of arms cannot be underestimated. It came with the right to be called gentleman and to wear a sword, both important signifiers of status in an age obsessed with class. In 1568 John Shakespeare, the playwright's father and High Bailiff of Stratford-upon-Avon, put in an application for a coat of arms, but for whatever reason, possibly the expense, he did not follow through with it. The claim was revived in 1596 when William Shakespeare, now prospering in London, tried again on behalf of his father. This time the application was successful with the heralds noting that John Shakespeare's great grandfather had done Henry VII 'faithful and approved service', possibly of a military nature. Three years later Shakespeare applied for the arms to be crossed with those of the Ardens at Park Hall.

Shakespeare's coat of arms is a yellow shield shot through diagonally by a black banner and silver spear. The accompanying motto is the defensive-sounding 'Non Sanz Droict', which is Norman French for 'not without right.' He clearly believed that the Shakespeare lineage merited this honour. Not everyone agreed. Ben Jonson, writing pettishly in the 1599 play *Every Man Out of His Humour*, misquotes the motto as *not without mustard* and has the character Sogliardo boast, 'I' faith I thank God I can write myself a gentle man now; here's my patent, it cost me thirty pound by this breath.' Jonson is teasing Shakespeare as a bourgeois social climber. When Shakespeare visited in 1596, utmost in his mind would have been the desire that the name Shakespeare be finally recognised. He needn't have worried on that score.

The building that he knew was built in the late fifteenth century and was formed of a quadrangle. It was home to Margaret Beaufort from 1500 and was eventually gifted to the College in 1555. A carved portcullis can still be seen on the wall which Pevsner says may date from Margaret Beaufort's time.

*Visitor information*

The College of Arms is located at 130 Queen Victoria Street, London EC4V 4BT. Tel: 0207 248 2762.

It is open to the public and welcomes visitors free of charge from Monday to Friday 10:00–16:00. Highlights include the Earl Marshall's Court and an outstanding portrait collection of the Officers of Arms. With prior notice it is sometimes possible to arrange for one of the heralds to be there and answer questions. Guided tours or groups of up to twenty people can also be arranged.

# St Helens Bishopsgate

*Tax dodger*

The lives of illiterate people in early modern England usually went unrecorded unless they were getting married or were about to be punished. Scores of ordinary citizens living unremarkable lives have disappeared without written trace, as if they had never existed. Shakespeare, for all his reams of poetry, left so little in the way of personal evidence behind him it is as if he too wanted to fade into the same obscurity. Unlike the garrulous Robert Greene, Thomas Nashe and Ben Jonson, he did not write any long, rambling, self important pamphlets. His letters to Anne Hathaway – and he must have written them – have all disappeared. This has made it difficult at times to place his whereabouts at certain stages in his career but thankfully for us, in the years 1597 and 1598, he found himself on a list of tax dodgers in the parish of St Helen, Bishopsgate. The collectors were unable to find him at his address and listed him as an evader. This is our first record of Shakespeare's residence in London.

Located in the north east of the City, Bishopsgate was an area of transience and movement. Several large coaching inns lined Bishopsgate Street serving those travelling to and from far off counties such as Suffolk and Cambridgeshire. It was also conveniently close to Shoreditch and The Theatre. Shakespeare, newly arrived from the country and perhaps still getting his bearings, would have had a short stroll out of Bishopsgate, up Norton Folgate where Kit Marlowe had lived, and into the fields beyond where the playhouses stood.

The buildings have changed beyond anything that Shakespeare would recognise but if he came back today and ventured down Bishopsgate turning left into Great St Helen's, he would recognise the medieval parish church. It stands stoically beneath the giant Gherkin building, a silent witness to centuries of change and regeneration. Shakespeare would have attended St Helen's during his residence in the parish so it is well worth a visit, not least to view the Shakespeare window of 1884 in which he stands resplendent in a red doublet and white ruff, a book in one hand and his green cloak slung rakishly over one shoulder. The church itself is an unusual shape. It has the appearance of two churches that have been pushed together, side by side, which in a way is exactly what happened. When a Benedictine nunnery was founded within the grounds of the parish church in 1210, the nuns extended the church by building their own nave next to the existing one so that the local congregation could worship alongside them, albeit separated by a screen. The nuns were evicted in 1538 during the Dissolution of the Monasteries, and the screen was taken down a few years later.

Stepping inside St Helens is like entering a miniature Westminster Abbey. Elizabethan monuments such as the tomb chest of Sir Thomas Gresham and that of Sir William Pickering, suitor to Elizabeth I, lie in the shadows beneath the arches. Another tomb remembers the rich city merchant Sir John Crosby who died in 1476. Crosby owned the magnificent Crosby Place, located nearby. He rented it to Richard, Duke of Gloucester, who kept his household there in the days before he became Richard III. Shakespeare, living in his new Bishopsgate digs, would have been familiar with Crosby Place. The grand merchant's house was evidently a source of fascination because he mentions it several times in the early play *Richard III*. Here is Richard instructing the hired thugs who are about to drown Clarence in a vat of malmsey:

Gloucester: Are you now going to dispatch this deed?
First murderer: We are, my lord, and come to have the warrant,
That we may be admitted where he is.
Gloucester: Well thought upon; I have it here about me.
(*Gives the warrant*)
When you have done, repair to Crosby Place.

*Richard III*: Act I, Scene III

In 1908 Crosby Place was moved brick by brick from its Bishopsgate location and re-sited in Cheney Walk, Chelsea, where it is now in private hands, augmented by the addition of mock-Tudor wings on each side of the fifteenth-century building.

As for Shakespeare and the tax collectors, they eventually caught up with him just over the river in the county of Surrey where he duly paid his outstanding debt. This was a time of great change for Shakespeare. The Chamberlain's Men were about to lose the lease on the land in Shoreditch. It was time to move to Bankside.

*Visitor Information*

Great St Helens is an active church which holds lots of classes and reading groups so its opening hours are limited to Monday to Friday, 9:30–12:30. It also opens on the occasional afternoon on Mondays, Wednesdays and Fridays. Entrance is through the church office where a friendly guide will welcome you and show you into the nave, allowing you to soak up the wonderfully Gothic thirteenth-century atmosphere. For up-to-date opening times call 0207 783 2231.

The nearest tube is Liverpool Street Station. Close by is the church of St Andrew Undershaft, most of which dates from around 1520. Its unusual name derives from the huge maypole outside which towered above the church. St Andrew was literally under the shaft. Following the 'Evil May Day' riots of 1517 the maypole was taken down and later destroyed as a pagan idol. Inside can be seen the memorial bust of John Stow, who wrote the *Survey of London* of 1598. This was his parish church and he described it as 'fair and beautiful.' The bust shows him sitting at a desk, eyes cast downwards as he writes. In his hand is a real feather quill pen. Every three years his livery company, the Merchant Taylors, replaces the pen in a solemn ceremony attended by the Lord Mayor.

The church is administered by its neighbour, the church of St Helen's Bishopsgate who use it for meetings and classes, therefore it is not generally open to the public but visits can sometimes be arranged with prior notice. Call the St Helen's office for more information.

# The Rose

What's in a name? That which we call a rose by any other name would smell as sweet.

*Romeo and Juliet*: Juliet, Act II, Scene II

## Blood and Beauty

We saw earlier how The Theatre and The Curtain have ongoing planning applications to bring them back into some kind of use. One archaeological project which remains defiantly open to visitors, despite the odds, is The Rose on Bankside. Usually associated with the enigmatic and tragic figure of Christopher Marlowe who pioneered blank verse and whose hubristic flights of fancy gave us Doctor Faustus and Tamburlaine, there is also evidence that the theatre hosted Shakespeare in the early days of his career.

Built in 1587 by the entrepreneur and property developer Philip Henslowe on the site of a Bankside tenement, The Rose was the first purpose-built playhouse south of the Thames. It was an astute choice of location. Elizabethan Bankside was London's entertainment district, a heady underworld of brothels, gambling houses and bear-baiting rings where citizens flocked to indulge their pleasures.

With all this bloodlust and illicit activity it is tempting to imagine the arrival of Bankside's first theatre as having a civilising effect on the district. This would be a mistake. We know from Henslowe's diary that one of the plays performed there was Shakespeare's gruesome tragedy, *Titus Andronicus,* on 21 January 1594. With all its murders and mutilations, *Titus* perfectly complimented the offerings found elsewhere on Bankside

> Titus Andronicus: Will't please you to eat?
> Tamora: Why hast thou slain thine only daughter thus?
> Titus Andronicus: Not I; 'twas Chiron and Demetrius:
> They ravished her, and cut away her tongue;
> And they, 'twas they, that did her all this wrong.
> Saturninus: Go fetch them hither to us presently.
> Titus Andronicus: Why, there they are both, baked in that pie;
> Whereof their mother daintily hath fed.
> Eating the flesh that she herself hath bred.
> 'Tis true, 'tis true; witness my knife's sharp point.
> (*Kills Tamora*)
>
> *Titus Andronicus*: Act IV, Scene III

The Elizabethan drama scene was as much a theatre of blood as anything found in the bear pits.

It is also fair to say that The Rose was a proving ground for Shakespeare. Writers such as Stephen Greenblatt convincingly suggest that the young playwright was influenced by Marlowe's blank verse style. Perhaps Shakespeare was among the audience at The Rose in 1592, watching with a critical eye as *The Jew of Malta* unfolded on stage. In that same year, *Henry VI, Part I* was part of the repertoire at The Rose. There is no documentary evidence to say that Shakespeare and Marlowe ever met but London was a small world and it would be surprising if two playwrights, both working from the same venue did not occasionally rub shoulders. Marlowe was stabbed in the eye the following year.

For a period of approximately thirteen years The Rose enjoyed its heyday as the premier playhouse of Bankside. This came to end in 1599 when the Chamberlain's Men muscled in and built The Globe almost next door. Henslowe could not compete and moved his company north to Shoreditch where he started again with a brand new playhouse, The Fortune.

Excavations by MOLA (Museum of London Archaeology) in 1989 revealed The Rose to be polygonal in shape with a central yard where the groundlings would stand. It had tiered galleries for those who could afford a seat. The team also uncovered a string of rosary beads, a gentleman's ring, a cuttlefish, grape seeds and numerous discarded nutshells. Such personal items are a poignant reminder that this was a place where humans gathered together to hear stories, to learn and be entertained.

Thanks to the effort of fundraisers and volunteers, The Rose today is no empty shell. It hosts theatre companies on a regular basis ensuring not only that this delicate space retains its original purpose but also raises vital funds for its continuing preservation. Approximately two-thirds of the site has been uncovered and The Rose Theatre Trust hopes to raise the funds needed to uncover the remaining third. At present the site is open only once a week but the aim is to turn the site into a permanent exhibition. The Shakespeare in Love musical company recently held a fundraising gala with one anonymous individual making a £10,000 donation.

*Visitor Information*

The Rose Theatre Trust holds open days each Saturday when visitors can view the archaeology and enjoy a talk by one of the expert guides. Entry is free but they welcome donations. If you come to see one of the many theatre productions hosted here, be sure to wear plenty of layers; this being a delicate archaeological site there is no heating and it can get quite chilly. For the same reason there are no public toilets so the venue advises patrons to use the loos at the nearby Globe before settling down to enjoy the show.

To reach the site on foot from the direction of The Globe, turn right onto Bear Gardens and follow the chalky arrows along the cobbled lane until you reach the Globe Education Sackler Studios on the left. Turn left onto Park Street and within a few yards, just before the bridge you will see its black door festooned with theatre flyers and a blue plaque on the grey wall. Call 0207 261 9565 for details or visit www.rosetheatre.org.uk.

## Shakespeare's Globe

> Nor shall this peace sleep with her; but as when
> The bird of wonder dies, the maiden phoenix,
> Her ashes new create another heir
> As great in admiration as herself.
>
> *Henry VIII*: Cranmer, Act V, Scene V

*This Wooden 'O'*

Shakespeare never set foot in our next location but its wooden walls and galleries are so steeped in his spirit it would be a strange thing to omit it from this book. Shakespeare's Globe is the successor to the playhouse raised in 1599 by Richard and Cuthbert Burbage, whose brilliant father James, founder of The Theatre, had died two years previously.

The story of how the Burbages fell out with Giles Allen, the owner of the Shoreditch land upon which The Theatre stood, is like something out of a dark comedy. Imagine a cold and frosty night in December 1598. A group of players stands guard outside The Theatre, their swords drawn defensively in case anyone should try to interfere in this night's work. Behind them a team of carpenters work quickly and without fuss, carefully dismantling the playhouse and stacking the timbers onto a waiting cart. The mood is decisive. If Giles Allen will not renew the lease on the land, they will simply take their playhouse elsewhere. The landlord is left fuming; a profitable enterprise has been swiped from under his nose and there is nothing he can do about it, except plead his case, unsuccessfully, at court. The vision of an angry cartoon character hopping from foot to foot is hard to resist.

The Chamberlain's Men erected their new playhouse, The Globe, on Bankside using the timbers from The Theatre. It was a new start for them. The Latin inscription above the door read, *'Totus mundus agit histrionem'* which roughly translates as *'All the world's a stage'*, echoing Jaques' line in *As You Like It* which was written in the same year. There is some disagreement as to which play was performed first at the new venue but thanks to the Swiss tourist Thomas Platter, we know that *Julius Caesar* was performed that September. Platter, who had crossed over to Bankside after lunch, described it as an 'excellent performance' with 'a cast of some fifteen people.'

We have more certainty as to which play was in progress on the day The Globe burned down. It was 29 June 1616 and the King's Men were performing *Henry VIII*. As the afternoon wore on, and Henry VIII entered Cardinal Wolsey's house, a cannon was fired in honour of the king. So thrilling was the spectacle that no-one noticed a stray spark land in the thatched roof. It began to smoulder, but according to eye witness Henry Wotton, the audience thought it '*but an idle smoak*' and had '*eyes more attentive the show.*' In less than an hour the whole edifice had burned to the ground. It was hastily rebuilt only to be torn down again by the Puritans in 1644.

Shakespeare's Globe, the modern replica, was constructed with as much doggedness and determination as Burbage had shown in 1598 when he was forced to dismantle The Theatre and bring it over to Bankside. It owes its existence to the vision and tenacity of Sam Wanamaker, the American actor who had been appalled to find nothing but a grimy old plaque on the approximate site of The Globe.

The designers cleverly built up a picture of what the original Globe would have looked like using scraps of evidence from contemporary sketches and prints as well as clues from within the plays, for example the wooden 'O' described in the prologue of *Henry V*, and of course the archaeology of the newly discovered Rose. With its lime-washed walls of English oak, reed-thatched roof, and hard wooden benches (you'd be advised to hire a cushion if you're sitting) Shakespeare's Globe is a good approximation of its forebear. Thankfully, modern health and safety standards mean that there is little chance of the building catching fire as it did in 1616. The walls are coated with fire retardant materials and before each performance the volunteer stewards do a fire drill and check all the passages and stairs for hazards.

A great emphasis is placed on authenticity and plays are often performed using original practices and pronunciation. As a patron, whether sitting in the galleries with a glass of wine or standing in the yard with the groundlings, this is as close as we can get to an authentic Elizabethan play-going experience and for that reason alone it is a must for anyone in search of Shakespeare.

*Visitor Information*

Performances in the outdoor theatre run from April to October. The recently opened Sam Wanamaker Playhouse is located downstairs and is open during the winter months with occasional summertime performances. Its design is based on Shakespeare's indoor playhouse at Blackfriars and its use of candlelight gives an eerily atmospheric quality to proceedings. Outside on the piazza there are stunning views of the River Thames and St Paul's Cathedral. The refreshment stalls on the piazza sell a range of drinks including Pimms, wine, beer and coffee. You may wish to eat at the Swan restaurant which has outdoor seating on the piazza and serves excellent food.

The Globe Exhibition has some very interesting displays which showcase early modern London and Shakespeare's place within it. Included in the ticket price is a tour of the theatre. Tickets: Adults, £13.50; Seniors, £12.00; Students, £11.00; Children aged between 5 and 18, £8. Opening hours: 9:00–17:30 every day except Christmas Day and Christmas Eve. The tours run every twenty minutes with the first at 9:30 and the last at 17:00. Contact: 0207 401 9919.

# St John's Gate

> Art made tongue tied by authority,
> And folly, doctor-like, controlling skill,
> And simple truth miscalled simplicity,
> And captain good attending captive ill.
>
> From Sonnet 66

*Passing the Censor*

Shakespeare's writing was scrutinised not just by playgoers at the Globe but by an establishment terrified of how it was portrayed to the masses. Our next location is a reminder of this unwelcome side to his working life.

St John's Gate is a picturesque anomaly seemingly dropped at random amidst the modern offices and studios of trendy Clerkenwell. Dating from 1504 when Henry VII was on the throne, it is all that remains of the medieval Priory of St John of Jerusalem which fell victim to the Dissolution of the Monasteries during the reign of the thrifty king's son, Henry VIII. It is only by a miracle that the gatehouse survives. In the 1550s, Edward Seymour had the priory church blown up so he could use the bricks to build Somerset House, his grand new palace on the Thames. Fortunately, the gatehouse was left intact and went on to have a very interesting Shakespearean connection.

Up until the mid-twentieth century the Lord Chamberlain acted as state censor and no play could be performed in public until it had passed his beady eye. Elizabethan and Jacobean playwrights had to present their work to the Master of the Revels who performed the office of censor on behalf of the Lord Chamberlain. For most of Shakespeare's working life, this official was a man called Edmund Tilney who was based within the priory complex. He had the power to veto performances and could authorise the imprisonment of anyone flouting his censorship. In practice this meant that when Shakespeare had written a play he, or a member of his company, would need to take it to St John's for perusal by Tilney. If he found anything within the text which could cause offence (especially to the monarch or the aristocracy) he would suggest changes. When the play was approved for performance, the company paid a fee for their license and rehearsals could begin.

It is sometimes suggested that Tilney was based within the gatehouse itself although this seems unlikely since he held such an important role and gatehouses were generally used by porters. It is more probable that he occupied one of the grander buildings within the precinct of the priory. What we do know is that Shakespeare, or one of his colleagues, would have walked beneath the archway en route to report to Tilney, perhaps anxiously clutching a rolled up manuscript and hoping it contained nothing to offend.

As you approach St John's Gate from Smithfield Market, passing the cafés and bars of St John's Street and turning left into the 'blink and you miss it' St John's Lane, you are suddenly greeted by the breathtaking, if incongruous, sight of its ancient stone archway complete with crenelations and Tudor bosses. Although the building's stone façade and interior were largely reconstructed by the Victorians, this is one London building which Shakespeare would be familiar with if he came back today.

*Visitor Information*

The gatehouse incorporates a museum dedicated to the work of the Order of St John and the history of the Knights Hospitaller from whom St John's Ambulance descends. Highlights of the museum include the Tudor era Council Chamber which lies directly at the centre of the gatehouse and which was used as a store room for hunting equipment by Henry VIII. Later, William Hogarth's father opened a coffee shop in the same room. It was a short-lived venture; its demise is possibly connected with the bizarre fact that customers were only allowed to communicate in Latin. For a peek inside join one of the informative and entertaining tours run by the volunteer guides. The tours include a peek into the Priory Church of St John, with its light, airy nave. The crypt dates from 1145.

The opening hours are from Monday to Saturday, 10:00–17:00.

Guided tours are held on Tuesdays, Fridays and Saturdays, at 11:00 and 14:30.

Entry is free but the museum suggests a donation of £5 for guided tours.

## Middle Temple Hall

I do not now fool myself, to let imagination jade me; for every reason excites me to this, that my lady loves me. She did commend my yellow stockings of late, she did praise my leg being cross gartered; and in this she manifests herself to my love ...

*Twelfth Night*: Malvolio, Act II, Scene V

*Twelfth Night*

On 2 February 1602, a student of the Middle Temple made a casual, throwaway entry in his diary. It was only a few lines, sandwiched between long accounts of the sermons he had heard at Paul's Cross, as well as family gossip, recipes for spring ale and a mysterious remedy for 'haymeroids' ('two ounces of shoemacke braide, and put it to halfe a pint of red rose water, warme them over the fire and bath the place with it').

For Shakespeare scholars, however, the most interesting entry is this

'At our feest we had a play called 'Twelve Night' or 'What you Will', much like the Commedy of Errores, or Menechmi in Plautus, but most like and neere to that in Italian called Inganni. A good practice in it to make the Steward believe his Lady the widdowe was in love with him, by counterfeyting a letter as from his Lady in general terms, telling him what she liked best in him, and prescribing his gesture in smiling, his apparaile, &c, and then when he came to practice making him beleeue they took him to be mad.

John Manningham had just witnessed what was possibly the first ever performance of *Twelfth Night*. In his excitement at remembering the cruel trick played on Malvolio he omits to tell us which part Shakespeare played that evening but we can be fairly certain that he was there in some capacity. The students' Candlemas 'feest' was held in Middle Temple Hall, a beautiful Elizabethan survival complete with double hammer-beamed roof. The walls are adorned with coats of arms and wood panelling from Windsor Forest. The dining table in the middle of the hall is known as the 'cup board' and the wood reputedly comes from Sir Francis Drake's galleon, the Golden Hinde. At the back of the hall is an ancient oak screen which dates from 1573. This would have served as the backdrop to the *Twelfth Night* performance. Two small doors in the screen led to a passage into which the players could duck between scenes. There they might hurriedly change costumes or check their cues. The passage of time has done little to alter this imposing space. Standing in the middle of the hall today it is easy to conjure images of that February evening in 1602 when Shakespeare and his company presented the farcical antics of Viola, Sebastian, Sir Toby Belch and Sir Andrew Aguecheek to a crowd of pleasure hungry students.

Nikolaus Pevsner, the archaeological historian, describes the hall as 'the finest Elizabethan building in Central London', and it is hard to disagree. Dating from around 1562 to 1570, the hall serves as a dining room for members of the Middle Temple, one of the four Inns of Court. The students, barristers and the Master of the Bench gather here to dine every lunchtime in a tradition which has endured since the completion of the building.

Outside, situated between the Middle Temple and the Inner Temple is the historic garden which stretches down towards the Thames. With its finely manicured lawns, fruit trees and fragrant herbs it offers a sense of timeless tranquillity. Originally an orchard, by the fourteenth century the garden had become renowned for its roses. An interesting scene in *Henry VI, Part I* imagines the nobility entering a garden, for privacy, and deciding which side to take in the Wars of the Roses

> Richard Plantagenet: Great lords and gentlemen, what means this silence?
> Dare no man answer in a case of truth?
> Suffolk: Within the Temple-hall we were too loud;
> The garden here is more convenient.
>
> *Henry VI, Part I*: Act II, Scene IV

The men go on to choose their allegiance in the conflict by plucking roses of their favoured side's colour; red for Lancaster and white for York. In the garden today that scene is remembered in the Long Border, a beautiful plantation of red and white roses.

Although the Middle Temple is technically within the City of London, in a quirky twist of history, it retains its own powers of local authority. The Knights Templar, who founded the Temple in the Middle Ages, and from whom the name derives, were subject only to the pope and therefore not answerable to local laws. The Temple still retains remnants of this autonomy and oversees functions normally held by local councils such as paving and lighting, licensing, water supply and public health.

The hall still plays host to theatre companies today; in 2011 Antic Disposition chose this venue to produce *The Tempest* in celebration of the play's 400th anniversary. Those familiar with the film *Shakespeare in Love* will also recognise the hall as the setting for the command performance of *The Two Gentlemen of Verona* in which the queen, played by Judi Dench, is shown laughing at the antics of the clown Will Kempe and Crab the dog. It is unknown how many other times Shakespeare himself performed at the Middle Temple, if indeed he did, but it is only thanks to John Manningham's care in writing about his 'feest' that we know about this occasion at all. The Chamberlain's Men are also known to have performed at Gray's Inn where they treated a raucous crowd to *The Comedy of Errors* but that hall is not open to visitors.

## Visitor Information

As well as the chance to see a Shakespeare performance in one of his original venues, Middle Temple Hall also conducts guided tours. They require a minimum of ten people per group and entry is £7 per person for one hour. For an extra £4 you can also enjoy lunch in the hall.

To locate the hall is an adventure in itself. My favourite route is entering via the Inner Temple Gateway off Fleet Street and walking down the narrow lane. To the left-hand side is the beautiful, sandy-coloured Temple church with its famous round nave. Dating from 1185 the nave is home to nine stone effigies of supporters of the Knights Templar including that of William Marshal, the 'best knight that ever lived', according to Stephen Langton, who was Archbishop of Canterbury during the reign of King John. Marshal was accepted into the ranks of Knights Templar on his deathbed. The church is often open to visitors but following Dan Brown's the *Da Vinci Code* and the massive interest it provoked, they now charge a small entry fee.

Continue south down Church Court and bear right into Elm Court. Walk straight ahead and through the entry onto Middle Temple Lane. The hall is straight ahead. Call 0207 427 4820 to book a tour. When there are no private functions taking place the garden is open to the public from 12:30–15:00 daily.

## Hampton Court Palace

> At Christmas I no more desire a rose
> Than wish a snow in May's new-fangled mirth;
> But like of each thing that in season grows.
>
> *Love's Labour's Lost*: Biron, Act I, Scene I

*Christmas Revels*

In 1603 Elizabeth I died and was succeeded by James VI of Scotland. The son of Mary Queen of Scots was an unknown entity in England but he successfully united the two crowns. South of the border he became known as James I. His succession gave a significant boost to Shakespeare's company when on 19 May 1603 they were translated from the Chamberlain's Men to the King's Men. It was unmistakeably a promotion. They were now entitled to wear the king's scarlet livery. As the king's servants, they were also expected to be ready to perform at his command.

In this section we must briefly leave what Shakespeare knew as London and head into the depths of Surrey where we shall join him and his king at Hampton Court Palace for the Christmas celebrations of 1603. Cardinal Wolsey's country mansion was built in 1515 on the pleasant banks of the River Thames, not far from the market town of Kingston. Such was the beauty and grandeur of the building that Henry VIII soon relieved him of it and turned it into a royal palace. He embarked on a programme of extension work to increase the living space for his courtiers, including apartments for Anne Boleyn. She would enjoy several visits to Hampton Court during her brief triumph as queen. Henry and Anne's daughter Elizabeth also spent time there with her favourite, Robert Dudley. Now it was James's turn. After a childhood spent in the wild and thistly Scottish landscape, James must have found southern England a vastly different prospect. With its sweet climate and gently rolling fields the countryside around Hampton Court was tame in comparison. It offered good hunting and he would use the palace as a royal playground. He also spent his first Christmas here. With plague in the city of London, this notoriously paranoid king fled to Hampton Court where the air was pure and the frightening mass of common people with their diseases and ill thoughts could not reach him. Over a fortnight of feasting and carousing, he was entertained by his new troupe of players, the King's Men.

The scene was the magnificent hammer-beamed Great Hall. The Story of Abraham, picked out in cloth of gold and silver thread on the huge tapestries which hung from the walls, would have gleamed in the flickering candlelight. Arranging themselves on the benches was a tableau of painted faces and white ruffs; a perfumed press of bodies dressed in gorgeous silks and furs. The king and his queen, Anne of Denmark, would have been seated on a raised dais in the centre of the hall. It is not known which plays the company performed that season but it can be assumed that the repertoire included some comedies. A letter from the courtier Dudley Carleton to his friend John Chamberlain says, 'On New Year's night we had a play of Robin Goodfellow', which indicates that they had seen *A Midsummer Night's Dream*. After an evening of magic and romance, the assembled courtiers would have listened to Robin Goodfellow, otherwise known as Puck, bring the play to a close

> And as I am an honest Puck,
> If we have unearned luck
> Now to 'scape the serpent's tongue,
> We will make amends ere long;

> Else the Puck a liar call;
> So good night unto you all ...
> *A Midsummer Night's Dream*: Puck, Act V, Scene I

It would be interesting to know what James thought of the performance. It is sometimes suggested that he had a short attention span when it came to plays and that the relative brevity of the 1606 play *Macbeth* was a purposeful device to hold his attention. The witches would also have been a point of interest, for James was obsessed with witchcraft. He believed that a Scottish woman, Agnes Sampson, had tried to kill him and his new bride by whipping up a sea storm as they sailed from Oslo to Edinburgh in 1590. James personally participated in her interrogation and she was burned at the stake. Nine years later, James wrote *Daemonology*, a treatise in which he outlined his support for witch-hunts. Shakespeare's writing took on a darker turn during James's reign – the comedies were broadly written in the Elizabethan half of his career. From 1603 onwards he wrote plays such as *King Lear, The Tempest, Othello, The Winter's Tale* and *Measure for Measure*, all of which deal with themes such as discord and injustice. It was around this time that the genre of revenge tragedy grew in popularity.

Shortly after the festivities, in January 1604, James hosted a meeting of church leaders and puritans at Hampton Court. The so-called Hampton Court Conference led to the composition of the vernacular King James Bible. A faintly nonsense theory says that Shakespeare contributed to this new translation of the Bible. In Psalm Forty-Six, the forty-sixth word from the start is 'shake' and the forty sixth word from the end is *'spear.'* In 1610 when the work was in progress, Shakespeare was forty-six years old. Realistically, this is unlikely to be anything more than coincidence. The King James Bible was translated by clerics and scholars; it is doubtful they would have enlisted a mere playwright.

Much of the Tudor fabric of Hampton Court Palace has been replaced over the years. Centuries of rebuilding work has changed its essential character and bestowed on posterity a richly layered history cake. In the seventeenth century Christopher Wren demolished the Tudor apartments to make way for a fine new building for William III and Mary II. The Great Hall, although restored, is still in much the same condition as it was when Henry VIII held court here and Shakespeare performed for King James. The tapestries are faded now but still hang from the walls, the ghostly shades of Abraham just visible. The gatehouse known as Anne Boleyn's Gateway was built by Henry VIII with the intention of housing his new queen in the apartments above. Sadly for Anne she did not live to see the finished result. In an attempt to erase all traces of her memory Henry ordered all emblems and signs of the disgraced queen to be destroyed and replaced with those of Jane Seymour. Evidently he missed some because on the ceiling of the archway is a carving of Henry and Anne's initials and her falcon crests.

Hampton Court Palace is said to have its ghosts. According to legend, the desperate spirit of Katherine Howard still races along the 'Haunted Gallery' in search of her husband Henry VIII; a doomed attempt to save herself from the fate that befell Anne Boleyn. If there are tragic ghosts here it would also be nice to think of the actor who played Robin Goodfellow in 1603 haunting the Great Hall and speaking his lines to a rapt audience

> If we shadows have offended,
> Think but this, and all is mended,

That you have but slumber'd here
While these visions did appear …
*A Midsummer Night's Dream*: Puck, Act V, Scene I

## Visitor Information

Hampton Court Palace is located in East Molesey, Surrey KT8 9AU, Tel: 0844 482 7777.

Opening hours are Monday to Sunday, 10.00–18.00. Admission prices vary depending on what season you are visiting. There are also standalone tickets available for the Maze and Gardens. Please call for up to date information or book online via www. hrp.org.uk/hamptonCourtPalace/hamptoncourtadmission

# St Giles

How now, brother Edmund! What serious
contemplation are you in?
*King Lear*: Edgar, Act I, Scene II

## The Outsiders

It is sometimes forgotten that William was not the only Shakespeare living in London and earning his living at the playhouse. Edmund Shakespeare, the playwright's brother, is known to have lived for a short time in the capital but the details of his life are even sketchier than William's. We know that he had an illegitimate son, Edward, who was still a baby when he died in 1607. We also know that Edmund followed him to the grave months later at the age of 27. What we don't know is when he came to London or how he and his son died. Thanks to the practice of only recording the father's name on baptismal records, we don't even know who Edward's mother was.

Although Edmund and William Shakespeare came from the same family and both worked in the same profession in the same town, the contrast in their circumstances is intriguing. Whilst William was making a good living as a shareholder on Bankside and building up a property portfolio, Edmund scratched a living as a jobbing actor, probably staying in rented digs. Like other members of the persecuted theatrical procession, he lived outside the City walls. His parish of St Giles-without-Cripplegate was handily close to Shoreditch and the northern playhouses. The 'Cripple Gate' itself formed one of the entrances, or exits, through the wall and the name has obscure origins, but one theory says it comes from the Anglo-Saxon word *cruple* meaning covered walkway or tunnel.

The church of St Giles, where little Edward was buried, still stands today and enjoys a position of glorious isolation within the Barbican complex. As you enter St Giles Terrace from Fore Street, you are suddenly in the midst of a wide open space, dominated by the church with its ragstone walls, battlements and red brick bell tower. A soothing water fountain echoes in the background. The remains of the Roman wall are still visible to one side of the church giving a sense of its proximity to the City. Dotted about the terrace are trees and late Victorian gas lamps. All this is overlooked by the 1960s Brutalist tower blocks of the Barbican. The whole area is a fascinating snapshot of the last two millennia.

There has been a church on this site since 1090. It was rebuilt and enlarged in 1394 but the current building dates from around 1550 when the medieval church was, in John Stow's words, 'sore burnt and consumed' by fire. As you step inside, seek out the stained glass East Window depicting important figures such as St Giles. To the right-hand side are traces of the medieval wall which have been left exposed for all to see. Another window of note is on the north wall and shows the stained glass image of Edward Alleyn, the great Elizabethan actor who played major roles such as Dr Faustus and Tamburlaine at The Rose, of which he was part owner. Forced out of business on Bankside by the arrival of The Globe, Alleyn and Philip Henslowe moved north to Cripplegate where they founded another playhouse, The Fortune. Alleyn was generous to the parish and founded alms houses for the poor. His memorial window, based on the famous portrait, depicts him as a prosperous figure dressed in a black cloak with the Fortune to one side and the alms houses nestling in his arms.

It is curious to think that Edmund Shakespeare chose to base himself in Cripplegate, close to Edward Alleyn and The Fortune, when his big brother William was enjoying huge success at The Globe, his Bankside hit factory. Perhaps he wanted to keep some distance, to assert his independence. Or maybe William was unwilling, or unable, to help. Some writers have suggested that they had a strained relationship. Why else would William have named the bitter, jealous, illegitimate brother in *King Lear* 'Edmund'? The idea of fraternal rivalry between the pair is a compelling one, ultimately a question to be reserved for fiction writers.

Whatever the truth of their relationship, it is easy to imagine William attending the funeral at St Giles Cripplegate on that day in August 1607 to see little Edward buried. He could not have known that by the end of the year he would also be burying his brother. On 31 December 1607 William lavished twenty shillings on Edmund's funeral 'with a forenoon knell of the great bell'. His last act of brotherly love was to ensure that this obscure young man was buried with dignity.

*Visitor Information*

The nearest tube stations are St Pauls, Barbican or Moorgate. St Giles Cripplegate is normally open Monday to Friday from

11:00–16:00. To check opening times before you travel, call 0207 638 1997.

As well as visiting St Giles you may also wish to stop by at the Barbican Centre, the former London home of the Royal Shakespeare Company, and a world class centre of performing arts. The complex houses an art gallery, a cinema and a library which has a superb theatre section. Built in the aftermath of the Second World War on a bomb-blasted wasteland, the Barbican Centre is surrounded by concrete tower blocks and apartments in the divisive Brutalist style of architecture.

The Museum of London is just a short stroll away and is free to enter. Its galleries tell the story of the capital from its pre-Roman dawn to the modern age. Look out for items of jewellery from the Cheapside Hoard and also the fascinating display of artefacts found at the site of The Rose. The museum bookshop stocks a wide range of local history titles, maps and offbeat gifts. When you have browsed to your heart's content, the café is next door and serves some delicious cakes and snacks.

## City of London Walking Tour

It is now time to walk in Shakespeare's footsteps, through the streets of the Old City. This self-guided walking tour goes off the beaten track and delves into some delightfully hidden corners. As you navigate through narrow lanes and shadowy courtyards you will discover the site of Shakespeare's lodgings on Silver Street, the site of the Blackfriars playhouse, and a memorial to the two men who arguably saved Shakespeare for posterity. This route has been carefully designed to help you get a sense of the topography of Shakespeare's London and takes approximately one hour to complete. I suggest taking the walk at the weekend when the offices are closed and the streets are semi-deserted. Most shops, cafés and bars are still open at weekends, especially around St Paul's. Free toilets are located in the shopping mall One New Change.

*Start: St Paul's Tube (Central Line)*

Leave the station via exit one. You are standing on the corner of Cheapside, the historical shopping hub of the City of London. The large, pinkish grey-coloured building across the road is One New Change, a modernist shopping mall built by Jean Nouvel which opened to great fanfare in 2011. This is part of an attempt by the City of London Corporation to attract shoppers from the West End and reinvigorate the City's mercantile heritage. The streets leading off from Cheapside echo the goods on sale here in the Middle Ages: Honey Lane, Milk Street, Wood Street and Bread Street among others.

Shakespeare gives Cheapside a name check, when Jack Cade and the rebels plan their next move:

> Dick: My lord, when shall we go to Cheapside and take up
> Commodities upon our bills?
> Cade: Marry, presently.
> All: O, brave!
>
> *Henry VI, Part II*: Act IV, Scene VII

In *Henry IV, Part I*, Falstaff's favourite pub is the Boar's Head Tavern in Eastcheap, literally the eastern end of Cheapside. By Shakespeare's day, Cheapside had come up in the world and was mainly occupied by affluent goldsmiths. Thomas Middleton's city comedy *A Chaste Maid in Cheapside*, written in 1613, pokes fun at this new middle class.

Walk past the water feature, turning left onto Foster Lane. Continue up Foster Lane, noting the nineteenth-century

Goldsmith's Hall on your right-hand side. The livery companies began in the Middle Ages and functioned as trade guilds. The Goldsmiths Company received its charter in 1327 and is responsible for hallmarking gold, silver and platinum.

## The City Walls

Cross Gresham Street and walk straight ahead, past the red-brick Wren church of St Anne and St Agnes on your left. Rebuilt by Sir Christopher Wren after the Great Fire of London, there has been a church on this site since 1137. Just beyond the church is a set of railings and the beginnings of a wooden walkway. Nestling among the wild flowers in the grounds below are the remains of the Roman wall and fort. The square shape in rough stone with the gravel in the middle is a corner bastion, or watch tower, of the Roman fort which was built here in around AD 110. It was a big rectangular fort with rounded corners and housed approximately 1000 soldiers. The city wall wrapped itself around the fort, so this spot represents the north western boundary of Shakespeare's London and gives a sense of how small his world was.

What you see now is a mixture of medieval and Roman brickwork. The foundations were only discovered after the Blitz in 1940 when a bomb destroyed the Victorian warehouses in the area. Until then, nobody, least of all Shakespeare and his contemporaries, had any idea of the fort's existence. As the author of *Julius Caesar* and someone who was clearly fascinated with antiquity, Shakespeare may have been interested to know that he lived within the bounds of the Roman fort. This brings us to our next stop.

## Shakespeare's Lodgings at 'Silver Street'

Continue up the wooden walkway which runs parallel to the city wall on the left. When you reach the end, turn right and walk into the little garden of St Olave Silver Street. Look for the little stone plaque on the wall with its sinister skull and crossbones. The faded writing beneath says 'this was the parish church of St Olave Silver Street, destroyed by the dreadfull fire of 1666.' In his 1598 *Survey of London*, John Stow dismisses the church as 'a small thing, and without any noteworthy monuments.' Six years after he wrote these dismissive words, that star of the future, William Shakespeare, moved into the parish and began attending services there. We know nothing about his religious beliefs, if indeed he had any, but it is safe to assume that he did go to church. All Elizabethans and Jacobeans were required to do so and if he had refused his name would have appeared on the recusancy lists.

He lodged with the Mountjoys, a French family of tiara makers who lived in a wooden house on the corner of Silver Street and Monkwell Street. Both streets have disappeared but Silver Street ran roughly parallel to London Wall whose traffic roars past the remains of the church. Centuries of development means the level of Elizabethan London is actually several feet below the surface, so Charles Nichol, in his excellent book, *The Lodger*, believes the closest we can get to the actual site of Shakespeare's lodging is the underground car park.

*The Lodger* details the court case of 1612 in which Stephen Bellott sued his father in law, Christopher Mountjoy, for his marriage dowry. Shakespeare, having lodged with the family at the time of Bellott's marriage to Mountjoy's daughter, was called to give evidence and testify as to how much money had been promised, a question he was unable to answer. It is thanks to this slightly grubby court case that we know of Shakespeare's residence here in what would have been a very quiet, salubrious corner of the city. The mystery is why he wanted to live so far away from his place of work, The Globe on Bankside.

Turn right onto London Wall and walk past the modernist building by Lord Rogers on your right, noting the colour-coded water pipes and air ducts on the outside of the building. Turn right again onto Wood Street. In front of you the Gothic tower of St Albans stands in splendid isolation in the middle of the road. It is all that remains of a Wren church destroyed in the Blitz and is now a private house.

Walk past the tower, turning left onto Love Lane and into the gardens of St Mary Aldermanbury.

### John Heminges and Henry Condell Memorial

These pretty gardens mark the site of the church of St Mary Aldermanbury, rebuilt by Sir Christopher Wren after the Great Fire of London and later destroyed in the Blitz. The grounds are a green and peaceful oasis in the midst of the city and are popular with workers who come here to enjoy their sandwiches. The city police horses are stabled next door at Wood Street Police Station. Sometimes the organic scent of manure wafts down on the breeze, a reminder that at one time horse manure would have been one of the city's dominant aromas. As well as horses, the station has a small museum which includes items such as uniforms, truncheons and Jack the Ripper paraphernalia. The museum is run by volunteers so the opening hours are variable and it is best to check the website for up-to-date information if you are making a special visit. See http://www.cityoflondon.police.uk/about-us/history/museum for details.

The stone footings in the lower level of the garden were preserved by Wren and date from the fifteenth century. Walking up the stone steps and into what was the churchyard, the visitor is greeted by the familiar face of William Shakespeare gazing down from a pink granite plinth. The bust was placed here by

Charles Clement Walker, a Victorian philanthropist, in memory of two local residents who did so much to preserve Shakespeare's work for posterity.

Shakespeare's friends and fellow actors John Heminges and Henry Condell lived in the parish of St Mary Aldermanbury and served as church wardens. They are best known for their heroic efforts in compiling the First Folio of *Mr William Shakespeare's Comedies, Histories and Tragedies*, thus saving them from obscurity. The work was published in 1623, seven years after Shakespeare's death, a fact which seems to have been a source of disappointment for the compilers. Here are Heminges and Condell in their introduction 'to the great variety of readers' of the First Folio:

> It had bene a thing, we confesse, worthie to have bene
> Wished, that the author himselfe had lived to have set
> Forth, and overseen his owne writings.

Shakespeare left money for Heminges and Condell to buy themselves memorial rings and the three men evidently enjoyed a close friendship. It is easy to imagine Shakespeare strolling round the corner from Silver Street to visit them.

The church itself had an interesting fate. After the devastation of the Blitz it was left to rot, abandoned and unloved, a sad testament to the City's post-war poverty. Rescue came in the 1960s when it was dismantled brick by brick and shipped off to Fulton, Missouri, where it was rebuilt to Wren's design in the grounds of Westminster College.

Walk down the steps and into Aldermanbury, keeping the Guildhall library to your left-hand side. Turn left at the church of St Lawrence Jewry and walk into Guildhall Yard.

## Guildhall

You are now standing in the vast space of Guildhall Yard, dominated by the medieval Great Hall with its Gothic arched windows and playful white Portland stone porch, added in 1788 by George Dance the Younger. The turrets and spirelet, or *flèche*, are from the nineteenth century and the roof was replaced after a bomb gutted the hall in the Second World War.

Shakespeare would have been familiar with this imposing edifice as it was the scene of his kinsman Edward Arden's trial on a charge of treason in 1583. Whether or not Shakespeare attended the trial is unknown but one can imagine him viewing the Guildhall with a shudder.

The hall is open to visitors and has free entry but it is a working building and sometimes closes at short notice to host official functions and council meetings. The entrance is via the glass doors to the left of Guildhall Yard and you may be asked to put any bags through the airport-style security conveyor belt. The security guards today are a friendly bunch – less sinister than those encountered by Edward Arden – and are happy to answer questions.

Still standing in Guildhall Yard, look at the large black circle on the ground. This marks the outline of the Roman Amphitheatre which was discovered during the construction of the Guildhall Art Gallery in 1988. Access to the amphitheatre is via the art gallery to the right-hand side of the hall. Completed in 1999 the gallery's semi-arched windows are designed to blend in with the Gothic style of its ancient neighbour. Look out for the busts of William Shakespeare, Samuel Pepys, Christopher Wren and Oliver Cromwell hidden in their shadowy niches outside. Facing the Great Hall is the church of St Lawrence Jewry, another Wren building. It takes its name from the fact that this was the medieval Jewish district. Stepping inside, the carpet of royal blue, the chandeliers and the gilded ceiling give the interior a palatial feel; perhaps this is to be expected since it is the official church of the Lord Mayor of London. St Lawrence has become known for its programme of music; the pleasing sound of piano recitals can often be heard wafting through the doors. The church is open daily 8:00–17:00.

With your back to the Great Hall, walk south with the church of St Lawrence Jewry to your right and cross Gresham Street. Turn right and walk several yards until you reach Milk Street. Turn left down Milk Street and cross over Cheapside, reaching the corner of Bread Street adjacent to the shopping Mall, One New Change.

*The Mermaid Tavern and Bow Lane*
Like all the plainly named streets off Cheapside, Bread Street was named for what was sold here in the Middle Ages. By Shakespeare's day, the street was inhabited by rich merchants and, according to Stow, 'divers fair inns', one of which was the Mermaid Tavern.

It seems a good bet that Shakespeare frequented the Mermaid since the proprietor, a man named William Johnson, witnessed his mortgage on the Blackfriars gatehouse in 1613. Ben Jonson and Francis Beaumont certainly drank here as evidenced by Beaumont's epistle to Jonson in which he remembers the evenings spent drinking and exchanging banter

> What things have we seen
> Done at the Mermaid? Heard words that have been
> So nimble, and so full of subtle flame,
> As if that every one from whence they came,
> Had meant to put his whole wit in a jest,
> And had resolved to live a fool the rest of his dull life.

Today the street is lined with nondescript office buildings so you may want to walk through the short alleyway into the courtyard of St Mary le Bow to see the statue of Captain John Smith, who founded Jamestown, Virginia in 1608. This was the year *Pericles* was entered in the Stationer's Register and the King's Men bought the Blackfriars playhouse.

St Mary le Bow was built by Sir Christopher Wren after the Great Fire. Tradition states that true Cockneys must be born within hearing distance of the church bells. In the Norman crypt downstairs is the Café Below which is open for lunch and dinner and serves delicious organic fare.

Walk to the other side of the churchyard into the pretty Bow Lane. The decorative paving stones on this narrow lane have been laid out to indicate how much narrower it was before the Great Fire of London. Turn right and walk a few paces down Bow Lane until you reach the tiny Groveland Court on your right. Tucked away inside is the Williamson's Tavern which dates from the seventeenth century. It served as the official residence of the Mayors of London until the middle of the eighteenth century when Mansion House, their current home, was built close to the Bank of England. The tavern stands on the site of an earlier building which was the home of the soldier Sir John Fastolf whose alleged cowardice in the Wars of the Roses may have inspired Shakespeare's character Falstaff.

At the end of Bow Lane, turn right past the Gothic church of St Mary Aldermary, and walk along Watling Street towards the baroque splendour of St Paul's Cathedral which looms ahead.

*Blackfriars*

At the end of Watling Street turn left and carefully cross New Change and Cannon Street until you are on Carter Lane, opposite the cathedral. Carter Lane was named for the carters who used to drop off their passengers at the many coaching inns which lined the lane. Keep walking down Carter Lane for approximately 100 yards. On the left, affixed to a nondescript grey building, is a plaque which marks the site of the Bell Inn from where one Richard Quiney wrote a letter to his Warwickshire pal Shakespeare in 1598. Quiney was asking for a loan of £30, a huge amount. Whether he got the money, we do not know. But the letter was found among Quiney's possessions after his death so he evidently decided not to send it.

Continue down Carter Lane and turn left into a small alley that leads to the tranquillity of Wardrobe Place, a small courtyard lined with Georgian houses. Look for the original foot scraper outside Number 4. In an age when the streets were filthy with horse manure and other waste it was used for wiping dirty shoes before entering the house. Until its destruction in the Great Fire of 1666 Wardrobe Place was the site of the King's Wardrobe which housed the royal tapestries, haberdashery, cloth and discarded outfits. It was here in 1604 that the King's Men came to be fitted with scarlet livery for the coronation procession of James I. The buildings are made up of serviced apartments and offices.

Exit Wardrobe Place and turn left down St Andrew's Hill. We are now in the Blackfriars area. At the bottom of the hill there is a cosy little pub called the Cockpit, named after the brutal cockfighting matches that took place there in the Victorian era. The bar still boasts an example of a cockfighting ring but happily there are no blood sports on offer today.

It would be understandable for anyone in search of Shakespeare to ignore this pub and head over the river to The Globe. The Cockpit is not on the tourist trail. But maybe it should be because it boasts a Tudor cellar which was almost certainly part of a house which Shakespeare bought in 1613, the house known as the Blackfriars Gatehouse. He paid £140 and his mortgage was witnessed by John Heminges, his fellow actor who later helped compile the First Folio of all Shakespeare's tragedies, histories and comedies in 1623.

So what exactly was this gatehouse? Well, the narrow alleyway which runs alongside it once led into a Dominican monastery, the Blackfriars, so called because of the black gowns worn by the friars. Shakespeare's gatehouse formed the entrance to the monastery. It's uncertain whether he ever lived in the house himself but we know that he bequeathed it to his daughter Susanna in his will. In an interesting twist, the gatehouse was next door to the scene of an illegal Catholic mass which took place in 1623 at the French Ambassador's house. Known as the Doleful Evensong, over 300 people had gathered in a room at the top when the floor collapsed. The congregation plunged to the ground and over ninety people were killed.

The gatehouse is just one connection Shakespeare had in this area. The next location on the trail is an unassuming and rather hidden away remnant of this area's religious and theatrical past. Although it does not feature on the main tourist itineraries it has borne witness to some of the most pivotal aspects of English history.

The narrow alleyway running down the side of the Cockpit is Ireland Yard. Halfway down, on the right-hand side is a small yard laid out on the footprint of an old ruined churchyard. St Ann Blackfriars was built within the grounds of the monastery after the dissolution and it served as the local parish church. It was destroyed in the Great Fire of London and never rebuilt. The yard is at a raised level from the ground so walk up the steps, keeping your eye on the old stone ruins behind the black railings on your right. This sad pile of rubble is all that remains of the Blackfriars Monastery. There were approximately 400 friars here between its foundation in the thirteenth century and 1538 when Henry VIII and Thomas Cromwell set about dissolving the religious houses. It was in the Great Hall of the Blackfriars that Henry held a court hearing to test the validity of his marriage to Catherine of Aragon in 1529. Shakespeare dramatizes the scene in the play *Henry VIII*, showing her heartfelt speech in defence of her marriage:

> Sir, I desire you do me right and justice;
> And to bestow your pity on me: for
> I am a most poor woman, and a stranger,
> Born out of your dominions; having here
> No judge indifferent, nor no more assurance
> Of equal friendship and proceeding. Alas sir,
> In what have I offended you?
>
> > *Henry VIII*: Queen Katharine, Act II, Scene IV

The speech in the play is based upon Catherine's own words. She delivered the speech on her knees in an attitude of submission, but this was no meek and feeble woman. After finishing what she had to say she rose and walked defiantly out of the door, ignoring the calls for her to return. She may have won the sympathy of the public but as we all know, the king got his divorce. A few years later he married Anne Boleyn and all the monasteries, priories and nunneries fell one by one.

After the Dissolution, parts of the Blackfriars Monastery were sold off piecemeal. That's how we have Shakespeare buying the gatehouse in 1613 and his theatre company, the King's Men, opening an indoor playhouse in the refectory, or dining hall. This posh new theatre attracted a higher class of clientele than the raucous Globe and the company could charge a higher entrance fee. They began to experiment with different music, using softer instruments such as the lute and the flute. This is where Shakespeare's final plays were performed – *The Tempest*, *The Winter's Tale*, *Pericles* and *Cymbeline*. And by poignant coincidence the play *Henry VIII* is also likely to have been performed here, re-enacting the tense events of Henry and Catherine of Aragon's divorce hearing which had taken place there eighty years previously.

As you come back down the steps, turn right and walk to the end of Ireland Yard. Look up at the street sign which recalls a lost era. It says simply, 'Playhouse Yard'. Church Entry is a narrow passage which leads past another section of St Ann's Blackfriars and back up to Carter Lane.

*Visitor Information*

The Cockpit Tavern is open Monday to Saturday 11:00–23:00 and Sunday 12:00–14:30 then 19:00–22:30. During quiet periods they are usually happy to show visitors 'Shakespeare's Cellar.'

The church of St Andrew by the Wardrobe across from the pub is an easily missed Wren church with dark-red bricks and large plain windows. In the gallery upstairs they have a monument to Shakespeare and the lute player John Dowland, his contemporary, which they are happy to show visitors upon request.

Current places to eat nearby include Café Rouge opposite St Paul's Cathedral and Pret A Manger in Paternoster Square.

Stationers' Hall, where plays were registered, is located nearby although not open to the public. You may wish to take a stroll about the precincts of St Paul's as this is where the early modern book trade was centred. Shakespeare's plays were sold by the booksellers here including *Henry V* which was sold from a shop on the corner of Carter Lane. Shakespeare himself would probably have enjoyed browsing for the latest pamphlet or book of poetry.

## Southbank Walking Tour

Our next walk takes us out of the City, where Puritans, bankers and merchants reigned, and across the river to the thrilling disorder of Bankside.

It has almost become a cliché to describe Bankside as the Elizabethan entertainment district but its status can convincingly be compared to the Soho of the 1950s. It was alive with bohemian verve. Actors and writers rubbed shoulders with thieves, prostitutes and beggars. The bull rings and playhouses were melting pots of humanity where a lowly apprentice fishmonger might find himself standing inches away from an earl and his train of aristocratic followers. On Bankside, reality could be suspended and identities blurred as we see with Moll Cutpurse, born plain Mary Frith, who dressed in men's breeches and smoked a pipe. She regularly appeared on stage, singing and exchanging ribaldries with the audience, and inspired two plays, *The Madde Pranckes of Merry Moll of the Bankside* by John Day and *The Roaring Girl* by Middleton and Dekker.

This playground culture developed thanks to the special status of Bankside as the waterfront to the Clink and Paris Garden 'liberties', two areas outside the jurisdiction of the City. The Clink encompassed an area to the west of London Bridge and was under the control of the Bishops of Winchester. In a strange hangover from England's Catholic past, this meant that criminals and refugees from justice could claim the right of sanctuary here. The Bishops took a pragmatic approach to the liberty's seedy nature and licensed the local brothels, or stews, taking a cut of the money and earning the women the nickname 'Winchester Geese.' The trade was tightly regulated and the 'stew holders' were bound by a list of rules laid down in the reign of Henry II, of which these are some examples:

> No single woman to be kept against her will that would leave
>> her sin.
> To take no more for the woman's chamber in the week than
>> fourteen pence.
> No stew holder to receive any woman of religion, or any man's
>> wife.

An attempt had been made to suppress the brothels in the reign of Henry VIII but this was clearly unsuccessful as John Stow names the stew houses as among the 'most notable' in Southwark, alongside establishments such as the Bishop of Winchester's palace and the bear gardens which were located further west in Paris Garden.

In later years, Bankside became industrialised then fell into decline after extensive bombing in the Second World War but the area has had a renaissance in recent years and is once more a centre of culture and fun. The National, Southwark Playhouse, the Old Vic, The Rose and, of course, Shakespeare's Globe are some of the theatres located in the area. The Tate Modern art gallery is an example of what can be achieved in a disused power station. There are medieval ruins and cobbled lanes, atmospheric old pubs and modern restaurants. The soaring spirit of Shakespeare's Bankside is everywhere.

A good way to start this walk is to cross the Millennium Bridge from St Paul's with the sweeping vista of Bankside before you. Straight ahead is the huge dark hunk of the Tate Modern with its looming tower. It is free to enter and you may wish to step inside and use the facilities or view the modern art before heading back to the sixteenth century.

If you are starting the walk straight away, turn right as you leave the Millennium Bridge. On the right-hand side there is Cardinal's Wharf where you will see a small terrace of seventeenth-century red-bricked houses. At the end of the terrace is Number 49, a tall, cream coloured house with a red door and an ambiguous history. The building bears a sign purporting to be the house where Catherine of Aragon stayed when she first arrived in London. Sadly this is almost certainly not the case as the house was only started in 1710, over two hundred years after her landing. Another, equally implausible legend says that Christopher Wren stayed at this house during the post-fire rebuilding of St Paul's Cathedral. In fact, Wren stayed at a house slightly further along. Next to the house is the intriguing Cardinal's Cap Alley, a dark and narrow alleyway which is disappointingly railed off. It dates back to the fourteenth century and led to a brothel called the Cardinal's Hat that, like the other red light establishments in Southwark, was licensed by the Bishop of Winchester. Shakespeare refers to the Cardinal's Hat in *Henry VI, Part I*. Here is the Duke of Gloucester insulting the Bishop of Winchester for his part in the trade:

> Stand back, thou manifest conspirator,
> Thou that contriv'dst to murder our dead lord;
> Thou that giv'st whores indulgences to sin:
> I'll canvass thee in thy broad cardinal's hat,
> If thy proceed in thy insolence.
>
> *Henry VI, Part* I: Gloucester, Act I, Scene III

A few steps along is the Shakespeare's Globe Exhibition which runs guided tours of the theatre. Next door is the riverside entrance to Shakespeare's Globe itself.

## Shakespeare's Globe
The Globe is a reconstruction of the original playhouse which was built close by in 1599. Take a look at the black wrought-iron

gates by Richard Quinnell which are decorated with emblems representing plants and creatures featured in Shakespeare's plays. Quinnell used apprentice blacksmiths from all over the world, supporting Sam Wanamaker's vision that The Globe should live up to its international name. A blue plaque to Wanamaker can be seen on the red-brick wall.

From this spot you can see the fine thatched roof of the theatre, the first of its kind since thatch was banned after the Great Fire of London.

A short flight of steps leads up to a white piazza, paved with stones bearing the names of those individuals who have helped to fund the running of the theatre. To gain entry to the piazza and the theatre, you can either join one of the tours, which start at the Exhibition Centre, or go to the box office around the corner and buy a ticket to one of the performances. For those who just want a quick glimpse inside and maybe a taste of the theatre in action, a good idea is to buy a groundling ticket. It costs £5 and allows you to wander in and out at will.

From the gates at The Globe, continue straight ahead with the river at your left-hand side until you reach Bear Gardens. Stop here and look at the side of the building which currently houses the Real Greek restaurant.

*The Wherryman's Seat*

Set in a shallow recess inside the wall is a genuine wherryman's seat. The wherrymen were vital to early modern Londoners. With only one bridge spanning the Thames, people hailed boats in the same way that we hail taxis. At one time the Thames waterfront was lined with stone benches upon which the wherrymen would sit and wait for their boats to fill with passengers. The example set into the wall of the Real Greek dates from the fifteenth century and is the only one we have left.

It was a tightly regulated profession overseen by a trade guild, the Company of Watermen. John Taylor, the self-styled 'Water Poet' was a well-known member and local character. He is mostly remembered for his attempt in 1622 to sail down the Thames in a paper boat, but his real passion was poetry.

In 1620 he published *The Praise of Hempseed*, which paid tribute to the lives of poets dead and gone, Shakespeare included

> In paper, many a poet now survives
> Or else their lines had perish'd with their lives.
> Old Chaucer, Gower, and Sir Thomas More,
> Sir Philip Sidney, who the laurel wore,
> Spenser, and Shakespeare did in art excel.

Taylor fancied himself as an equal to these men and to prove his worth, challenged the poet William Fennor to a battle of the wits at the Hope Playhouse in 1614. Fennor failed to show up, leaving Taylor to try and entertain the restive crowd alone. Unable to hold their attention, they began to riot. The resident company, the Lady Elizabeth's Men, were forced to step in and rescue the situation with a performance of their own.

With the wherryman's seat in front of you, turn right down Bear Gardens and walk down the cobbled lane. The Hope Playhouse was located approximately halfway down on the site of the old bear-baiting ring. At the end of the lane on the left-hand corner you will see the Globe Education Sackler Studios which house rehearsal space and Theo's Café. A wicker basket of apples is usually placed temptingly outside the door. Theo's is open Monday to Friday 9:00–19:00 and Saturday to Sunday 10:00–18:00.

## The Rose

Turn left onto Park Street, known as Maiden's Lane in Shakespeare's day, and walk straight ahead. Just before you reach Southwark Bridge, look out for the black door covered in theatre flyers and posters. A blue plaque announces that this is the site of The Rose Playhouse, built by Philip Henslowe in 1587. Plays performed here include *Dr Faustus*, *The Jew of Malta* and *Titus Andronicus*. The archaeological site still hosts theatre companies today and includes a fascinating exhibition as well as in-depth talks by expert guides. The centre is open on Saturdays from 10:00–17:00 and is free to enter. If you stop by, please consider dropping a donation in the tin. The Rose Revealed Project is in need of funds to help continue the excavation of this important site.

Continue along Park Street for a few yards, crossing the road once you have walked under the bridge.

## The Globe

In front of you is an attractive plaque bearing Shakespeare's image and information about The Globe. This is the site of the playhouse which burned down in 1613 and lies just 750 feet from the replica around the corner. The site was partially excavated in 1989 by archaeologists from MOLA (Museum of London Archaeology) who discovered signs of charring above the foundations. Fire was an everyday hazard in the seventeenth century and thatched roofs were finally banned after the Great Fire of 1666 which devoured the medieval city. Today's Globe is the first London building to be permitted a thatched roof since then.

It is possible to see the approximate location of the stair turret and outer walls by peeping through the black railings into the car park. The remains, preserved below ground, are picked out in clusters of red granite cobblestones. To the right-hand side is Anchor Terrace, an attractive row of houses built in 1834 which used to belong to the Anchor Brewery until 1981 when it was pulled down. The rest of The Globe lies underneath these houses which are now luxury apartments and protected by a Grade II listing.

Continue down Park Street, turning left at the end and walking past Vinopolis back towards the river. On your left-hand side is the Anchor, a sprawling pub, its dark brickwork brightened by a dash of red paint at the windows.

## The Anchor

This pub enjoys a beautiful position overlooking the River Thames. For this reason it is a popular haunt with both locals and tourists alike and can get very crowded. If you have time to stop it can be fun to while away an hour or so sitting on the terrace, enjoying the views of St Paul's over the river. The pub is also steeped in history. There has been a tavern of some description on this site since the thirteenth century and while it is not true that Shakespeare drank in this building – this latest incarnation dates from the nineteenth century – he would have been familiar with its Tudor predecessor.

When you have finished your drink, turn back the way you came and stroll through the railway tunnel noting the cobblestoned ground and the atmospheric rumbling of trains up above. A dancing fairy light effect on the walls gives the tunnel a magical feel and draws you onwards into the gloom. Straight ahead is the Clink Museum.

## The Clink

Come, let's away to prison;
We two alone will sing like birds I' th' cage.

*King Lear*, Act 5 Scene III

Despite the gibbeted skeleton hanging from the exterior wall and the eerie sounds which emanate from within, the costumed actors at the door of The Clink museum give this site a cartoonish air of fun and innocence. It was in the twelfth century that this notorious gaol was built within the grounds of Winchester Palace and over the centuries the evocative name 'Clink' has become synonymous with prison. With the cells situated below water level, the air was dank and unwholesome, disease rife. It quickly built a reputation as a death trap for the poor souls imprisoned there.

John Stow describes a typical inmate as those who 'should brabble, fray, or break the peace on the said bank'; in other words, the local drunks. The religious squabbles of the sixteenth century also ensured that The Clink became a stop gap for heretics on their journey through the legal system, often before finding themselves tied to a stake. In 1555 John Rogers was sent here after his trial for heresy. He became the first Protestant martyr in the reign of Mary I.

The prison was attacked several times over the years. The first occasion was in 1450 when Jack Cade's marauding rebels tore through Bankside and then in 1780 during the Gordon Riots when the building was burned down for good. The museum stands on the approximate site of the prison and is well worth a visit.

*Visitor Information*

The Clink is located at 1 Clink Street, London SE1 9DG. Tel: 0207 403 0900.

Opening times are 10:00–21:00 every day between July and September. The rest of the year it is open Monday to Friday 10:00–18:00 and weekends 10:00–19:30.

Continue along Clink Street for two minutes, passing Pret A

Manger on your right, then stop at the railings and absorb the tumbledown beauty of the remains of Winchester Palace.

## Winchester Palace

The west wall with its impressive rose window is a striking reminder of Bankside's medieval heritage. Started in 1144 by Henry of Blois, the palace served as the London base to the Bishops of Winchester. It was conveniently located close to London Bridge and the Thames giving the bishops easy access to court. Palace supplies and provisions were delivered via the nearby wharf then stored in a huge cellar beneath the great hall. In Shakespeare's day the palace complex was one of the most important sites on Bankside. With its own gardens and tennis court and, of course, prison, it was almost a little village in its own right. In the seventeenth century it fell out of use when Bishop Lancelot Andrewes died and was broken up into individual tenements. The building was finally devastated by fire in 1814. What we can see today dates from the fourteenth century; the site is now a Grade I listed monument and is overseen by English Heritage.

Continue to the end of Pickfords Wharf and stop at black galleon with its decorative red and yellow paintwork. Painted on the prow is a blue badge bearing the image of a white hind. This is a well-loved replica of the *Golden Hinde*.

## The Golden Hinde

In 1577 plain old Francis Drake set off on an epic sea voyage in a golden galleon named *The Pelican*. At some point as he sailed around the globe, braving the Atlantic and Pacific Oceans, the Straits of Magellan and the Cape of Good Hope, he decided to change the name of his vessel to the *Golden Hinde*, perhaps in tribute to his patron Sir Christopher Hatton, whose coat of arms featured the image of one. He also engaged in a spot of piracy, making Queen Elizabeth I very rich and very pleased with him. When he returned in 1581 the queen boarded the ship and gave him a knighthood. The swashbuckling legend of Sir Francis Drake was born. The ship remained docked at Greenwich where it became a tourist attraction and was eventually stripped of its timbers by souvenir hunters.

Drake is remembered for many things, the ignoble slave trade among them, but his curiosity about the world and his primal urge to test the known horizons made the great globe smaller than it had ever been. Along with Shakespeare, he was a champion of the English Renaissance.

The replica of the *Golden Hinde* was completed in 1973 and launched on its maiden voyage that year. Inside it feels very cramped and it is hard to imagine how such a small space could have accommodated Drake, his twenty officers and forty crew members. Docked permanently at St Mary Overies docks it is open for self-guided tours every day from 10:00–17:30. Tickets are £7 for adults, £5 for children and £20 for a family ticket. The venue sometimes closes for private events so call 0207 403 0123 beforehand if you're making a special visit.

Walk a few paces along Cathedral Street as it curves round towards Southwark Cathedral. The bustling Borough Market is to your right. Its mouth-watering array of street food stalls may tempt you to grab a bite to eat and take your place among the other foodies relaxing in the shadow of Southwark Cathedral.

### Southwark Cathedral

Take a moment to look up and appreciate the beauty of this timeless Southwark landmark. Like most of London's ancient churches it is a patchwork of rebuilding and restoration but it retains its Gothic character. The current building was started in the thirteenth century and began life as part of an Augustinian priory. It was known as St Mary Overie, the unusual name 'Overie' probably meaning 'over the river'. In 1539 the priory was dissolved and Henry VIII leased the church to the local population. Around this time it was renamed St Saviours and this was the name by which Shakespeare knew it.

If he lived in Southwark, as is generally believed, then he would have attended church services here. He would have been familiar with the gaudy green and red tomb of the fourteenth-century poet John Gower, a contemporary of Chaucer, who rented rooms within the priory. He was certainly familiar with Gower's work. The play *Pericles* has Gower narrating the prologues before each act. Here is Gower rising from the dead to introduce the play:

> To sing a song that old was sung,
> From ashes ancient Gower is come;
> Assuming man's infirmities,
> To glad your ear and please your eyes ...
>
> *Pericles*: Gower, Prologue

Gower's tomb is still an important and much-loved feature of the cathedral today. Another focal point for visitors is a humble flag stone on the floor of the choir. It bears the name of 'Edmond Shakespeare' who was buried at St Saviours on the morning of 31 December 1607. The funeral cost twenty shillings and included a 'forenoon knell of the great bell.' It is widely assumed that it was William who both arranged and paid for the lavish ceremony. It is not known exactly where Edmund lies within the cathedral but the high concentration of actors and playhouse personnel on Bankside meant that he was not alone. There are two other memorial stones near Edmund's which commemorate the playwrights John Fletcher and Philip

Massinger. St Saviours was also the final resting place of Philip Henslowe, who like Edmund Shakespeare, was buried with a tolling of the bell.

Shakespeare himself is remembered with a flamboyant stained glass window in the south aisle. The window shows figures from the plays including Prospero and Hamlet. Beneath the window Shakespeare himself reclines gracefully in a niche. He looks deep in thought and holds a quill pen as if he were in the middle of plotting a scene. The Shakespeare Memorial is the focus of celebrations each year on his birthday (23 April) when flowers and sprigs of rosemary, signifying remembrance, are strewn about his statue.

The cathedral has public toilets which can be accessed by paying 50p for a token at the little shop in the northern cloister. The cathedral itself is free to enter but welcomes donations and charges a small fee for interior photography. Opening hours are Monday to Friday 8:00–18:00 and Saturday, Sunday and Bank Holidays 9:00–18:00. Call 0207 367 6722 for more information.

Exit the cathedral from the south doors and turn left, walking eastwards through the churchyard towards the gate on the right-hand side. Pass the food stalls on your right and walk up the steps onto Borough High Street. Carefully cross the busy road towards London Bridge Station and turn right, continuing down Borough High Street until you reach a little courtyard called George Inn Yard on the left.

## The George

You are now standing in front of the George, a handsome old coaching inn of the type which used to line Borough High Street in Shakespeare's day. London Bridge was locked at night time so travellers wishing to cross over into London could stop here and refresh themselves overnight. There was no shortage of places to stay. Stow tells us that there 'be many fair inns, the Spur, Christopher, Bull, Queen's Head, Tabard, George, Hart, King's Head &c ...' Another example was the White Hart Inn which Shakespeare mentions in the play *Henry VI, Part II* as Jack Cade's rebels tear through Southwark. In this scene Cade pours scorn on an offer of pardon for his followers

What, Buckingham and Clifford, are ye so brave? And you, base peasants, do ye believe him? Will you needs be hanged with your pardons about your necks? Hath my sword therefore broke through London gates, that you should leave me at the White Hart in Southwark?

*Henry VI, Part II*: Cade, Act IV, Scene VIII

There has been an inn on the site of the George since the middle ages but the present building dates from 1676 when it was rebuilt following the Great Fire of Southwark which, having started in Borough High Street, quickly consumed hundreds of local houses. Although the building we see today has only one side, the rebuilt George had three galleried sides and formed a little courtyard following the footprint of the medieval inn. Coaching inns of this design were numerous across the country and gave the playing companies a convenient venue when on tour. Standing outside the George today and looking up at the wooden galleries gives the visitor a good idea of what the old inn yards looked like and how they used to function as theatrical spaces. The actors stood on a raised platform in the yard and the audience would gather round them like the groundlings at the purpose built playhouses. Patrons who happened to be staying at the inn were lucky enough to have a vantage point from the galleries outside their chambers. They could enjoy the show with an unimpeded view and in safety and comfort. The purpose-built playhouses such as The Theatre and The Globe were probably designed with this layout in mind.

In 1889 Great Northern Railway demolished the northern wings of the George to make way for warehouses. Despite all the changes it has seen, the pub is steeped in atmosphere. The George is now run by the National Trust and is a popular watering hole with both history seekers and locals alike. As we finish the Bankside walking tour, this is a good opportunity to take a seat and raise a glass to the spirit of Shakespeare and friends.

The pub is located at George Inn Yard, 77 Borough High Street, London SE1 1NH. Tel: 020 7407 2056. It is open daily from 11.00–23.00.

# A Journey into Shakespeare's Imagination

The poet's eye, in fine frenzy rolling,
Doth glance from heaven to earth, from earth to heaven,
And as imagination bodies forth
The forms of things unknown, the poet's pen
Turns them to shapes and gives to airy nothing
A local habitation and a name.
*A Midsummer Night's Dream*: Theseus: Act V, Scene I

## Such Shaping Fantasies

The previous chapters have been concerned with locations Shakespeare either knew or is thought to have known. We have quite literally been walking in his footsteps with an emphasis on the known facts of his life. It is now time to step away from biography and seek our inspiration from the lives of his characters and the settings of the plays.

As Shakespeare plotted his scenes, sending characters in diverse directions from London to Northumberland with the mere stroke of his pen, he may have had little idea about the geography of the locations he was writing about. Places such as Pontefract and Warkworth may have been just names to him. Based in London, he is very likely to have been familiar with the local play settings and could probably visualise them as he wrote. Let us imagine for a moment Shakespeare sitting at a desk in his digs at Bishopsgate. The year is 1592 and he is labouring over a scene in *Richard III*, trying to imagine the young Prince Edward standing outside the Tower of London with his guardians, then trustingly following them inside to what history knows will be his death. Shakespeare decides to go and have a look at the scene for himself. He lays down his pen, has a yawn and a stretch, and then heads out for some fresh air. Walking down Bishopsgate in the direction of the River Thames, he would have shortly reached the top of Cornhill, named for the crops which were sold there in the Middle Ages. Turning left at the Leadenhall, which as Stow tells us was 'employed and used as a granary for corn and grain', he would have exited the city via the Aldgate then walked down the Minories past the site of the old Franciscan nunnery before crossing the moat to the Tower of London. It was a place with a reputation; everyone knew that the Princes in the Tower had been murdered there on the orders of their wicked uncle. Shakespeare could have made a day of this imaginary trip to the Tower, stopping to see the beasts in the royal menagerie, like any other Elizabethan Londoner. On other jaunts around the city he may have walked past the London Stone, that mythical landmark which had captured his imagination in *Henry VI, Part II*. If he ever ventured to the town of Windsor he may have met the merry wives of that town and begun to form the idea for his next comedy.

The settings of his plays take us to some surprising corners of England, ranging from the traditionally beautiful to the slightly gritty. The locations seem suited to their characters, from the filthy streets of London through which Jack Cade and his fellow rebels marauded, to the regal splendour of Westminster Hall which hosted the wealthy, if corrupt, nobles who plotted and usurped their way into history.

Most of his English locations are found in the history plays. It is widely accepted that his historical knowledge of the Wars of the Roses came from two main sources. Edward Hall was a lawyer whose chronicle, *The Union of the Two Noble and Illustre Families of Lancaster and York*, was published in 1548, the year following his death. This told the story of England's turbulent history from the start of the reign of Henry IV in 1399 and finishing with the reign of Edward's own monarch Henry VIII. Shakespeare could also have referred to the second edition of Raphael Holinshed's *Chronicles of England, Scotland and Ireland* which was published in 1587. *The History of Richard III*, Sir Thomas More's work of Tudor propaganda probably inspired Shakespeare to paint the last Yorkist king as a child-killing hunchback. Despite the obvious bias of More's work, it was from the history books that Shakespeare learnt key facts such as where Richard II starved to death and where the Duke of York's head was displayed after his death in 1460. Other locations are used merely as creative backdrops to the drama. The Boars Head Tavern on Eastcheap was a real place that helped Shakespeare to paint Falstaff's character as a bon viveur with a healthy taste for sack and tall tales. The Great Park at Windsor framed the late night antics of Falstaff and the merry wives.

This section of the book is part-literary tour and part-history tour. We begin on the south coast of England where one of the most unsettling scenes in *King Lear* was set, and move slowly northwards where we end at the windswept coast of Northumberland. Along the way we meet Shakespeare's characters and explore some of the settings in which they played out their scenes. As before, visitor information is included at the end of each section along with ideas to get the most out of your trip.

# Dover

> Gloucester: *Know'st thou the way to Dover?*
> Edgar: *both stile and gate, horse-way and foot-path.*
> *King Lear*: Act IV, Scene I

### Shakespeare's Cliff

Despite the lack of satnav in the early years of the seventeenth century, Shakespeare and the King's Men certainly knew the way to Dover. The King's Men are recorded as performing in the town on two occasions, once in 1605 and then again in July 1610. It was probably on his first visit on 4 October 1605 that Shakespeare found inspiration in the dramatic landscape that features in the play *King Lear*. The White Cliffs of Dover are an iconic English landmark and Shakespeare describes one of the cliffs in fairly good detail. In this scene the blinded Gloucester is asking his son Edgar to lead him to the top of the highest cliff in Dover. He intends to take his own life by jumping off it

> There is a cliff, whose high and bending head
> Looks fearfully in the confined deep:
> Bring me but to the very brim of it,
> And I'll repair the misery thou dost bear
> With something rich about me: from that place
> I shall no leading need.
> *King Lear*: Gloucester, Act IV, Scene I

Later in Act IV, Edgar takes advantage of his father's blindness and leads him to safety along a flat stretch of ground. He manages to fool him into thinking they are climbing the cliff

> Gloucester: When shall we come to the top of that same hill?
>
> Edgar: You do climb up it now: look how we labour.
>
> Gloucester: Methinks the ground is even.
>
> Edgar: Horrible steep
>
> Hark, do you hear the sea?
>
> *King Lear*: Act IV, Scene VI

The coastal atmosphere is written so vividly it is hard not to conclude that Shakespeare spent some time wandering about the clifftops, perhaps in between performances. After soaking in the sights and sounds he may have made notes while the imagery was still fresh in his mind. Here is Edgar describing the view from the top of the 'cliff':

> Come on sire, here's the place: stand still. How fearful
>
> And dizzy 'tis, to cast one's eyes so low!
>
> The crows and choughs that wing the midway air
>
> Show scarce so gross as beetles: half way down
>
> Hangs one that gathers samphire, dreadful trade!
>
> Methinks he seems no bigger than his head:
>
> The fishermen, that walk upon the beach,
>
> Appear like mice: and yond tall anchoring bark,
>
> Diminish'd to her cock: her cock, a buoy
>
> Almost too small for sight: the murmuring surge,
>
> That on the unnumber'd idle pebbles chafes,
>
> Cannot be heard so high. I'll look no more;
>
> Lest my brain turn, and the deficient sight
>
> Topple down headlong.
>
> *King Lear*: Edgar, Act IV, Scene VI

The sensation of vertigo is described with what must be first-hand knowledge. Perhaps Shakespeare felt his own brain 'turn' with a sudden dizziness, as he peered down at the fishermen below. The samphire gatherers which Edgar refers to were picking a species of this perennial plant which could be found growing from cliff faces. It was a delicacy and was usually eaten pickled. The gatherers risked their lives dangling down the cliff face from long ropes, buffeted by the raw coastal winds; it was as Shakespeare said, a 'dreadful trade.'

It is possible to retrace Gloucester and Edgar's footsteps today. To the west of Dover Harbour is Shakespeare Beach, an isolated stretch of shingle which connects the Admiralty Pier to Shakespeare Cliff, thought to be the very cliff described in *King Lear*. The beach is accessible by steps and a footbridge leading down to the beach from Shakespeare Cliff. With no commercial development here and few visitors, in the depths of winter it is a place of bleak beauty. As you stand at the base of the cliff, listening to the seagulls and the howling wind, you can almost hear Gloucester's plaintive cry as he prepares to jump:

> O you mighty gods!
> This world I do renounce, and, in your sights,
> Shake patiently my great affliction off.
>
> *King Lear*: Gloucester, Act IV, Scene VI

Running west from Shakespeare Cliff is an unusual feature called Samphire Hoe which was named in tribute to Edgar's mention of the plant in *King Lear*. Stretching from Dover to Folkestone, this man-made nature reserve was created with spoil from the Channel Tunnel digging. The biodiversity on the site is second to none with butterflies and rare plant species. Cattle and sheep graze freely in the meadows. This is a brilliant

*Above left*: 1. Droeshout Portrait. This engraving appeared as the First Folio frontispiece.

*Above right*: 2. Jester Statue. Touchstone frolics at the top of Henley Street in Stratford-upon-Avon.

*Below*: 3. The Birthplace. Shakespeare was born here in 1564.

*Above:* 4. Hall's Croft. The home of Dr John Hall and his wife Susanna, Shakespeare's eldest daughter.

*Below left:* 5. Holy Trinity, Stratford-upon-Avon. The medieval church in which Shakespeare was baptised and buried. (Courtesy of Holy Trinity, Stratford-upon-Avon)

*Below right:* 6. Shakespeare's Grave, Holy Trinity, Stratford-upon-Avon. 'Cursed be he who moves my bones'. So far nobody has dared to defy Shakespeare's curse. (Courtesy of Holy Trinity, Stratford-upon-Avon)

*Left:* 7. Falstaff Statue. A cheerfully sotted Falstaff; part of the Gower Memorial in Stratford.

*Right:* 8. Hamlet Statue. 'Alas, poor Yorick!' The Hamlet statue at the Gower Memorial represents Philosophy.

9. Mary Arden's House. The childhood home of Shakespeare's mother.

10. Riverside Walks in Bidford. A hungover Shakespeare may have appreciated this sign pointing in the direction of home after his date with the Bidford Sippers.

11. Charlecote House, National Trust. The home of Sir Thomas Lucy. Legend says that a young William Shakespeare went poaching on his land. (Courtesy of the National Trust)

12. Anne Hathaway's Cottage. The pretty cottage where Anne Hathaway grew up.

13. Hoghton Tower. Legend says a young Shakespeare served here as a schoolmaster or household actor. This vintage image shows the upper courtyard.

CLEAR SPAN OF ROOF 23'10"
SIX PRINCIPALS IN LENGTH OF
HALL ABOVT 6'6 C-C

RVFFORD OLD HALL.
LANCASHIRE

*Left:* 14. Rufford Old Hall. A vintage drawing showing the Great Hall where Shakespeare may have entertained Sir Thomas Hesketh.

*Below:* 15. John Norden's Map of London. The London of 1593 was small and compact with a population of almost 200,000 people.

*Right:* 16. Claes Visscher's Panorama of London (1600). This detail shows houses in Southwark.

*Below:* 17. Execution site, Smithfield. Heretics used to be burnt at the stake on this site. Edward Arden was hanged, drawn and quartered here.

18. Shakespeare's Globe. Sam Wanamaker's vision made real. This reconstruction of The Globe has staged performances since its opening in 1997.

*Left:* 19. St Andrew Undershaft. Old and new worlds collide. The Elizabethan historian John Stow is buried here.

*Right:* 20. St John's Gate. Tradition says Edmund Tilney, the Master of the Revels, was stationed here.

*Above:* 21. Middle Temple Hall. A rare Elizabethan survival in the City of London. The Chamberlain's Men performed *Twelfth Night* here in 1602.

*Below left:* 22. Hampton Court Palace. The King's Men entertained King James and Anne of Denmark in the Great Hall during the Christmas of 1603.

*Below right:* 23. St Giles Cripplegate. Shakespeare's brother Edmund buried his son here in 1607.

*Above left:* 24. Heminges and Condell Memorial. Located in the gardens of St Mary Aldermanbury, this memorial is dedicated to the two men who compiled the First Folio of Shakespeare's works. *Above right:* 25. St Helen Bishopsgate. A sight Shakespeare would recognise from the period of time he spent lodging in the parish. *Below (inset):* 26. Richard Quiney's letter. Whilst lodging at the Bell Inn on Carter Lane Quiney wrote to his fellow Stratford man William Shakespeare in 1598 asking for a loan. *Below:* 27. Carter Lane and the site of the Bell Inn. Carter Lane was lined with coaching taverns including the Bell Inn from where Thomas Quiney wrote a letter to Shakespeare.

*Above left:* 28. The Cockpit. This Victorian pub marks the approximate site of the gatehouse Shakespeare purchased for £140.

*Above right:* 29. Wherryman's Seat. The only surviving example of a wherryman's seat on Bankside.

*Below:* 30. Plaque outside the site of The Globe. Close up of the attractive plaque located on a wall outside the location of the original Globe Playhouse.

31. Southwark Cathedral. Ancient stones gleaming in the midday sun. Shakespeare buried his brother Edmund here.

32. George Tavern. An example of the coaching inns which used to line Borough High Street. Performances would be held in the yard with patrons watching from the galleries.

33. Shakespeare Memorial, Southwark Cathedral. The Bard lies beneath his magnificent memorial window at Southwark Cathedral. (Courtesy of Southwark Cathedral)

34. Shakespeare Cliff, Dover. Shakespeare describes this cliff vividly in *King Lear*.

IN THE CASTLE GROUNDS, PONTEFRACT

35. 'Pontefract Castle. Pomfret, Pomfret! O thou bloody prison …' The castle was the scene of Richard II's death.

36. Warkworth Castle. The Northumbrian home of Henry 'Hotspur' Percy.

*Left:* 37. The footpath to Bosworth. The walk from Market Bosworth to Bosworth Field Heritage Centre makes for a pleasant day out.

*Right:* 38. Leicester Guildhall. One of the oldest buildings in the city, this is where members of the trade guilds met in the Middle Ages.

*Above:* 39. Wilton House. The home of Mary Sidney Herbert. Shakespeare's company performed *As You Like It* here in December 1603.

*Below left:* 40. *Seven Ages of Man.* All the world is a stage at Baynard House. The church of St Andrew in the Wardrobe can be seen in the background.

*Below right:* 41. Shakespeare statue, Leicester Square. Shakespeare watches over the revellers.

example of what can be achieved for nature with a bit of willing and imagination.

## Visitor Information

These days Dover tends to be the place we pass through on our way to the continent but it is worth lingering in the area to explore a coastline steeped in history. For families there is plenty of seaside fun. The area around Dover Harbour is popular with water sports enthusiasts who enjoy windsurfing, sailing and kayaking from the Dover Sea Sports Centre. For those looking for a sedate stroll, a pretty promenade lines the shingle beach.

Enjoying a stunning location on a hill set back from the clifftop is Dover Castle. There has been a fortress on this site since Saxon times but the present building's history can be dated back to the twelfth century in the reign of Henry II who added state apartments for entertaining guests. Over the centuries the castle became an important defence against invaders coming from the English Channel and in the sixteenth century Henry VIII added the Moat's Bulwark to help protect the harbour. Today the site is managed by English Heritage and it is open to visitors. Inside the Great Tower, Henry II's state apartments have been recreated to give a sense of life inside a medieval royal palace. Look out for the age-battered Roman lighthouse within the grounds. It has stood here since around AD 46, a few years after the invasion. At nights it would have been lit with a beacon of fire to guide home any boats sailing in from the Empire.

Dover Castle is located at Castle Hill, Dover, Kent CT16 1HU. Tel: 01304 211067.

Opening times to the castle vary depending on the season so please call or check www.english-heritage.org.uk/visit/places/dover-castle.

Admission is £18.00 for adults, £10.80 for children, £16.10

for concessions and £46.80 for a family ticket comprising two adults and up to three children.

To enjoy a sea view of the famous white cliffs of Dover it is possible to take a boat cruise complete with guided commentary from Dover White Cliff Tours who also run a 'Dover Rover' bus tour to the top of the cliffs. See www.doverwhiteclifftours.com for details or call 07971 301379.


# Tower of London

### Death and Disappearances

The Tower of London is one of the highlights of the capital. It was designated an UNESCO World heritage site in 1988 and attracts endless swarms of visitors who come to see this fine example of a Norman fortress. From its position just outside the City of London, it squats on the river bank and was surely an imposing and gloomy view for anyone unfortunate enough to have been locked within its walls. This is where a quick succession of tragic queens met their ends; Anne Boleyn, Katherine Howard and Lady Jane Grey. It seems that we in the twenty-first century have an endless fascination for the Tower's grim past. The passage of time has reduced the horrors of beheading and torture to mere words on a page but for the Tudors it was all too real.

Shakespeare is almost silent on the subject of the Tower of London but some interesting scenes in *Richard III* could reveal something of his feelings about it. In Act III, Scene I, young Prince Edward speaks plainly: 'I do not like the Tower...' He is a doomed little boy who, along with his brother, will shortly be swallowed up within its stone walls and disappear from history. He is inquisitive and he asks Buckingham about the old building, wondering if it was built by Julius Caesar. Buckingham replies that it was indeed built by Caesar and at this point the reader wonders if this is another amusing example of Shakespeare's dodgy grasp of history. The anachronistic game of billiards in *Antony and Cleopatra* springs to mind. For Elizabethans, however, the origins of the Tower were hazy. Squatting just outside London, at the south-eastern boundary, it seemed integral to the City walls which dated back to the Roman occupation. Shakespeare's contemporaries knew the White Tower as 'Julius Caesar's Tower.'

Of course, we know different. Started in 1078 the great stone fortress was built by William the Conqueror to consolidate his victory over the English and to keep the population in awe of his might. Comprised of two defensive walls, one outer and one inner, the Tower of London is in fact a series of towers encircling the oldest structure in the complex, the White Tower. With its fifteen-foot thick walls of Kentish rag stone, the White Tower presents a grim, impregnable face to the world. The entrance is approximately fifteen feet up the side of the building and is still reached via a wooden staircase of the type which could be removed if the castle walls were penetrated by an enemy army. The half-timbered Queen's House nearby is one of the official residences of the monarch but also houses the Lieutenant of the Tower. It was built around 1540 in the reign of Henry VIII.

By Shakespeare's day the Tower was a contradictory place; on one hand it functioned as a tourist attraction with visitors flocking to see fearsome beasts such as leopards and bears at the royal menagerie. On the other hand it was still very much a royal palace. It was also a prison. The Tower was a place where the unlucky, the brave and the foolish went to suffer and die.

In November 1583, Tower diaries state that Edward Arden, kinsman to Shakespeare, was tortured upon the rack following his son-in-law John Somerville's arrest. Somerville himself was found strangled inside his cell. In 1601, Robert Devereux, the Earl of Essex, was beheaded on Tower Green for his failed uprising against the queen. Perhaps unwittingly, Shakespeare's company had played a role in the rebellion by agreeing to perform *Richard II* at The Globe, complete with the deposition scene in which the king is shown giving up his crown.

Visitors to the Tower today can see pitiful graffiti etched into the walls, testament to the lost souls who had short stays there prior to execution or who pined away for years, forgotten behind bars. In the Beauchamp Tower the name Jane is etched into the stone, possibly carved by Guildford Dudley, husband to Lady Jane Grey. The couple were executed on 12 February 1554; Guildford outside in public on Tower Green and Jane within the privacy of the Tower walls. Also on the wall of the Beauchamp Tower is the florid signature of Philip Howard, the Earl of Arundel, a Catholic convert. He was imprisoned in 1585 after trying to leave the country. After his capture he was sentenced to death and spent the rest of his life in a desperate limbo, unaware that Elizabeth I had not signed the death warrant. He died of dysentery in 1595.

Although escape from the Tower was not unheard of, it was very rare and difficult to achieve. One of the most celebrated successes was that of the priest John Gerard who managed to slither out of the Salt Tower and across the moat with the help of some good friends and a length of rope. In *Richard III,* the imprisoned Clarence tells Brackenbury of a dream in which he'd broken from the Tower and set sail for Burgundy. It is an eerie premonition of his subsequent drowning in a vat of malmsey:

> As we paced along
> Upon the giddy footings of the hatches,

Methought that Gloucester stumbled; and, in falling,
Struck me, that thought to stay him, overboard,
Into the tumbling billows of the main.
Lord, Lord! Methought, what pain it was to drown!

*Richard III*: Clarence, Act I, Scene IV

In Act IV of the same play, Queen Elizabeth stands before the Tower and thinks with concern about her two boys, the young princes, trapped inside:

Stay, yet look back with me unto the Tower.
Pity, you ancient stones, those tender babes
Whom envy hath immured within your walls!
Rough cradle for such little pretty ones!
Rude, ragged nurse, old sullen playfellow
For tender princes, use my babies well!
So foolish sorrow bids your stones farewell.

*Richard III*: Queen Elizabeth, Act IV, Scene I

Like his character Elizabeth, William Shakespeare may also have thought of the Tower with sadness and with dread, knowing what had happened to Edward Arden in there. His relative silence on that most infamous building seems eloquent, and considering that he was one of the few playwrights of his age to avoid imprisonment, his silence also appears to be a part of his wisdom.

Visitors enter the complex via the Middle Tower which leads onto a walkway over the grass moat. In 2014 the lawn was filled with ceramic red poppies in remembrance of those who died in the First World War. The walkway leads through the Byward Tower. After passing beneath its arched doorway, you will see the Bell Tower on the left. It was in here that Sir Thomas More was held prior to his execution in 1535. The following year the poet Thomas Wyatt was also held in here after his arrest on suspicion of adultery with Anne Boleyn. A memorial to Anne in the form of a glass cushion is located at the reputed site of her execution on Tower Green near the White Tower. On the other side of the White Tower are the sixteenth-century Queen's House and the Bloody Tower with its grisly exhibition on the instruments of torture used within. The Crown Jewels are kept in the Jewel House and include items such as the Coronation Spoon which has been used for anointing monarchs at their coronations for over 800 years.

Near the Wakefield Tower are the raven lodgings where the Tower's black ravens – Bran, Porsha, Erin, Merlina, Munin, Hugine, Rocky, Gripp and Jubilee – are housed. These birds are treated as employees and can be dismissed for bad conduct as in the case of Raven George who was sent packing in 1986 after attacking television aerials. As befitting local celebrities, they enjoy a rich diet comprised of fresh meat, cheese, grapes and cod liver oil. Legend has it that if the ravens ever left the Tower, the kingdom would fall. Each bird has one wing clipped to keep them safely within its walls.

The Tower is also famous for its Yeoman Warders, who can be seen patrolling the grounds in their distinctive tunics of dark blue with red trimmings. They are commonly known as Beefeaters, a nickname of uncertain origin. They are all retired forces personnel with at least twenty-two years of impeccable service. Although their official function is to guard the Crown Jewels they have a wealth of knowledge about the Tower and are among the most entertaining tour guides in London, interspersing their grisly tales with cheeky repartee. They and their families live in the Tower apartments.

*Visitor Information*

Tower Hill station is on both the Circle and District Lines and is located just over the road from the ticket booths. As you leave the station, walk straight ahead into the pretty Trinity Park. This was Tower Hill, the site of numerous sixteenth-century executions. A small plaque at the far end of the park marks the site of the scaffold and remembers victims such as Sir Thomas More, Thomas Cromwell and Robert Devereux, Earl of Essex. Exit the park via the nearby gate and cross the busy road at the traffic lights. Straight ahead and to the right are the Tower of London ticket booths. After purchasing your tickets walk down the slope until you reach the entrance on the left-hand side. The public loos behind the ticket booths charge 50p so you may wish to hold on until you get inside the Tower. There are cafés located within the Tower and also outside near the ticket booths.

After hearing all those tales of torture and execution, you may be in need of a drink. The perfect pub in which to revive your spirits is the aptly named Hung, Drawn and Quartered which is located round the corner at 26–27 Great Tower Street.

The nearby church of All Hallows by the Tower was built in the fifteenth century but stands on the site of a much older foundation. The bodies of Sir Thomas More and Bishop Fisher were temporarily housed here after their executions in 1535 before being laid to rest in the chapel of St Peter ad Vincula within the Tower. It was from the church tower that Samuel Pepys stood and watched the Great Fire of London. In the crypt there is a superb museum which contains artefacts from the original Saxon church as well as part of a Roman floor.

Those interested in the diarist Samuel Pepys may wish to cross back over Tower Hill and head towards Seething Lane where he lived in a house owned by the Navy Office. In the little park opposite is a bust of the man himself. He attended the nearby church of St Olave Hart Street, described by Dickens as 'St Ghastly Grim' because of the stone skulls above the archway. Pepys was an avid theatre goer and recorded seeing *A Midsummer Night's Dream* on 29 September 1662. His review was fairly critical:

> Michaelmas Day. And then to the King's Theatre, where we saw 'Midsummer Night's Dream', which I had never seen before, nor shall ever again, for it is the most insipid ridiculous play that ever I saw in my life. I saw, I confess, some good dancing and some handsome women, which was all my pleasure.

Ouch.

The Tower of London is open Tuesday to Saturday 9:00–17:30 and Sunday to Monday 10:00–17:30. Last admission is at 17:00. Admission to the Tower of London: Adult, £24.50; Children between five and fifteen, £11.00; Concessions, £18.70; Family, £60.70.

Hung, Drawn and Quartered is open Monday to Saturday 11:00–23:00 and Sundays 12:00–18:00.

All Hallows by the Tower offers free guided tours from April to October most weekdays between 14:00–16:00. The adjoining Kitchen @ Tower café serves a range of delicious meals including full English Breakfasts, sandwiches, homemade burgers and fish and chips. Opening hours are Monday to Friday 8:00–17:30, Saturdays 9:00–17:30 and Sundays and Bank Holidays 10:00–17:30.

## Cannon Street and Eastcheap

> If there were anything in thy pocket but tavern reckonings, memorandums of bawdy houses, and one poor penny worth

of sugar candy to make thee long winded, if thy pocket were enriched with any other injuries but these, I am a villain.

*Henry IV, Part I*: Prince Henry, Act III, Scene III

## Jack the Lads

At numbers 33–35 Eastcheap in the City of London is a building that the architectural writer Nikolaus Pevsner called 'one of the maddest displays in London.' He may well have been right about 'mad' but, at the same time, this particular building shows us the care with which the Victorians balanced pragmatic function and playfulness. Built in 1869 to house a vinegar warehouse, the red-brick façade is eerily Gothic. The windows are topped by a 'frenzy of sharp gables.' Underneath the central arch a boar's head can be seen peeping through the decoratively carved foliage. This is in remembrance of the tavern where Shakespeare set some of the funniest scenes in the plays *Henry IV, Parts I & II.* The Boar's Head stood near this site between two vanished thoroughfares, Small Alley and St Michael's Lane. Its date of construction is unknown but it is known to have existed in the sixteenth century so maybe Shakespeare spent the odd evening there, nursing a pot of ale and observing the local life.

Eastcheap is a short but busy stretch of road just to the north east of London Bridge. One of the oldest streets in London, Eastcheap dates back to around 1100 when it was the site of a medieval marketplace. It was called 'East' cheap in those days to distinguish it from Westcheap, which is now known as Cheapside. According to the Elizabethan historian John Stow, the street was inhabited by butchers who had moved in from elsewhere in the city; Shakespeare's Eastcheap would have been ripe with the smell of freshly cut meat. One imagines flies hovering over pools of blood and scrawny curs begging for scraps. At the very least it was a down to earth neighbourhood, hardly fit for royals. Yet, this is where Shakespeare imagines the heir apparent, Prince Hal hanging out. Here he is, settling down at the Boar's Head, boasting about how he knows all the local bar staff

> Prince Henry: ... Sirrah, I am sworn brother to a leash of drawers; and can call them all by their Christian names, as Tom, Dick and Francis ... and when I am king of England, I shall command all the good lads in Eastcheap.
>
> *Henry IV, Part I*: Prince Henry, Act II, Scene IV

The same scene goes on to show Prince Hal and his sidekick Poins teasing Francis the tapster. The clientele of the Boar's Head is similar to pubs up and down the country; there is usually someone propping up the bar telling tall tales. When Falstaff enters he begins to relate an exaggerated story of the trouble he had at Gads Hill when he was set upon by a gang of robbers. As his story progresses, the number of assailants he was forced to defend himself against gradually increases from two to eleven. Prince Hal, one of the two robbers, can take no more:

> Prince Henry: These lies are like their father that begets them; gross as a mountain, open, palpable. Why, thou clay brained guts, thou knotty pated fool, thou whoreson, obscene, grease tallow-catch –
> Falstaff: What, art thou mad? Art thou mad? Is it not the truth?
>
> *Henry IV, Part I*: Prince Henry, Act II, Scene IV

In Act III, Scene III, Falstaff accuses the hostess Mistress Quickly of keeping pickpockets in her house. She in turn accuses him of owing her money in unpaid bar tabs.

Like most of London's Tudor-era buildings the tavern was destroyed in the Great Fire of London but it was rebuilt in 1668, this time in brick, with a carved boar's head above the window bearing the landlord's initials. Here it stood until 1831 when it was demolished to make way for the rebuilding of London Bridge. The sign of the boar's head was rescued and is now on display at Shakespeare's Globe on Bankside. The building that Pevsner called one of the 'maddest' in London now houses offices.

Just to the south of Eastcheap is the Monument, a fluted pillar erected by Sir Christopher Wren after the Great Fire of London. It stands 202 feet high, just feet away from Pudding Lane and the scene of the accident. The summer of 1666 had been long and hot. It had not rained at all. The timber houses that crowded the narrow streets of the city were like a tinderbox waiting to go up. In some ways the accident was inevitable; all it needed was a stray spark. In the end it was a careless maid at Thomas Fariner's bakery who failed to douse the ovens; this led to a fire which rampaged out of control, killing at least six people including the maid who was too scared to leave the burning building. Over three days it all but destroyed the medieval city.

Across the busy junction from the Monument is Cannon Street which leads in a straight line to St Paul's. The name Cannon Street signifies candles rather than cannons. In the Middle Ages it was known as Candelwrichstrete after the local candle makers; by Shakespeare's day the name had evolved to the much snappier Candlewick Street and the candle makers had been joined there by drapers. The name Cannon Street dates from the seventeenth century.

Halfway down and hidden behind a grubby pane of glass at street level is the mysterious London Stone. The shop window in which it resides belongs to a branch of WH Smith on the north side of the street. In Shakespeare's day the stone was located on the south side and, according to Stow, was something of a hazard to passing traffic. He describes it thus:

On the south side of this high street, near unto the channel, is pitched upright a great stone called London Stone, fixed in the ground very deep, fastened with bars of iron, and otherwise so strongly set, that if carts do run against it through negligence, the wheels be broken, and the stone itself unshaken.

The origins of the stone were hazy and Stow was intrigued. By examining church records and documents he managed to trace its existence back to the twelfth century. He was curious about what it could have been used for and examined various theories, one of which suggested that the stone may have been a meeting place for debtors to meet their creditors, or that it was named after 'John and Thomas Londonstone dwelling there.' He dismissed that theory on the reasonable grounds that John and Thomas are more likely to have taken the name of the stone than the stone being named for them. Even today nobody really knows what the stone is, although it is sometimes suggested that it was a Roman milestone or, given its proximity to the Roman governor's palace, a part of that building. In 1450 when Jack Cade led his 5,000 rebels into the city he is said to have struck his sword against the stone as he proclaimed himself Lord of the City. By this time it must have been a highly symbolic landmark as Shakespeare shows Cade taking possession of the stone

> Now is Mortimer lord of this city. And here, sitting
> Upon London-stone, I charge and command that, of the
> City's cost, the pissing-conduit run nothing but
> Claret wine this first year of our reign. And now
> Henceforth it shall be treason for any that calls
> Me other than Lord Mortimer.
>
> *Henry VI, Part II*: Cade, Act IV, Scene VI

After looting and beheading their way around the city Cade is eventually slain and the rebellion quashed. Today, Cannon Street hums with the sound of traffic and diggers. City workers dash about in a hurry. Nobody seems to notice the white stone hidden behind its grill. In 2012 it was nearly moved by developers but various heritage organisations protested and, for the time being at least, it remains in its place, a quiet and unobtrusive remnant of a more mystical age.

*Visitor Information*
Monument Tube Station, on the Central, Circle and District Lines, is located between Eastcheap and Cannon Street. Those brave enough to climb the narrow, spiral staircase to the top of the Monument itself will enjoy far-reaching views of the city and beyond. Opening hours are 9:30–18:00 from April to September and 9:30–17:30 from October to March. Tickets cost £4.00 for adults, £2.70 for concessions and £2.00 for children under sixteen. For details call 0207 626 2717 or see www. themonument.info.

# St Magnus the Martyr, Fish Street Hill and London Bridge

> What say ye, countrymen? Will ye relent,
> And yield to mercy whilst 'tis offered you;
> Or let a rebel lead you to your deaths?
> *Henry VI, Part II*: Clifford, Act IV, Scene VIII

*A Church by the Thames*
The rebel Jack Cade rampages through several scenes in the play *Henry VI, Part II*. He and his fellow rioters turn up in locations

all over the city causing mayhem and havoc wherever they go in a doomed attempt to overthrow the king's councillors. Shakespeare of course embellished and dramatized these scenes for the consumption of Elizabethan playgoers but they are loosely based on historical facts; this was a rebellion which rocked London. The causes of Jack Cade's uprising were complex and varied but they can be briefly outlined here. The population had been growing weary with the seemingly endless wars in France. Those in southern counties such as Kent felt vulnerable to attack from the Continent. This very real fear was exacerbated by the high taxes levied to pay for the conflicts combined with a growing resentment at perceived corruption among the king's advisors. All these tensions resulted in an explosive uprising.

The Kentish Cade is an obscure figure; almost nothing is known about him. He used several aliases including the provocative 'Mortimer', a name loaded with significance. The king's rival Richard, Duke of York, had Mortimer ancestry. He also had a claim to the throne so Cade's use of that particular name can only have been seen as a threat. In May 1450, Cade and his rebels set out from Kent to march on London. They stopped briefly at Blackheath then arrived at Southwark where they stayed at the White Hart Inn on what is now Borough High Street. On 3 July they entered the city via London Bridge. Initially the citizens gave them a warm welcome; Cade had promised there would be no looting or destructive behaviour. It seems however that, drunk on power, he and his followers could not restrain themselves. At this point the level-headed merchants and traders of the city turned against them.

Shakespeare seems to have had a lot of fun portraying Cade's bolshy pride with his characteristically blunt instructions to his men

Up Fish Street! Down Saint Magnus Corner! Kill
and knock down! Throw them into the Thames!

*Henry VI, Part II*: Cade, Act IV, Scene VIII

Cade delivers these lines when the rebels are losing their
momentum. They have retreated to Southwark where the king's
men, Buckingham and Clifford, come with offers of pardons.
Cade's men realise which way the tide is turning and desert him.
After a bit more blustering, Cade wisely flees.

Fish Street was safe for now. There would be no more 'killing
and knocking down' or even 'throwing in the Thames'.

It was London Bridge which finally defeated Jack Cade. After
looting his way around the city he retired to the White Hart in
Southwark and the citizens closed the bridge against him. On
8 July a battle commenced between Cade's followers and the
city officials. It would last all night and took place partly on
the bridge itself where Cade's decapitated head would shortly
be set on a spike. It was a decisive end to one of London's most
dramatic episodes.

When Cade urged his men 'up Fish Street' he was talking
about what we know as Fish Street Hill, a cobbled lane which
opens out at its centre point to make room for the Monument,
Wren's memorial to the Great Fire. The street was first laid out
by the Romans and led from the forum to their river crossing,
whatever form that took. Shakespeare knew it as the street
leading down towards London Bridge from the north of the city.
John Stow describes the area, 'In New Fish Street be fishmongers
and fair taverns on Fish Street Hill and Grass Street, men of
divers trades, grocers, and haberdashers.' It was a place of brisk,
noisy commerce carried out in the shadow of the bridge. St
Magnus' Corner was located just to the east of Fish Street Hill
at the north end of London Bridge. In the Middle Ages this spot

functioned almost in the same way as Paul's Cross with public announcements and gatherings. Standing nearby was the church from which it took its name. The present St Magnus the Martyr is a baroque Italianate-style creation dating from 1688 when Wren rebuilt it after the Great Fire. In contrast to many of the plainer city churches, St Magnus the Martyr is High Church in character; the services are enhanced by early sacred music; the smell of incense hangs in the air. Ironically, this is the resting place of Miles Coverdale, a man of puritan leanings who served as rector at the church in 1546. He translated the Bible into English and was a fierce critic of anything resembling religious flummery. The pre-fire church – and the one known by Shakespeare and Coverdale – was according to Stow a 'fair parish church ... in the which church have been buried many men of good Worship, whose monuments are now for the most part utterly defaced.' He was presumably talking about the iconoclastic vandalism of the reformation when images of the Virgin Mary were smashed.

St Magnus the Martyr's situation at the north end of London Bridge meant that this was the first church to greet travellers entering the city from the south. Its spire can still be seen today, nestling against the riverbank as you walk over the bridge. Every weekday morning like clockwork an endless stream of commuters walks across London Bridge on their way to work in the city. The spectacle is repeated in reverse as they head back the same way to the train station to make the journey home. With their suits and smartphones it looks like a thoroughly modern phenomenon but these hardy souls are enacting a ritual which has endured since the earliest days of London's history.

London Bridge was first built in stone during the reign of Henry II as an act of penitence for the murder of Thomas à Becket. Work started in 1176 and took over thirty years to complete, partially funded by public donations to 'God and the Bridge'. To the commissioners of the project and to medieval Londoners, the work was seen as a religious duty. To that end the Bridge House Estates was founded to facilitate public giving. By making careful investments and by raising taxes from the numerous shops which began to appear on the bridge, its wealth increased exponentially. The Bridge House Estates is still in existence today and continues to fund the upkeep of London's bridges using money which has accumulated over the last thousand years.

Appropriately for a project of such piety, the architect of Old London Bridge was a priest. Peter de Colechurch designed a fine stone crossing supported by twenty arches. In the middle was a chapel dedicated to St Thomas à Becket at which pilgrims would stop and pray on their way to Canterbury. Over the years mercantile Londoners began to fill the bridge with shops and houses which effectively turned the bridge into a street on water. Stow describes it in admiring terms, 'All the bridge is replenished on both the sides with large, fair, and beautiful buildings, inhabitants for the most part rich merchants, and other wealthy citizens.' At only twenty-six feet wide the passage would have been crowded with shoppers and travellers. Those in a hurry to catch a play on Bankside may have preferred to cross the river by wherry, a method which would also have allowed them to avoid the sight of the par-boiled traitors' heads set on spikes above the southern entrance.

Old London Bridge endured for over 600 years during which time it witnessed the lives of generations of Londoners going about their business – whether that was shopping, travelling or rioting. As time progressed and the population grew, the decision was made to replace it with something more fit for purpose. In 1799 submissions for a new design were invited with the Scottish engineer John Rennie winning the competition. His creation was simple and elegant; he designed a wide stone bridge with five rounded arches through which the river traffic could navigate safely. It was built slightly further upstream to Old London Bridge and work was completed in 1831.

In the 1960s, to avoid costly repairs, the Court of Common Council sold Rennie's bridge to a wealthy American. It was dismantled and shipped off to Lake Havasu City in Arizona where it still stands. The urban legend that the buyer thought he was purchasing Tower Bridge is sadly unfounded.

The modern London Bridge is of a rather less romantic design than its predecessors. Completed in 1972 with liberal use of concrete it is utilitarian and plain; its long evolution for now, complete.

*Visitor Information*

St Magnus the Martyr is located at Lower Thames Street, London EC3R 6DN. Tel: 020 7626 4481.

St Magnus the Martyr is one of the most fascinating, yet overlooked, churches in the City of London. Possibly due to its tricky location on the wrong side of the thundering Lower Thames Street, it does not attract the attention it deserves. In the small churchyard there remains one of the stone arches at the foot of Old London Bridge. Another remnant of the bridge can be found in a more unusual location. At the eastern tip of Victoria Park in the east end of London one of its alcoves has been turned into a shelter with a stone bench within.

# St Etheldreda

> Beauty, truth and rarity.
> Grace in all simplicity,
> Here enclos'd in cinders lie.
> Lines taken from *The Phoenix and the Turtle*

*Martyrs and Strawberries*

Newgate Street in the City of London is a long, unlovely stretch which bisects the Smithfield and St Paul's areas. The sound of diggers competes with the roar of passing traffic. Stony-faced office workers stride purposefully to and from the offices and heaven help the poor tourist who stands in their way. Despite passing some of London's richest heritage sites, this is without a doubt a thoroughfare and not a place to loiter. The pedestrian cannot help but be swept along at the same frantic pace as everyone else. What a relief then to arrive at Ely Place. Located just off Charterhouse Street and Holborn Viaduct, this is a quiet cul-de-sac of grand terraced houses, some of which date back to 1773 when the street was laid out. It is unusual in that it is privately owned; indeed the guardhouse at the entrance used to be manned by security guards in top hats up until the 1980s. Today it is looked after by a governing body of commissioners and beadles. It is worth seeking out because halfway up on the left-hand side is one of those hidden gems of London. Often overlooked by visitors, yet loaded with history, is the church of St Etheldreda's. Started around 1290 by John de Kirkeby during the reign of Edward I, this is one of England's oldest Catholic churches, coming second after St Leonard and St Mary in Malton.

From outside the church the first thing you notice is the huge Gothic arched window which dominates the eastern façade. Stepping inside, a long corridor leads you past the crypt and into the cosy chapel where the noise of the street suddenly fades into near silence. Lined along the two side walls, high above the pews are eight statues representing English martyrs who died for their faith in the sixteenth century. They gaze down like watchful guardians. Margaret Ward is depicted in Elizabethan dress, holding a basket. She was a lady's maid who was executed in 1588 for helping a priest escape from Bridewell Prison. Her partner in crime was the boatman John Roche who helpfully swapped clothes with the priest and was arrested in his stead. Roche is depicted wearing a plain brown jerkin and hose. The Carthusian monk St John Houghton is dressed in the long white flowing robes of his order. He was the prior of the Charterhouse monastery and was executed in 1535 for refusing to swear an oath to the Act of Supremacy which asserted that Henry VIII, and not the pope, was head of the Church in England.

Two of the other St Etheldreda martyrs are loosely connected to Shakespeare. Swithin Wells was a schoolmaster who was hanged, drawn and quartered outside his house on Grays Inn Lane in 1591 for the crime of allowing Catholic Masses to be held there. During the late 1570s he had acted as tutor to the young Henry Wriothesley, the Earl of Southampton. Shakespeare would later dedicate his two narrative poems *Venus and Adonis* and *The Rape of Lucrece* to the earl. Another interesting character is Anne Line who is shown wearing a long brown dress with dark cap and ruff. She was employed by the Jesuits to run safe houses for their priests. She and her husband Roger were parted from each other when he moved to Flanders after being banished in 1594. He died in exile. Some writers suggest that Shakespeare's poem *The Phoenix and the Turtle* contains allusions to their deaths:

> Death is now the phoenix' nest;
> And the turtle's loyal breast
> To eternity doth rest,
> Leaving no posterity,
> 'Twas not their infirmity,
> It was married chastity.
> Truth may seem, but cannot be:

> Beauty brag, but 'tis not she;
> Truth and beauty buried be.
> To this urn let those repair
> That are either true or fair;
> For these dead birds sigh a prayer.

The church of St Etheldreda was constructed as part of a complex which housed the Bishops of Ely who needed a London base for the occasions when they were called to attend the king or Parliament. It was a huge, sprawling site spread over fifty-eight acres with the Bishop's Palace and the chapel at the centre. John of Gaunt moved into the palace after his Savoy Palace was burnt down during the Peasants' Revolt of 1381. He spent his last years there before his death at Leicester Castle in 1399. It is at Ely Palace that Shakespeare has a fading Gaunt giving his 'Scepter'd Isle' speech:

> This royal throne of kings, this scepter'd isle,
> This earth of majesty, this seat of Mars,
> This other eden, demi-paradise...
> > *Richard II*: John of Gaunt, Act II, Scene I

The palace grounds included orchards and gardens which were well known for their strawberries. In *Richard III* Gloucester meets the Bishop of Ely at the Tower of London and has a sudden hankering for some of them:

> Gloucester: My lord of Ely, when I was last in Holborn
> I saw good strawberries in your garden there.
> I do beseech you send for some of them.
> Bishop of Ely: Marry and will, my lord, with all my heart.
> > *Richard III*: Act III, Scene IV

The prospect of shortly eating some delicious strawberries ought to have put history's favourite villain in a good mood. However, in the same scene he turns on his old friend Hastings and has him executed. St Etheldreda's continues the fruit association with its annual charity Strawberry Fayre in which visitors can sample a variety of strawberries with cream.

In 1578 Sir Christopher Hatton took up residency in the palace with the help of his close friend Queen Elizabeth I. She exerted pressure on its dismayed resident Bishop Richard Cox who eventually yielded to Hatton a twenty-one year lease of the apartments and the gatehouse along with fourteen acres of grounds. Hatton enjoyed all this for the token rent of ten pounds, ten loads of hay and a single red rose per year. He used the crypt of St Etheldreda's chapel as a tavern. The nearby jewellery district of Hatton Garden, which takes its name from that lucky courtier, lies just to the west of Ely Place on a stretch of land that he rented from the bishop. The two are connected by Ely Court, a tiny, yet curious passageway which is home to an equally small pub. Ye Olde Mitre was first built in 1546 in the grounds of the palace to serve the bishop's household. The present building dates from 1772, around the same time as the palace was destroyed and the houses in Ely Place were built. From the outside it looks like a quintessential English watering hole with its oak frontage, potted flowers and decorative beer barrels on the terrace. In a corner of the bar is the trunk of an ancient cherry tree and legend has it that Elizabeth I danced around the tree on her visits to Christopher Hatton. In a strange hangover from the days when the Mitre was on Ely Palace land, the pub landlords used to have to apply to the authorities in Cambridgeshire for their licence.

All in all Ely Place is a delightful corner of Holborn, full of quirks and tales.

*Visitor Information*

Ye Olde Mitre is located at 1 Ely Court, Ely Place, London EC1N 6SJ. Tel: 0207 405 4751. They serve excellent cask ales as well as a varied menu of bar snacks that they are proud to say does not include chips. Opening hours: Monday to Friday 11:00–23:00, closed at weekends. More information can be found at www. yeoldemitreholborn.co.uk.

St Etheldreda is located at 14 Ely Place, London EC1N 6RY. Tel: 020 7405 1061. The doors of St Etheldreda's are generally open, although be aware that services are held here on a regular basis so it is best to avoid those times if you are just visiting. Downstairs in the crypt there is an interesting model of Ely Palace as it used to look. Henry VIII attended a feast in the crypt in 1531. He was accompanied by his soon-to-be estranged wife Catherine of Aragon and, according to John Stow, they sat in separate chambers. More information can be found at www. stetheldreda.com.

As you exit Ely Place and find yourself once more in the land of harried commuters and car fumes, you may wish to turn right and cross Holborn Circus heading up High Holborn towards Grays Inn where the Chamberlain's Men performed *The Comedy of Errors* in 1594. One of the four Inns of Court, previous members include Shakespeare's patron Henry Wriothesley, the Earl of Southampton and the playwrights Thomas Middleton and George Chapman.

# Westminster Hall

> For God's sake, let us sit upon the ground
> And tell sad stories of the death of kings
>
> *Richard II*: Richard II, Act III, Scene II

*The Deposition Scene*

It is no exaggeration to say that Westminster Hall is one of the finest great halls in the whole of Europe. Started in 1097 by William Rufus as part of his new palace of Westminster, the hall has occupied a place at the beating heart of English state affairs for over 900 years. The first meeting of Parliament took place here in 1265 when the rebel baron Simon de Montfort summoned representatives from each borough to have a parley, or discussion. At 240 feet long by 67 feet wide the hall is an impressive sight. The thick stone walls are topped by a series of rounded windows that let light stream into the vast space. Much of what we see today is down to the remodelling work carried out in the late fourteenth century by Richard II, a man who understood the power of imagery and used it to create an image of himself as a ruler touched by God. In 1393 he commissioned the huge hammer-beam roof that we see today, a ruinously expensive job paid for in part by exiles and outlaws to whom he promised safe passage back to England if they contributed funds. Carved into the roof are a flight of winged angels. They bear shields decorated with the *fleur de lis* of France, the country of Richard's birth, and the three lions of England. A set of thirteen statues of Richard's kingly predecessors, from Edward the Confessor onwards, stands in niches on the south wall and along the windowsills. At one time their crowns were gilded and would have glinted brightly in the candlelight. Richard's symbol, the white hart, also features in the carvings. The embellishments in the hall sent out a clear statement of his power and glory, creating around the king an untouchable air of mystique. Richard was the first monarch to insist on being addressed as 'majesty.'

The reasons for his inevitable downfall read like a list of 'how not to rule the country.' This book is not the place to explore

Richard's life in detail but it is safe to argue that his exiling of the popular Henry Bolingbroke, who was at that time a loyal subject, was ill-advised and wrongheaded. When he disinherited Bolingbroke during his banishment, he created a fatal mistrust among other landowners. For which noble could trust the king now? Richard's reliance on small cliques of advisors and his downright aloofness could hardly have helped. In 1399 Richard's world came crashing down when Henry Bolingbroke sneaked back into the country while Richard was in Ireland. The English nobility flocked to Bolingbroke's cause and Richard was sent to the Tower of London.

In the play *Richard II* Shakespeare sets the deposition scene inside Westminster Hall. He portrays Richard as a broken man, hardly able to believe that his illusion of immortality is over. The smoke has cleared and Richard is just a mortal like any other. His public humiliation is hard to bear as he gives up his crown in a hall resplendent with the symbols of his rule. This is one of the most controversial scenes of the Shakespeare canon:

> Henry Bolingbroke: Are you contented to resign the crown?
> King Richard II: Ay, no; no, ay; for I must nothing be;
> Therefore no no, for I resign to thee.
> Now mark me, how I will undo myself;
> I give this heavy weight from off my head
> And this unwieldy sceptre from my hand,
> The pride of kingly sway from out my heart;
> With mine own tears I wash away my balm,
> With mine own hands I give away my crown ...
>
> *Richard II*: Act IV, Scene I

Northumberland then urges him to read aloud the list of

accusations against him so that the public would know he had been justly removed from power. Richard is unwilling

> Must I do so? And must I ravel out
> My weaved up folly? Gentle Northumberland,
> If thy offences were upon record,
> Would it not shame thee in so fair a troop
> To read a lecture of them? If thou wouldst,
> There shouldst thou find one heinous article,
> Containing the deposing of a king ...
>
> *Richard II*: Richard II, Act IV, Scene I

Richard's response here shows that although he has given up the crown, he is likely to bear the grudge forever. He asks Henry Bolingbroke to let him go, but is sent to the Tower of London instead where he wastes away, forgotten. Any potential risk he might pose to the new order has been neutered.

For a man living in the paranoid Elizabethan police state, Shakespeare had written quite a daring scene. Showing a monarch, any monarch, losing his crown on the public stage was sailing close to the wind and it was too much for the Master of the Revels. When *Richard II* was first performed in 1595 this scene was omitted. Elizabeth I was another monarch who knew how to use imagery and symbols as armour.

Until the nineteenth century Westminster Hall was used as a law court and over the years it has witnessed some of the most important state trials in history, including that of Sir Thomas More who was found guilty of treason for refusing to swear the Act of Supremacy in 1535. More would later be the subject of a play thought to have been written in collaboration with several writers, including Shakespeare. In January 1606, eight men, one of them weak with torture, were rowed down the river from their cells in the Tower of London to be charged with a much more serious crime. Guy Fawkes, who had been caught red-handed in the cellars with thirty-six barrels of gunpowder and a lit fuse, pleaded not guilty to the charge of attempting to blow the place up. To this day the Yeoman of the Guard conducts a ceremonial search of the cellars beneath the House of Lords before the State Opening of Parliament.

### Visitor Information

Tours of Parliament can be arranged by booking in advance. For UK residents it is possible to book a free tour by contacting your local Member of Parliament. They will arrange for you to join a tour led by a qualified Blue Badge guide on certain dates. Bear in mind that the tours are extremely popular and can get booked up six months in advance. It is advised to book early and to be flexible with your dates. Both UK and overseas residents can pay for the public tours by booking online or calling 0207 219 4114. Dates available depend on whether or not Parliament is in session so see www.parliament.uk/visiting for up-to-date information and prices. Included in the tours are Westminster Hall, the Royal Gallery, the Central Lobby, the Commons Chamber and St Stephen's Hall.

Outside, the picturesque Parliament Square is alive with a mix of visitors, suited parliamentary workers and, quite often, some form of protest. Open-topped buses zoom around the square, their tour guides giving sparkling commentary about the visual feast on every side. Westminster Hall is dwarfed by the neo-Gothic palace buildings, started by Charles Barry in 1840. Six years previously, a fire had destroyed the medieval buildings and Barry was the winner of a competition to design its replacement. The Elizabeth Tower is more commonly known as Big Ben, a misnomer as Big Ben is the clock not the tower. It was named after Elizabeth II in 2012 who celebrated her Diamond Jubilee that year. The white church between Westminster Palace and the Westminster Abbey is St Margaret's and has stood here since 1523. Inside is a beautiful stained glass window dating from 1509 which commemorates the betrothal of Henry VIII and Catherine of Aragon. Sir Walter Raleigh was buried here after his execution in Old Palace Yard in 1618. The church is open to visitors Monday to Friday 9.30–15.30, Saturday 9.30–13.30 and Sundays 14.00–16.30.

On Abingdon Street around the corner is a remnant of the medieval Westminster Palace. The Jewel House dates from 1365 and functioned as a storage space for Edward III. Along with Westminster Hall it survived the fire which devastated the rest of the palace and is now overseen by English Heritage. It is sometimes overlooked but is well worth a visit to see its fourteenth-century carved ceilings and the exhibition inside. Opening hours are variable so check before travelling. Admission is currently £4.20 for adults, £2.50 for children between five and fifteen, £3.80 for concessions and £11.00 for a family ticket. Call 0370 333 1181 for up-to-date information.

Across the road from the palace is Westminster Abbey. Started by Edward the Confessor in 1042 the church is a 'royal peculiar' meaning that it falls under the jurisdiction of the monarch and not the local diocese. Its labyrinthine passageways are crammed with ancient tomb chests belonging to a glittering array of celebrated British monarchs. The tomb of Elizabeth I lies beneath the canopy of an ornate burial monument. Her successor James I placed her on top of the tomb of her half sister Mary I. The question of whether or not those feuding women wished to spend eternity in such close proximity seems not to have bothered James. At the base of the monument are the words, 'Partners in throne and grave, here we sleep Elizabeth and Mary, sisters in hope of the Resurrection.' The tomb shared by Richard II and his wife Anne of Bohemia is located in the shrine. In Poet's Corner is a white marble memorial to Shakespeare. Erected in 1741 it depicts the poet leaning thoughtfully on a pile of books. In 1599 Shakespeare may have been among the poets who attended the funeral of Edmund Spenser, the aristocratic author of *The Faerie Queene*. According to William Camden, the men took turns to read elegies to Spencer before throwing their papers and pens into the tomb. His friend Ben Jonson is also buried in the abbey. Owing to his poverty in later life he was unable to afford a horizontal position and is buried standing up. A small stone on the wall marks the spot. It has the inscription, 'O, rare Ben Johnson'.

Westminster Abbey is open to visitors from Monday to Saturday but hours are variable so check www.westminster-abbey.org/visit-us for up-to-date information. Ticket prices are as follows: Adults, £20; Concessions £17; Children between the ages of six and sixteen, £9; Children under the age of five go free. There are also family tickets available. The abbey offers daily verger-led tours for £5 per person. Starting from the North Door the tours last for ninety minutes and include Poets Corner, the Cloisters, Nave and the Royal Tombs. The times are variable so the abbey recommends asking about availability on arrival. Alternatively the Blue Badge tour guides are qualified to work inside the abbey and you may wish to book one for a private tour. See www.guidelondon.org.uk to find a guide.

# Windsor

Let's consult together against this greasy knight. Come hither.
*Merry Wives of Windsor*: Mistress Page, Act II, Scene I

## The Merry Wives

The 'greasy knight' is of course Sir John Falstaff; that loveable rogue who first featured in both parts of *Henry IV*. He must have delighted the crowds because the epilogue of *Henry IV, Part II* promises to resurrect the character

> One word more, I beseech you. If you be not too much cloyed with fat meat, our humble author will continue the story, with Sir John in it, and make you merry with fair Katherine of France: where, for anything I know, Falstaff shall die of a sweat, unless a' be already killed with your hard opinions.
>
> *Henry IV, Part II*: Dancer, Epilogue

The epilogue seems to hint that Falstaff will reappear in *Henry V*. In the end however, it seems Shakespeare chose to keep him well away from the action of that play, killing him off in a scene which takes place offstage. The first time Falstaff is even mentioned is when his boy enters and interrupts an argument between Pistol, Nym, Bardolph and Mistress Quickly. He begs them to attend his dying master. Nym and Pistol know who is to blame for their old friend's demise:

> Nym: The king hath run bad humours on the knight; that's the even of it.
> Pistol: Nym, thou hast spoke the right;
> His heart is fracted and corroborate.
>
> *Henry V*: Act II, Scene I

They are implying that Falstaff's heart broke – fracted – when King Henry rejected him upon his coronation.

Whilst large parts of *Henry IV, Part I* are given over to slapstick fun, the play *Henry V* has a different feel to it, dealing with the serious themes of leadership and war. Perhaps, like Hal, Shakespeare felt there was no room for the comic antics of a fat, dissolute knight.

By contrast there was plenty of room for him in *The Merry Wives of Windsor*. A cloud of uncertainty hangs over the dating of the play but an appealing legend says it was commissioned by Elizabeth I who wanted to see Falstaff in love. Shakespeare set his comedy firmly in middle England. Its homely cast of characters is made up of ordinary, recognisable types – housewives and their husbands, a country parson, a doctor, gentlemen of leisure and various servants. There was nothing here to frighten the horses. This was safe, uncontroversial fun. Perhaps by locating the play in Windsor he was paying tribute – consciously or unconsciously – to the queen, whose castle dominated the town. He is also likely to have visited the town himself. Located on the pleasant banks of the River Thames, the town of Windsor lay approximately twenty-two miles from London. It would have been easy for Shakespeare to travel there and indeed he shows some local knowledge in the play, mentioning sites such as the nearby Frogmore. He also mentions the Garter Inn which was located on the High Street. The diarist Samuel Pepys stayed there in February 1666 but the inn was later destroyed by fire. It is at the Garter that Shakespeare sets the scene in which Falstaff tells Pistol and Nym of his intention to seduce Mistress Ford and Mistress Page. He seems to think he's in with a chance

I have writ me here a letter to her: and here another to Page's wife, who even now gave me good eyes too, examined my parts with most judicious oeillades; sometimes the beam of her view gilded my foot, sometimes my portly belly.

*The Merry Wives of Windsor*: Falstaff, Act I, Scene III

Of course he only wants their money and when Mistresses Ford and Page compare the letters Falstaff sent them, they discover his plan and plot revenge. Mistress Page knows just the spot in which to humble him:

> There is an old tale goes that Herne the hunter,
> Sometime a keeper here in Windsor forest,
> Doth all the winter time, at still midnight,
> Walk round about an oak, with great ragg'd horns;
> And there he blasts the tree and takes the cattle
> And makes milch-kine yield blood and shakes a chain
> In a most hideous and dreadful manner
>
> *The Merry Wives of Windsor*: Mistress Page, Act IV, Scene IV

They plan to lure Falstaff to Herne's Oak on the pretence of a romantic assignation. Falstaff will come dressed as Herne the Hunter with a pair of horns upon his head. Just as he is about to make his move a gang of local children dressed as angry fairies will then set about him, pinching him and burning him with tapers. Then, when he has explained his poor behaviour, they will 'mock him home to Windsor.' As an act of revenge, it is certainly creative. The legend of Herne the Hunter has obscure origins. Tradition has it that he was a local man who was hung from an oak tree after being caught poaching. Herne's Oak died in the 1790s and blew down in 1863 during a gale.

When Mistress Page speaks of Windsor Forest she is talking about what we know as Windsor Great Park. Spanning 4,800 acres, the park was enclosed as a royal hunting ground in the fourteenth century and still provides vast open spaces for dog walkers, horse riders and walkers. As you progress up the famous Long Walk, a straight avenue of elm and plane trees, the impressive stone range of Windsor Castle comes slowly into view. Started in 1070 by William the Conqueror, the castle was initially intended as a fortress to help him secure his new kingdom. Situated upstream from London it was ideally placed to guard the capital from any attacks coming from the west. It also had the happy bonus of being near a Saxon hunting ground which one imagines William would have made full use of. His castle was built of wood but successive generations rebuilt and modernised it, turning it into a royal palace of splendour and comfort. Both Elizabeth I and James I of England stayed there, James for the hunting, Elizabeth for the sense of security it offered. The stone battlements still speak of its original defensive purpose. The famous Round Tower, a defensive keep in the central ward of the complex, was started in the twelfth century during the reign of Henry II.

Henry IV stayed at Windsor over the Christmas of 1399 while Richard II, the man whose crown he had usurped, languished at Pontefract Castle. The final scene of *Richard II* is set in Windsor Castle. Sir Pierce Exton has just murdered Richard and enters with the dead king's coffin. Henry Bolingbroke, having got what he wanted, is now wracked with guilt about his death. He blames Exton for murdering Richard and vows to make amends for what has happened in the manner of a typical medieval king:

> I'll make a voyage to the Holy Land,
> To wash this blood off from my guilty hand:
> March sadly after; grace my mournings here;
> In weeping after this untimely bier.
>> *Richard II*: Henry Bolingbroke, Act V, Scene VI

In the Lower Ward of the castle is St George's Chapel whose origins date back to the reign of Edward the Confessor. It became the mother church of the Order of the Garter and was substantially rebuilt in the late fifteenth century by Edward IV. Every June there is a service in honour of the members of the order. The banners of the Knights of the Garter can be seen hanging in the choir. It is also the resting place of Henry VIII and his third wife Jane Seymour. They lie side by side in tombs beneath the black and white tiled floor along with Charles I. For such a flamboyant king the site of his burial is a muted affair. All that marks the spot is a black memorial stone on the floor.

Although Windsor Castle is of ancient design much of the fabric of the building is the result of rebuilding work done in the nineteenth century by the architect Jeffry Wyatville. Its recent history has not been without trauma: the devastating fire of 1992 contributed towards what Elizabeth II memorably called her '*annus horribilis*.' After a controversy about who would pay for the renovations it was decided to raise funds by opening the castle to the public.

The town of Windsor was blessed from the beginning. Its location on the banks of the River Thames gave it an enviable trading position allowing it to prosper and thrive. Civic pride was in evidence during the sixteenth century with the local ordinance of 1585 requiring the citizens to pave the patch of ground in front of their houses. Today it remains a clean and pleasant town in which to while away the hours. The cobbled streets of the old town hug the outer walls of the castle. The main shopping district located off the High Street and Peascod Street offers an array of high street store and cafés. The town has a well heeled and prosperous air. Besides the coach loads of tourists, the streets are populated with a familiar cast of housewives, shoppers and ladies who lunch. If Shakespeare returned today and looked past the modern dress he might have a moment of recognition. In Windsor, Mistress Page, Mistress Quickly, Dr Caius and Nym live on.

*Visitor Information*

Windsor is served by two train stations: Windsor and Eton Riverside, and Windsor and Eton Central. The castle is the first thing you see on exiting the Riverside station and is a big draw for visitors. The castle is open March to October, 9:45–15:15, November to February, 9:45–16:16. The last admissions are forty-five minutes before closing. Be aware that the castle sometimes closes for state functions so check before travelling. Admission to the castle is £19.20 for adults, £17.50 for concession and £11.30 for those under seventeen and the disabled. Family tickets are available for £49.70. Check www.royalcollection.org.uk/visit/windsorcastle/plan-your-visit.

For refreshments you might want to pop into the Harte and Garter on the High Street. Located on the site of Shakespeare's Garter Inn, this is a lovely place to stop and enjoy a bite to eat. The brasserie is open daily for breakfast, lunch, dinner and afternoon tea and is a somewhat more upmarket venue than that haunted by Falstaff, Pistol and Nym.

On the High Street look out for the Market Cross House, a half-timbered black and white building which leans perilously to one side. The building from 1687 and its strange stance can be attributed to the fact that the builders used green wood. There has been a market house on this site since 1592. On market days the traders would meet here.

To enter the famous Long Walk and gain access to Windsor Great Park, follow the High Street south past the parish church of St Baptist until you reach Park Street. Cambridge Gate, which leads into the park, is straight ahead. On the left-hand side is the tiny and historic Two Brewers pub, housed in a building which dates from 1709.

Across the river is the town of Eton. The long High Street is lined with antique shops and upmarket boutiques from which union flags flutter in the breeze. The high street bank is Coutts. Eton is of course famous for its ancient college. Founded in 1440 during the reign of Henry VI, it has educated generations of privileged boys and boasts a long succession of British prime ministers as its alumni. An Old Etonian of the sixteenth century was Sir Thomas Hoby. A strict Puritan, Hoby is sometimes suggested to have been the inspiration for Malvolio in *Twelfth Night*.

# Bury St Edmunds Abbey

> Our kinsman Gloucester is as innocent
> From meaning treason to our royal person
> As is the sucking lamb or harmless dove
> > *Henry VI, Part II*: Henry VI, Act III, Scene I

## *The Weakness of a King*

Our next location is one of those picture-perfect market towns whose outward serenity belies a dramatic past. Visitors who venture to the town of Bury St Edmunds in Suffolk enjoy a visual feast of abbey ruins and medieval civic architecture. Its history dates back to the time of the Saxons and is washed through with the blood of martyrs and kings. The town was very much the creation of the Benedictine monks who founded a monastery here in AD 633. The brothers laid out the streets in a grid pattern and grew wealthy by charging trade tariffs in town. A further boost to their finances came when King Edmund was laid to rest within the abbey walls in AD 903. He had been murdered by the Danes after refusing to renounce his Christian faith. It was said that after they had riddled him with arrows, the Danes threw Edmund's head in the woods where it was watched over by a protective wolf. The relics of martyrs were good for business and Edmund attracted a steady stream of pilgrims over the years, including King John. The abbey found itself once more at the centre of history in 1214 when John met his barons here for a meeting. A year later they would meet at Runnymede to seal the Magna Carta.

During the writing of the play *Henry VI, Part II* Shakespeare took inspiration from the abbey's more recent history. Henry VI visited the abbey over Christmas 1433 and seems to have enjoyed the hospitality so much that he stayed on until the following April. Just over ten years later, he held a parliament in the refectory. This event was scarred by the arrest of Henry's uncle, Humphrey, Duke of Gloucester, on charges of treason. The accused man died in mysterious circumstances three days later. There was no outward mark on his body and it was put about that he had died of apoplexy, or a stroke. If this sounds suspiciously convenient – one only has to think of Edward II or Richard II, both of whom died amid rumours of murder – it was also a source of perplexity for Henry VI. Gloucester was popular and well thought of by the citizens; a hero of Agincourt and the brother of Henry V. His downfall stemmed from his rivalry with the Beauforts. Despising the fact that Gloucester was heir to the throne, they concocted a plan to remove him. They started by accusing his wife Eleanor of witchcraft, a charge which would have seen her burnt at the stake had Henry not intervened to save her life. Instead, Eleanor was kept under house arrest. In the meantime, Gloucester had been tainted by association and Beaufort was able to remove him.

Shakespeare dramatizes the moment of Gloucester's arrest in a tense scene at Bury St Edmunds Abbey. Margaret of Anjou is, yet again, the villain of the piece. Here she is batting away Henry's protestations of Gloucester's innocence:

> Ah, what's more dangerous than this fond affiance!
> Seems he a dove? His feathers are but borrowed,
> For he's disposed as the hateful raven:
> Is he a lamb? His skin is surely lent him,
> For he's inclined as is the ravenous wolf.
> Who cannot steal a shape that means deceit?
> Take heed, my lord; the welfare of us all
> Hangs in the cutting short that fraudful man.
>
> *Henry VI, Part II*: Queen Margaret, Act III, Scene I

As for Gloucester himself, for a wronged man, he seems to take his arrest with bold cheer,

> Well, Suffolk, thou shalt not see me blush
> Nor change my countenance for this arrest:
> A heart unspotted is not easily daunted.
> The purest spring is not so free from mud
> As I am clear from treason to my sovereign.
>
> *Henry VI, Part II*: Gloucester, Act III, Scene I

Bury St Edmunds Abbey endured until 1539 when it was dissolved along with religious houses up and down the land. In the succeeding centuries the fabric of the building was stripped and plundered for material to build new houses. Large fragments of its remains stand within the picturesque parkland setting of the Abbey Gardens. Look out for the stone wall which bordered the abbot's garden and the delightful medieval era houses built into the west front. Their unvarnished façades have the look of elegant decay.

The entrance to the abbey complex is almost as grand as it would have been in the days of Henry VI. Visitors still use the imposing Great Gate which has stood here since the fourteenth century. It is remarkably unscathed by time and gives a sense of the abbey's great wealth and standing in the town. The modern Bury St Edmunds is a tranquil and sedate jewel in the East Anglian flatlands; it is strange to think that its abbey was once the centre of courtly intrigue, hosting royalty and parliaments. For the likes of King John, Henry VI and Margaret of Anjou, Bury was a place of power brokerage and plots.

### Visitor Information

The abbey grounds are open during daylight hours and entry is free. The ruins enjoy a central location to the east of the town centre. Call 01284 764667 with any queries or for directions.

In the town centre is the thirteenth-century Guildhall, built by the abbot. At the time of writing it is closed to the public but its custodians are applying for a heritage lottery fund to pay for its restoration and eventual reopening. It is hoped that this historic venue will eventually be brought back to life with exhibitions, live actors and interactive displays.

## Kimbolton Castle

> Griffith: How does your grace?
> Katharine: O Griffith, sick to death!
>
> *Henry VIII*: Act IV, Scene II

### A Neglected Queen

The play *Henry VIII* dates from around 1613, the same year The Globe caught fire during what would have been one of its first performances. By this time King James had been on the throne for ten years and Elizabeth I was a fading memory. Shakespeare must have finally deemed it safe to write about the Tudors. He had covered English history from Richard II onwards and now it was time to put Henry VIII on stage. The Tudors still fascinate and appal us today so the reign of Henry VIII must have been an irresistible subject for a playwright living closer to the events. The king's 'Great Matter' had convulsed Tudor England and changed the cultural and religious landscape forever. Here was a ruler who defied the pope and the emperor to put aside his long-standing wife Catherine of Aragon, a much-loved figure in the country, and marry a commoner. The controversial figure of Anne Boleyn has a small part but Shakespeare treats her kindly, probably in deference to her recently departed daughter. Far from being a quick-tempered temptress, scheming her way onto Catherine of Aragon's throne, she is modest and demure, the very image of idealised early-modern womanhood. Here she is in an unlikely scene, expressing sympathy for the queen:

> Here's the pang that pinches:
> His highness having lived so long with her, and she
> So good a lady that no tongue could ever
> Pronounce dishonour of her; by my life,
> She never knew harm doing ...
>
> *Henry VIII*: Anne, Act II, Scene III

In reality, Anne despised Catherine and her daughter Mary. The Imperial Ambassador Eustace Chapuys reported her as saying 'she wished all Spaniards were at the bottom of the sea' and 'that she cared not for the queen or any of her family, and that she would rather see her hanged than have to confess that she was her queen and mistress.' From these unkind words a less sympathetic character emerges than the one portrayed by Shakespeare.

The play *Henry VIII* was a collaborative effort between Shakespeare and his colleague in the King's Men, John Fletcher,

and it is one of his least-performed pieces of work. In comparison
to Shakespeare's earlier work this has rather a plodding, pedestrian
feel to it. It lacks the usual richness of his imagery although there
are one or two flashes of brilliance:

> I am about to weep; but, thinking that
> We are a queen, or long have dream'd so, certain
> The daughter of a king, my drops of tears
> I'll turn to sparks of fire.
>
> *Henry VIII*: Queen Katharine, Act II, Scene IV

In 1533 Catherine of Aragon's marriage was declared void and
she was exiled to Kimbolton Castle in Cambridgeshire where
her health quickly began to fade. She died on 7 January 1536,
heartbroken and alone except for a few of her loyal servants and
her friend Maria de Salinas. Act IV, Scene II of the play takes
place at Kimbolton. Catherine lies in bed bewailing her ill health.
She speaks about the downfall of Cardinal Wolsey before falling
asleep to some 'sad and solemn music'. As she sleeps she is visited
by a vision of peace: A lengthy stage direction describes six
dancers in golden vizards, curtseying and waving bay garlands
over her sleeping form. As she dreams, she holds her hands up to
heaven. Her final words before exiting the stage are as follows:

> When I am dead, good wench,
> Let me be used with honour: strew me over
> With maiden flowers, that all the world may know
> I was a chaste wife to my grave: embalm me,
> Then lay me forth: although unqueen'd, yet like
> A queen, and a daughter to a king, inter me.
> I can no more.
>
> *Henry VIII*: Queen Katharine, Act IV, Scene II

Kimbolton Castle began its existence as a medieval fortress but began its transformation into a comfortable manor house in the fifteenth century. The owners of the house during Catherine's unhappy stay were the Wingfield family. Henry VIII had granted it to the courtier Sir Richard Wingfield in the 1520s as an expression of gratitude for years of loyal service as ambassador to France. The present building is a fine example of the early eighteenth century fondness for classical architecture. In a token of respect for its beginnings as a fortification the architects Sir John Vanbrugh and Nicholas Hawksmoor incorporated crenallations on the rooftop. The gatehouse was designed by Robert Adam.

Parts of the Tudor building have been retained and are visible behind glass panelling outside the chapel.

Catherine was laid to rest in nearby Peterborough Abbey (now Peterborough Cathedral) in a service presided over by the Bishops of Rochester, Ely and Lincoln. Her corpse was brought into the abbey on a wagon draped with black velvet followed by a train of her ladies. Henry VIII did not attend. In 1986 a memorial tablet was placed at Catherine's tomb bearing the poignant epitaph, 'A queen cherished by the English people for her loyalty, piety, courage and compassion.' The tomb attracts a steady stream of visitors who leave fresh flowers by its side.

*Visitor Information*

Kimbolton Castle now houses a school, located in Huntingdon, Cambridgeshire PE28 0EA. It is possible to organise a guided tour outside of term time. There are also regular open days when the general public are invited to visit between the hours of 13.00–16.00. Members of the Kimbolton Local History Society are on hand to answer questions as you move from room to room. To arrange a visit call 01480 860505.

Peterborough Cathedral has served as a place of worship since AD 654 when it was founded as part of an abbey. The overwhelming beauty of the current building is a testament to the genius of its Norman architects. The western façade is a stunning Romanesque creation of soaring arches and pinnacles. It seems a suitable resting place for Catherine of Aragon, a defiantly Catholic queen who was raised amid the flamboyant architecture of Spain. Dating from 1118 the cathedral suffered damage in the Civil War when Parliamentarian soldiers destroyed the stained glass and furnishings such as the choir stalls. The cathedral interior underwent extensive restoration in the eighteenth and nineteenth centuries. Opening hours are Monday to Friday 9.00–17.00, Saturdays 9.00–15.00 and Sundays 12.00–15.00. Admission is free but the cathedral welcomes donations. Guided tours are available at 14.00 Monday to Friday and 11.30 on Saturdays.

## Pontefract Castle

Tis a vile thing to die, my gracious lord,
When men are unprepared and look not for it.
*Richard III*: Catesby, Act III, Scene II

*Dying Like a Beast*
Pontefract Castle in West Yorkshire is a picturesque ruin, having fallen victim to damage caused in the Civil War. Walking around the remains today it is hard to believe that this was once one of England's most fearsome and bloody fortresses. It was a place of dread, where political prisoners disappeared behind its thick stone walls and battlements, never to be seen again.

Richard II was imprisoned here in late 1399 after his forced deposition and his death was announced in February 1400, a few short months later. Nobody seems to know how he died but the most popular theory is that his keepers starved him to death. It seems a cruel and cowardly way to dispose of an enemy but perhaps they believed this method offered a degree of separation from the killing of a king. After all, nobody would need to lay hands on him. It hardly bears thinking about; Richard wasting away in a long drawn out agony during the coldest months of the year. Shakespeare offers an alternative theory and allows Richard to precede his death with a long soliloquy; the king is left alone with his thoughts and appears to find the solitude maddening:

> I have been studying how I may compare
> This prison where I live unto the world:
> And for because the world is populous
> And here is not a creature but myself,
> I cannot do it; yet I'll hammer it out.
>
> *Richard II*: Richard II, Act V, Scene V

He goes on to draw comparisons between his essential feebleness and the hardness of the walls which enclose him:

> Thoughts tending to ambition, they do plot
> Unlikely wonders; how these vain weak nails
> May tear a passage through the flinty ribs
> Of this hard world, my ragged prison walls,
> And, for they cannot, die in their own pride ...
>
> *Richard II*: King Richard II, Act V, Scene V

Mercifully, Shakespeare does not inflict upon him the torment of starvation but ends it quickly. A keeper arrives with a plate of food for Richard. Normally the keeper would taste it first but this time Sir Pierce of Exton has forbidden him to do so. Richard suspects poison and beats the man. Exton hears the commotion and enters the cell. Richard kills several servants before Exton 'strikes him down'. Exton is full of remorse for killing a king but earlier in the play the usurper Bolingbroke, soon to become Henry IV, had urged someone to do it. Exton merely picked up the hint:

> Exton: Didst thou not mark the king, what words he spake,
> 'Have I no friend will rid me of this living fear?'
> Was it not so?
> Servant: These were his very words
>
> *Richard II*, Act IV, Scene IV

As well as witnessing the death of kings, Pontefract Castle also provided lodgings for prisoners such as James I of Scotland and Charles, Duke of Orleans, who was brought to England after his capture at the Battle of Agincourt in 1415.

On 9 April 1483 King Edward IV died. The heir to the throne was his thirteen-year-old son Edward who was then residing at Ludlow Castle in Wales. The boy was to be escorted to London by his uncle Anthony Woodville, Earl Rivers but the party only got as far as Stony Stratford in Buckinghamshire. Here they met with Richard of Gloucester, nominated as Edward's Protector by the king during his son's minority. The two parties dined together but in the morning Richard arrested Woodville and sent him to Pontefract Castle where he was beheaded. Little Edward and his brother Richard were taken to the Tower of London where they disappeared. Richard of Gloucester would soon become Richard III. Historians argue heatedly about Richard's intentions and some say that Shakespeare took his cue from Sir Thomas More in perpetuating Tudor propaganda about Richard as a child-murdering hunchback. The following lines in the play

*Richard III* are not complimentary and in the context of his opening speech, full of Machiavellian scheming, appear to link his outward appearance with his inward nature:

> I, that am curtail'd of this fair proportion,
> Cheated of feature by dissembling nature,
> Deformed, unfinish'd, sent before my time
> Into this breathing world, scarce half made up.
>
> *Richard III*: Richard III, Act I, Scene I

Shakespeare was not entirely incorrect in his description of the king's physical characteristics. From the recent discovery of Richard's bones we now know that he suffered from scoliosis, or curvature of the spine. On the matter of his treatment of prisoners and the justness of his claim to the throne, scholars will simply have to argue it out.

Shakespeare however was in no doubt that Richard was a tyrant. In moving scenes set at Pontefract Castle, Anthony Woodville bewails the injustice of his situation:

> Sir Richard Ratcliffe, let me tell thee this:
> Today shalt thou behold a subject die
> For truth, for duty, and for loyalty.
>
> *Richard III*: Rivers, Act III, Scene III

At the height of its power as a stronghold, Pontefract Castle was more commonly known as Pomfret, as illustrated by poor Woodville. Here he is reflecting on its bloody history and the death of the unfortunate Richard II:

> O Pomfret, Pomfret! O thou bloody prison,
> Fatal and ominous to noble peers!

Within the guilty closure of thy walls
Richard the Second here was hack'd to death;
And for more slander to thy dismal seat,
We give thee up our guiltless blood to drink.

*Richard III*: Rivers, Act III, Scene III

The castle was started by one of the Conqueror's companions, Ilbert de Lacey in 1070. Located at the top of a rocky outcrop overlooking the Anglo-Saxon settlements of Tanshelf and Kirkby, its earliest incarnation was probably a wooden structure which was gradually rebuilt in stone. With defence being the main consideration Pontefract was built in the concentric style. This meant that unlike the simple motte and bailey layout of other fortresses, Pontefract had two layers of protection – an outer wall and an inner wall with a series of towers built at intervals along the inner wall. Intruders would have much difficulty in gaining entry to Pontefract. Of course this also meant that it was difficult for prisoners to escape. In the winter of 1530 an escort of guards made a stop at Pontefract Castle. Their captive was Cardinal Wolsey, a sick and feeble shadow of the haughty churchman who had started Hampton Court Palace. He was in ill health on the long journey southwards, suffering crippling bouts of dysentery. Perhaps mercifully, he would never make it to London where nothing but a show trial and the executioner's block awaited. The party stopped at Leicester Abbey where he slipped away.

The castle's martial credentials were put to the test in 1536 during the northern uprising known as the Pilgrimage of Grace. Led by Robert Aske, this was a series of insurrections in protest at the recent religious and political changes in the country such as the Dissolution of the Monasteries. The rebels took Pontefract Castle, with the connivance of its resident commander Lord

Darcy. For his treachery he was executed on Tower Hill. Five years later, Henry VIII made a royal progress to the north and stopped at Pontefract. He did not know it at the time, but during their visit his fifth wife Katherine Howard spent her time conducting an illicit affair with Thomas Culpepper, one of Henry's gentlemen of the bedchamber.

Pontefract was the scene of three sieges during the Civil War and it passed back and forth between Royalist and Parliamentary hands. After Oliver Cromwell's forces eventually prevailed, and Charles I had been safely executed, he had the troublesome castle destroyed. The grounds were put to more peaceful use in later years when a liquorice farm was established on the site.

Fortunately, Cromwell's destruction of the castle was not total. The remains of the thirteenth-century keep can still be seen, as well as parts of the curtain wall and towers. Thirty-five feet below ground are some rather eerie tunnels which have been used both as a military store and a prison. Graffiti bearing the names of some of the unfortunates who found themselves locked up inside is etched into the walls. It is not known exactly where Richard II was held as he wasted away.

The town of Pontefract itself developed out of Tanshelf and Kirkby which were two separate settlements lying in the shadow of Ilbert de Lacey's castle. The name Pontefract comes from the Latin for 'broken bridge' – 'Pons' meaning 'bridge' and 'fractus' meaning 'broken.' The bridge in question was a crossing over the nearby River Aire which was destroyed in the time of William the Conqueror by Anglo-Saxon rebels. Today it is a working market town and is well worth a visit. Look out for Pontefract Cakes, a local sweet made from liquorice. Each tablet is stamped with the image of Pontefract Castle where the town's liquorice was originally grown.

The castle may no longer hold the same terror for visitors as it once did but Shakespeare knew its reputation and used it to dramatic effect. It is partly thanks to him that the stories of its victims are forever seeped into the fabric of its decaying remains.

### Visitor Information

Pontefract Castle is located at Castle Chain, Pontefract, West Yorkshire WF8 1QH. Tel: 01924 302700.

Entry to the grounds of Pontefract Castle is free but there is a small charge for entry to the underground military store. Admission is £2.50 for adults and £1.50 for children; this includes a guided tour.

The Pontefract Museum at 5 Salter Row tells the story of the town's history and houses the Ackworth Hoard, a collection of Civil War era treasure found in someone's garden. Probably belonging to a Royalist it includes gold and silver coins and a ring. Opening hours are Monday to Friday 10.00–16.30 and Saturday 10.30–16.30. Call 01977 722740 for details.

# York

> Welcome, my lord, to this brave town of York.
> Yonder's the head of that arch-enemy
> That sought to be encompass'd with your crown:
> Doth not the object cheer your heart, my lord?
>
> *Henry VI, Part III*: Queen Margaret, Act II, Scene II

### Northern Hospitality

In a sign of 'health and safety gone mad', visitors to York are no longer greeted with the sight of severed heads. Shakespearean queens no longer stand by the city gates, cackling over their dead enemies. York, however, still has plenty of medieval charm to tempt the visitor and this section aims to lure you to what is one of the most handsome cities in England.

In Shakespeare's lines above, the warrior queen Margaret of Anjou is greeting her husband Henry VI to York by showing him the head of his enemy, Richard, Duke of York. She has just helped to slay the duke during the Battle of Wakefield. Ungracious in victory, she mocks the dead man's remains by placing a paper crown on his severed head then sticking it on a spike above Micklegate Bar in York. Although Shakespeare embellished the historical facts of York's death – it was not Margaret who killed him – he was accurate about the fate of the head; its sightless gaze welcomed visitors to the city; a grisly warning to any others who would seek to take Henry VI's crown.

In the play, before Margaret stabs York, she mocks him by offering him a handkerchief soaked in the blood of his murdered son, the Earl of Rutland. Shakespeare's Margaret is portrayed as an unnatural creature, ruthless and cold, nourished by the blood of her enemies. As York prepares to die he tells her just what he thinks:

> O tiger's heart wrapt in a woman's hide!
> How couldst thou drain the life-blood of the child,
> To bid the father wipe his tears withal,
> And yet be seen to bear a woman's face?
>
> *Henry VI, Part II*: York, Act I, Scene IV

Having defeated her arch-enemy York, where better to display his head than at the entrance to his own city? The Battle of Wakefield was a fleeting victory for Margaret and Henry. The following year, in 1461, York's son Edward would take the crown.

Micklegate Bar still forms one of the entrances to York and it has not changed much since the Wars of the Roses. Started in the twelfth century as the southern entrance to the city, its towering battlements and stone arches offer a formidable face to approaching travellers. The upper stories of the bar date from the fourteenth century during the reign of Edward III whose coat of arms appears on the outer wall along with that of an eighteenth-century Lord Mayor of York. The façade is a pleasing mishmash of medieval and Roman stone work. The narrow arrow-slits facing out towards Blossom Street speak of its defensive purpose in repelling invading armies. Micklegate was also the official entrance to York for visiting monarchs, and still is today. It is just one of six gates, or bars as they are known, into the city. After the Romans arrived in AD 71 they surrounded their settlement in a defensive wall which was gradually rebuilt and developed over the succeeding centuries. The embattled walls stretch for two and half miles around the city and it is possible to walk almost the entire perimeter enjoying the changing cityscape as you progress. Those with vertigo should take care; in places, the wall is narrow and unfenced with a steep drop below.

There is plenty within the city itself to please the history lover. The oldest street in York is the Shambles which achieved the award of 'Britain's Most Picturesque Street' in 2010. It is easy to see why such an award might have been bestowed upon it. The medieval name 'Shambles', from the old English word for 'shelves', evokes a time when this narrow cobbled lane was a river of blood and animal entrails; the butchers displayed their wares on the shelves outside their shops. Look out for the meat hooks which can still be seen outside some of the buildings. Also notice how the pavements form a channel in the middle of the lane where the butchers would wash away the remnants of their trade. The nature of the lane has changed entirely since then. The butchers have been replaced with pleasant tea rooms and boutiques. The half-timbered buildings, some of which date back to the fifteenth century, still have old-fashioned hanging signs outside, giving the lane an air of timeless antiquity. At Number 10 is the former home of the Elizabethan martyr Margaret Clitherow who was crushed to death with heavy stones on Ouse Bridge in 1586 for harbouring Catholic priests. Her shrine is located in a medieval building across the street.

Nearby is York Minster; the stunning Gothic façade dominates Deangate. Started in 1230 on the site of the Roman Basilica, the present building was built in the Gothic style. It took over 200 years to complete. Next door the little church of St Michael le Belfrey is dwarfed in comparison. Built in 1525, this is where the conspirator Guy Fawkes was baptised in 1570.

The historic centre of York has a holiday feel to it. Tourists stand rustling their maps in the shadow of the Minster and the air is filled with the sounds of buskers. How different the atmosphere is to 600 years ago when the heads of traitors rotted above the city gates and butchers slaughtered livestock on the Shambles. The Wars of the Roses seem a long way off.

*Visitor Information*
York Minster is located at Deangate, York YO1 7HH. Tel: 01904 557200.

Opening hours are Monday to Saturday 09:00–17:00 and Sundays 12:45–17:00. York residents enjoy free access on production of proof of address. For everyone else there is a range of prices depending on whether you wish to enter the Minster and Tower or just the Minster itself. Please call for up-to-date information.

Micklegate Bar where the Duke of York's head was displayed is now a museum housing an exhibition about the reign of Henry VII. The Henry VII Experience is open seven days a week from 10:00–17:00 in summer and 10:00–16:00 in winter. You may want to team the visit with a trip to the Richard III Experience inside another of York's city gates, the Monk Bar. Admission to both these museums is £5.00 for adults, £3.00 for children between five and sixteen, £3.50 for concessions, £22.75 for a family of four and £23.75 for a family of five. Call 01904 615505 for details.

## Bosworth Field

Here pitch our tents, even here in Bosworth field.
My Lord of Surrey, why look you so sad?
*Richard III*: Richard III, Act V, Scene III

### The Death of Richard III

It is sometimes said that Shakespeare would have made a great writer for radio. The lines above illustrate how he painted instructive images with words and how he allows characters to speak without saying anything. The Lord of Surrey does not say how he is feeling; Richard notices.

Surrey has every reason to look sad. It is the eve of the Battle of Bosworth Field. Richard III and his men are preparing for what might be their last night on earth; in the morning they will ride out to defend the crown against the challenger Henry Tudor. Nobody knows which side fortune favours and nerves are beginning to fray. Surrey tries to put a brave face on it, protesting that he feels much lighter than his heavy looks would suggest. By contrast Richard III appears to be in a chipper mood. He points out that they have three times as many men as their enemies and the benefit of having a king among them:

> Why, our battalion trebles that account:
> Besides, the king's name is a tower of strength,
> Which they upon the adverse party want.
> > *Richard III*: Richard III, Act V, Scene III

In this fleeting show of bravado Richard seems to forget that kings, too, are mortal.

Later in the evening his sleeping form is haunted by the ghosts of those he has murdered. One by one, Clarence, Anthony Rivers and the Princes in the Tower come to his bedside and rain their curses down upon him. Here are the ghosts of the young princes:

> Dream on thy cousins smother'd in the Tower:
> Let us be led within thy bosom, Richard,
> And weigh thee down to ruin, shame and death!
> > *Richard III*: Princes, Act V, Scene III

In turn, each spirit tells the king to despair and die on the battlefield. At the same time they also visit Richard's enemy, Henry Tudor, and tell him to flourish. When Richard wakes from his dream he is out of sorts and begins a long struggle with his conscience, ending with this lament:

> There is no creature loves me;
> And if I die, no soul shall pity me:
> Nay, wherefore should they, since that I myself
> Find in myself no pity to myself?'
> > *Richard III*: Richard III, Act V, Scene III

Within hours, Richard will be dead.

The idea that nobody loved or pitied Richard can only have been wishful thinking, or perhaps naiveté, on Shakespeare's part. After all, like most Elizabethans, Shakespeare would have been exposed to plenty of Tudor propaganda. One of his sources for the play was Thomas More's *The History of Richard III* which painted the king as a tyrant. Like More, Shakespeare was writing under the watchful eye of the victorious Tudor dynasty. Henry Tudor was Elizabeth's grandfather. It would not do to go off-message. Whatever the Elizabethans thought of Richard III, nobody could accuse him of being unloved in the twenty-first century. Since 1924 the Richard III Society has worked to rehabilitate his reputation and defend him from what they see as Tudor smears. His fan base is fiercely loyal and often vociferous in its attempts to bring some balance to the debate. If the modern admiration for Richard sometimes verges on idolatry it could be argued that after Shakespeare's hatchet job on his character, he should be allowed to enjoy his moment in the sun.

A well-organised tourism industry has grown up around this most controversial of kings. As well as visiting Richard's tomb in Leicester Cathedral, devotees can also make an easy pilgrimage to the scene of the battle where the anti-climax of Richard's reign took place on 22 August 1485. Located in Leicestershire, close to the Warwickshire border, the Bosworth Battlefield Heritage Centre is based approximately two miles from where Richard's and Henry's forces met. Through the medium of guided walks and an exhibition it attempts to interpret the drama of that day in a way that appeals to all age groups. Started in 1974 the centre was built on Ambion Hill where it was assumed the battle took place. Something about this theory did not sit well with historians who realised that the battle took place near marshy ground. In 2009 researchers undertook geological surveys and metal detection in a field near the appropriately named Fenn Lane Farm. There they found a tiny silver badge on the site in the shape of a boar – Richard's emblem – which would have been worn by one of the king's supporters. The team also uncovered a large number of cannonballs and coins. Rather than shifting its base to the new site, the heritage centre remained where it was and devised a Battlefield Trail complete with information boards telling the story of the skirmish which marked the beginning of the Tudor dynasty.

Even without its extraordinary history the trail makes for a lovely walk. The landscape is gorgeously rural and undeveloped. Cornfields and meadows stretch for as far as the eye can see. In summer the bright blue sky glimmers over the fields, while insects chirrup among the wildflowers. As you wander around the trail, stopping every now and then to read the information boards, it is not hard to imagine the rural ambience being shattered by the clash of steel and the thunder of hooves. Amid the carnage a lone voice crying out in desperation: 'A horse! A horse! My kingdom for a horse!'

*Visitor Information*

The Bosworth Battlefield Heritage Centre is located at Ambion Lane, Sutton Cheney, Nuneaton, Warwickshire CV13 0AD. Although the centre is actually sited in Leicestershire, the postal address is, slightly confusingly, in Warwickshire. Tel: 01455 290429.

The centre is open Monday to Sunday 10:00–17:00 and the Country Park is open from 07:00–20.00. Admission to the heritage centre is £7.95 for adults, £4.75 for children aged three to fifteen, £17.50 for family tickets and £7.00 for seniors.

Although there are no direct bus routes to the site and most people arrive by car, non-drivers should not despair. The site can be easily reached on a pleasant day trip from Leicester. Take the Number 153 bus from St Margaret's Station to the small market town of Market Bosworth. The scenic journey takes just over an hour and stops in the pretty market place. Market Bosworth dates back to Anglo-Saxon times when the settlement was known as Bosa's Worth. In the thirteenth century the village began to host a market on Wednesdays and was henceforth known as Market Bosworth. Look out for the street signs, each of which displays the image of either a boar (for Richard III) or a dragon (for Henry Tudor). Some of the historic buildings in the market place are adorned with large shields bearing the coats of arms of noblemen who fought at the Battle of Bosworth Field. To reach the Bosworth Battlefield Heritage Centre from here you can either call for a local taxi to take you the three-mile distance, or walk. Those who are opting for the walk will enjoy an extremely pleasant, well signposted ramble through the fields. From the Market Place, descend from the bus and turn left, walking around the corner to Sutton Lane, a quiet lane lined with houses at the top end. Walk down the hill towards the gate and step through the gap on the left-hand side into the lane proper. At this point the houses fall away and you are surrounded by unbroken country on both sides. Continue down Sutton Lane, enjoying the wide grass verges strewn with wild flowers. After approximately ten minutes you will reach the sign of a footpath on the right-hand side. This leads you across the cornfields to the entrance of the heritage centre. On the final stretch you will be guided in by the sight of two huge flags snapping in the breeze. These represent Richard III and Henry Tudor. The whole walk takes approximately forty minutes from start to finish. The route is flat and gentle with no hills to contend with. The bright yellow waymarks make navigation a doddle.

The two flags are located at the top of the hill towards the entrance. Beneath them is a sundial enclosed by red and white rose bushes which represent the houses of York and Lancaster. From the top of the hill there are far reaching views of the gently rolling countryside.

At weekends the heritage centre offers guided walks of the Battlefield Trail and a 'Meet the Birds' event during which visitors can try their hands at flying birds of prey. Inside is an exhibition, a gift shop and the Tithe Barn restaurant which serves hot and cold food.

To extend the visit you may wish to visit the nearby village of Sutton Cheney. Tradition says that Richard III stopped here to pray at the church of St James on the eve of the battle. The church is a plain, yet handsome building which dates from the fourteenth century and is usually open at weekends.

# Warkworth

> The spirit within thee hath been so at war
> And thus hath so bestirr'd thy sleep,
> That beads of sweat have stood upon thy brow
> Like bubbles in a late-disturbed stream.
> > *Henry IV, Part I*: Lady Percy, Act II, Scene III

*Hotspur Percy*

Thirty miles north of Hadrian's Wall, nestling in a loop of the River Coquet, is Warkworth Castle. It stands on a hill overlooking the pretty village which shares its name, surrounded on all sides by green fields. Visible a mile to the east is the wind-blasted coast of Northumberland. There is not much left of the castle; centuries of war and conflict have ravaged the fabric of the building but in its medieval heyday this was the stronghold of the powerful Percy dynasty whose military strength helped to secure the north against the Scots. One of Shakespeare's best-loved characters has an illuminating scene at Warkworth in the play *Henry IV, Part I*. Henry Percy, better known as Hotspur, is planning a rebellion against the king but refuses to tell his wife what is going on. The scene tells us much about Hotspur's character:

> Lady Percy: Come, come, you paraquito, answer me
> Directly unto this question that I ask:
> In faith, I'll break thy little finger, Harry,
> An if thou wilt not tell me all things true.
> Hotspur: Away, away, you trifler! Love! I love thee not,
> I care not for thee, Kate: this is no world
> To play mammets and to tilt with lips:
> We must have bloody noses and crack'd crowns ...
>
> *Henry IV, Part I*: Act II, Scene III

For some reason Shakespeare calls Hotspur's wife 'Kate' when her name was actually Elizabeth. As for Hotspur himself, it was the Scots who gave him that nickname on account of his mercurial character; his quick readiness to fight. Indeed, Shakespeare depicts Hotspur as a rash youth; hot headed and impatient for action. His rebellion against Henry IV forms the backdrop to the play. Having helped Henry to usurp the crown from Richard II in 1399, the historical Hotspur and his father, the 1st Earl of Northumberland, had quickly grown disillusioned with the new king. In 1403 they formed alliances with other disaffected nobles and attempted a rebellion. The list of grievances was partly concerned with money – unpaid wages for their part in securing the border from Scottish raids and the royal insistence on Hotspur handing over valuable prisoners – but was also tinged with wounded family pride. Hotspur's brother-in-law Edmund Mortimer had been held prisoner by the Welsh rebel Owain Glyndwr since 1402. Despite the Percy family's pleas, Henry IV refused to allow them to pay the ransom to free him, possibly suspecting that their kinsman was not an unwilling captive. It was certainly a comfortable imprisonment for Mortimer – he married Glyndwr's daughter and was clearly treated with respect, but that was not the point. The king had irritated the Percy family. He had to go.

Shakespeare had fun dramatizing Hotspur's attempted rebellion and the fallout. His nemesis in the play is the king's son, Prince Hal. Although the historical Hotspur was older than Hal, the two men are portrayed as being the same age. In the play the king is disappointed with his feckless son – while Prince Hal spends all his time hanging around in taverns with Falstaff, Hotspur displays all the warlike qualities of an heir to the throne. Shakespeare sets them against each other throughout the action of the play culminating in the Battle of Shrewsbury of 1403. There can only be one winner.

Things begin to go wrong for Hotspur when his father the Earl of Northumberland fails to join him on the battlefield. He pleads sickness and leaves Hotspur hopelessly outnumbered. Historically it is not known why Northumberland's forces failed to appear. Neither do we know who struck the final blow or fired the arrow that killed Hotspur. What Shakespeare shows us is a fearless hothead who meets Hal on the battlefield for a face-to-face showdown. Prince Hal knows there is no room on this earth for the two of them and manages to deliver his rival a fatal blow, cutting off Hotspur's dying words with a heartfelt farewell:

> Fare thee well, great heart!
> Ill weaved ambition, how much thou art shrunk!
> When that this body did contain a spirit,
> A kingdom for it was too small a bound ...
>
> > *Henry IV, Part I*: Prince Hal, Act IV, Scene IV

Prince Hal may have been of royal blood but Hotspur was his equal in bravery.

The prickly subject of Hotspur's death is revisited in *Henry IV, Part II*. Back home at Warkworth Castle, the Earl of Northumberland is about to join yet another rebellion against the king. Hotspur's widow begs him to reconsider, reminding him of how he failed his son at the Battle of Shrewsbury:

> And him, O wondrous him!
> O, miracle of men! Him did you leave,
> Second to none, unseconded by you,
> To look upon the hideous god of war
> In disadvantage; to abide a field
> Where nothing but the sound of Hotspur's name
> Did seem defensible: so you left him.
>
> > *Henry IV, Part II*: Lady Percy, Act II, Scene III

To his credit, Northumberland feels shamed by her speech. His wife advises him to go to Scotland and wait there in safety until he knows which side is winning, to which suggestion he agrees.

Warkworth Castle lies just over thirty miles south of the Scottish border. The historical earl stayed in Scotland for a short time before re-entering England in rebellion and dying at the Battle of Bramham Moor in 1408. The crown took over the ownership of the castle until 1416 when Prince Hal, now crowned as Henry V, returned it to Hotspur's son. It was time to heal old wounds and start afresh.

The castle is now a well-preserved ruin in the care of English Heritage. It is believed the castle may have been started in the twelfth century by one Roger Fitz Richard, who was granted the land in a charter by Henry II. The increasingly powerful Percy family took ownership of the castle from 1345 when the widow of John de Clavering, the previous resident, died. Like many of our ancient castles, Warkworth suffered damage in the Civil War but the keep underwent restoration in the nineteenth century. In 1850 Algernon Percy began work on the Great Tower in whose upper storeys he built the duke's rooms which the family would visit in summer. Surrounded by a dry moat, the walls of the castle are mostly intact. A wooden bridge leads through the thirteenth-century gatehouse and into a grassy enclosure dotted with the stone footprints of the interior. The interesting cross-shaped keep was added in the fourteenth century by Hotspur's father. Look out for the carved angels bearing shields at the top. Another recurring symbol of Percy dominance is their lion badge which appears throughout the castle grounds; the unfading legacy of those heroes of the north.

*Visitor Information*

Warkworth Castle is located at Castle Terrace, Warkworth, Northumberland NE65 0UJ. Tel: 01665 711423.

The castle is open every day from 10.00–18.00. Admission is £5.40 for adults, £3.20 for children between five and fifteen, £4.90 for concessions and £14.00 for a family ticket. These prices also include admission to the Hermitage, a peaceful cave located half a mile away on the banks of the River Coquet. It is thought to have been built by the 1st Earl of Northumberland as a private chapel; presumably he chose this secluded site because it is only accessible by boat. Carved into the sandstone, it includes a chapel equipped with an altar and a carved image of an angel.

The village of Warkworth itself is also worth visiting for its riverside walks, shops and restaurants. At the other end of the village from the castle is the handsome church of St Lawrence whose present building dates from 1132.

# Miscellaneous Sites Related to Shakespeare

The following are a carefully chosen selection of sites which did not fit neatly into the main Acts of the book but which continue to tell his story through the medium of travel. Each location has its own quirky connection to Shakespeare, his works or his friends. We shall visit a stately home in Somerset whose previous incarnation the King's Men visited to perform for King James in 1603. From kings and courtiers we delve into the Clerkenwell underworld to meet some candidates for the title of Shakespeare's 'Dark Lady.' We also stop by at some Roman remains in the city of Leicester said by legend to be the site of King Lear's burial. First, however, we go back to London where statues, monuments and a medieval church await us.

Think of these sections as an epilogue to the main action; some closing scenes to ease us back into the twenty-first century.

## St Bartholomew the Great

> Death makes no conquest of this conqueror;
> For now he lives in fame, though not in life
> *Richard III*: Prince Edward, Act III, Scene I

*Shakespeare on the Silver Screen*

Shakespeare's fame continues down the ages, aided mostly by the theatre world which carefully tends the flame of his genius and keeps it burning. In recent years he has also been the subject of films and for our next location we visit a site that ardent Shakespeare fans may recognise. The church of St Bartholomew the Great in Smithfield has provided a backdrop to scenes in many of the world's best known films. Productions such as *The Other Boleyn Girl, Robin Hood, Prince of Thieves, Amazing Grace, The Mystery of Edwin Drood* and *Elizabeth: The Golden Age* have all used it as a filming location. With its visually stunning Norman architecture it is easy to see why producers love it here. Started as a priory in the twelfth century, the chancel still has a dark, monastic feel to it. Weak shafts of light stream in through the high windows and a shadowy arcade of rounded Romanesque arches skirts the sides of the building. The effect is pleasingly Gothic.

In 1998 the *Shakespeare in Love* crew arrived for filming. Shakespeare, played by Joseph Fiennes, is seen in the church praying for forgiveness. He has just heard about the murder of Kit Marlowe, and blames himself since he was the intended victim. Lord Wessex had earlier promised revenge upon Shakespeare for chasing after the love interest, Viola. When Wessex asks Shakespeare for his name, presumably so he can have him killed at a more convenient time, Shakespeare instinctively calls himself Marlowe and the murderers go on to stab the wrong man. It is all good fun and certainly not intended to be taken as truth or to provoke any conspiracy theories. Productions such as the BBC drama *A Waste of Shame* and the film *Anonymous* have also sought to show us aspects of his life, to varying degrees of plausibility. *Anonymous* made the ludicrous assertion that the works of Shakespeare were written by the Earl of Oxford.

The tangled web of conspiracy theories which have sprung up as a result of the 'authorship question' is a source of amusement to those who believe in the man from Stratford. To those who question how the son of a country glove maker could write scenes set at court or in foreign countries, the counter question must be posed: Could an earl know – or even care – enough about the lives of ordinary folk to create characters such as Bottom, Flute, Starveling, Bardolph, Constable Dull and Corin the shepherd?

To misquote Ben Jonson then, it is probably best to seek the real Shakespeare in his books rather than through fiction. The excellent *Hollow Crown* series of 2012 included adaptations of *Richard II*, *Henry IV, Parts I & II*, and *Henry V*. It was in St Bartholomew the Great that Sir Patrick Stewart, as an ailing John of Gaunt, was filmed giving the 'Scepter'd Isle' speech in *Richard II*. Gaunt is sweating with fever as he goes on to spit fury upon the king:

> John of Gaunt: Landlord of England art thou now, not king:
> Thy state of law is bondslave to the law; And thou ...
> Richard II: A lunatic lean-witted fool ...
>
> *Richard II*: Act II, Scene I

The church is clearly recognisable and is a natural stand in for Ely Palace where Shakespeare originally set the scene.

The story of the founding of St Bartholomew the Great is a colourful one. Rahere was a minstrel and jester at the court of Henry I who went on pilgrimage to Rome and contracted malaria. With his life in serious danger, and possibly suffering from fever, he made a solemn vow. He swore that if his life was spared, if he recovered from this terrible disease his first action would be to found an Augustinian priory. He would dedicate it to Saint Bartholomew whose spirit had come to him in a vision. It was a perfectly reasonable promise to make, for haven't we all made similar vows whilst languishing on our sick beds? The ailing Rahere meant every word. He returned to London and in 1123 founded the priory along with a hospital for the poor on a site outside the city walls. The priory survived until 1539 when it was dissolved and broken up. The nave was destroyed and the grounds granted to Sir Richard Rich who moved into the prior's house. The hospital continued to serve the poor thanks to a petition by the citizens begging Henry VIII to give it a legal standing and financial support. In 1546, the year before Henry died, he granted the hospital to the city. It has continued in its original function ever since, making what is now known as Bart's Hospital the oldest of its kind in the country. Remarkably for a hospital, the first physician, Dr Roderigo Lopez, did not arrive until 1567. Lopez was a Portuguese Jew who went on to become the queen's personal physician. He would later be hanged, drawn and quartered on malicious charges of treason.

In recognition of the man who saved the hospital after nearly destroying it, the portly statue of Henry VIII stands in a niche above the western entrance. Erected in 1702, this is the only exterior statue of Henry VIII in London.

Smithfield's location outside the city walls protected it in 1666 when the Great Fire engulfed the rest of the city in flames. It is thanks to this piece of small fortune that so many remnants of medieval London survive in this little corner of the city. We can see exactly how far the flames reached. On the corner of Cock Lane and Giltspur Street, just across the road from the hospital, is the famous statue of the Golden Boy of Pye Corner. He is a mean and chubby looking child who stands defensively with his arms crossed. Set high in a niche in the wall he represents gluttony and marks the spot where the Great Fire ended. The writing engraved beneath him reads, 'This Boy is in Memmory Put up for the late FIRE of LONDON Occasion'd by the Sin of Gluttony.'

If only Londoners of the mid-seventeenth century had watched their diet.

Crossing the road and entering the grounds of Bart's Hospital via the King Henry VIII gate on Giltspur Street the visitor is greeted with the tiny church of St Bartholomew the Less. Its fifteenth-century stone tower is a remarkable survival as the rest of the church was rebuilt in the 1820s. It later suffered bomb damage in the Second World War and underwent further restoration. St Bartholomew the Less is the only chapel within the hospital to have survived the Dissolution and offers a quiet space for hospital staff, patients and their visitors. As you step through the door into the vestibule, turn left up the little steps and peek beneath the rug on the floor. There you will find the fourteenth-century brass effigies of a local couple, William and Alice Markeby. Entering the light and airy nave, look out for the stained glass window with its image of St Bartholomew in a red cloak wrapping a protective arm around the hospital's founder. Rahere is dressed in the black garb of an Augustian prior, his hair tonsured. Beneath his flowing robes can be seen a flash of his multi-coloured jester's tights.

The museum at Bart's Hospital is also well worth visiting. Located in the North wing it houses ancient documents relating to Rahere and Henry VIII, as well as a display of historical surgical instruments.

*Visitor Information*
The churchyard of St Bartholomew the Great is entered via the half-timbered Tudor gatehouse at Smithfield. Built in 1595 by

Sir Philip Scudamore, the gatehouse is a distinctive part of the local landscape. A short footpath leads you into the church porch where payment is taken for entry. Admission is £4.00 for adults, £3.50 for concessions and £10.00 for a family group. The church opening hours are variable so please call 0207 600 0440 for up-to-date details. There is also a very good café in the cloisters. There is no entrance charge for St Bartholomew the Less.

Outside the church is the historic Cloth Fair which was laid out in 1590 on the grounds of the old priory. At Number 41 is a house which dates from 1597. Until the 1920s the whole lane was lined with Tudor houses but their dilapidated state was a cause of concern to the authorities. The buildings were subsequently destroyed as a public health hazard – a sad loss indeed. Recent construction on Cloth Fair has sought to echo the architectural style of the Tudor era with a development of gabled apartments. A small warren of narrow alleyways lies off the lane, giving a sense of the wonderful jumble that characterised Early Modern London. Shakespeare would have known Cloth Fair as a meeting place for the traders and merchants who gathered here during Bartholomew Fair which took place at Smithfield every August until 1855. His friend Ben Jonson immortalised the area in the 1614 play *Bartholomew Fair*. Number 43 Cloth Fair is the former home of the poet John Betjeman. Look out for the blue plaque.

St Bart's Hospital museum is open from Tuesday to Friday, 10.00–16.00. It is recommended to call ahead before travelling as opening hours can be subject to the availability of the volunteer staff. Call 0203 465 5798 for details.

With its central location it is easy to get to Smithfield but my favourite route is by leaving St Paul's tube station from Exit Two and crossing Newgate Street heading towards the ruins of Christchurch Greyfriars. The church, of Wren's design, was destroyed in the Second World War and is now a very pretty garden with award-winning floral displays. The central footpath represents the church aisle, while the plant beds to either side represent the pews. Depending on the season you may see roses or wild flowers wrapping themselves around the wooden pergolas, which mark the position of the church pillars. Isabella of France, wife to Edward II, is buried here and her mournful ghost is said to drift around the ruins clutching her dead husband's heart. From the garden, continue up Newgate Street until you reach Giltspur Street. On the corner across the road is the church of St Sepulchre made famous by its grizzly tradition of ringing the execution bell on hanging days. The bell is on display within the church. Turn right up Giltspur Street and continue into Smithfield, once the site of mass burnings. It was here that the first Protestant martyr John Rogers was burned in 1555. Other forms of execution carried out here included hanging, drawing and quartering. Shakespeare's kinsman Edward Arden was a victim of this method and died here in 1583. William Wallace, the Scottish rebel – or freedom fighter – was also dispatched at Smithfield. Look out for the plaque to his memory on the wall of Bart's Hospital. It is usually always decorated with flowers and the Saltire flag.

Smithfield is the backdrop to Act IV, Scene VII in the play *Henry IV, Part II* when the optimistic rebel Jack Cade announces that the gang's next move will be to burn down the Savoy, after which he will make all of England's laws.

If all this talk of riots and executions has not affected your appetite, there is a gluttony of great restaurants, cafés and bars in the area.

# Clerkenwell

> My mistress' eyes are nothing like the sun;
> Coral is far more red than her lips' red;
> If snow be white, why then her breasts are dun;
> If hairs be wires; black wires grow on her head.
>
> From Sonnet 130

*The Dark Ladies*

The lines above come from a sequence of Shakespeare's sonnets which intrigue and excite the imaginations of scholars. Sonnets 127–152 explore the poet's passion for a mysterious 'Dark Lady', a figure whose identity has never been conclusively proven. Several names have been put forward over the years: Could she have been Mary Fitton, a lady-in-waiting at the court of Elizabeth I? A famous beauty, Fitton had several affairs with courtiers including William Herbert, who is sometimes alleged to be the Fair Youth of the sonnets. Another theory is put forward by the writer Dr Aubrey Burl in his book *Shakespeare's Mistress: The Mystery of the Dark Lady Revealed*. Burl argues that Shakespeare's Dark Lady was the translator John Florio's wife and that they may have conducted their affair at Titchfield, the home of Shakespeare's patron, the Earl of Southampton, where Florio lived for some time.

The list of candidates for the Dark Lady is imaginative and encompasses all levels of Elizabethan society.

Lucy Negro, sometimes known as Black Luce, was a Clerkenwell brothel keeper. The details of her life are sketchy but she was known to her contemporaries as a notorious and lewd person. Her house of ill repute was raided on at least one occasion. She has been suggested as the Dark Lady by several scholars including Dr Duncan Salkeld whose 2012 book

*Shakespeare Among the Courtesans* explores the depiction of prostitution in Early Modern drama. Salkeld partly bases his theory on the fact that Shakespeare and Lucy had mutual acquaintances such as Philip Henslowe. Along with Lucy, another local brothel keeper was Gilbert East, who as Salkeld points out was an acquaintance of both Lucy and Henslowe. East's brothel was located on Turnmill Street. Perhaps it was Clerkenwell's location outside the city walls, away from the prying eyes of the London Aldermen which helped it to evolve into something of a red light district. If Lucy Negro was indeed the mystery woman it would mean that Shakespeare must sometimes have ventured beyond the city walls to stalk its seedy lanes and alleyways.

The name Clerkenwell is a contraction of Clerks Well. This well was built into the wall of a nunnery and took its name from the parish clerks who performed in the medieval mystery plays which were held on the green. In the Middle Ages Clerkenwell was a semi-rural district with an unmistakeably monastic flavour. No fewer than three religious houses were situated in the area including the Priory of St John and the Charterhouse, home to the austere Carthusians. By Shakespeare's day it was starting to get more built up but was still a popular route for cattle drovers on their way to market at Smithfield; they would steer their beasts down Cow Cross Street, passing the Charterhouse monastery and southwards into Smithfield itself.

Lucy Negro's rival for the title of the Dark Lady is the poet Emilia Lanier who also had Clerkenwell connections. She was the daughter of Baptiste Bassano, a Venetian musician who had played at the court of Henry VIII. A miniature portrait by Nicholas Hilliard purporting to be Emilia shows a dark-haired beauty whose knowing gaze is framed by a huge white ruff. For several years until 1592 Emilia was the mistress of Henry Carey, the first Lord Hunsden. When she became pregnant by him he paid her off with a pension and she married a court musician, Alfonso Lanier. She and Shakespeare would have had ample opportunities to cross paths through their mutual connections to men such as Hunsden and the Earl of Southampton. She came from a musical family which Shakespeare may have been alluding to in Sonnet 128:

> How oft when thou, my music, music play'st,
> Upon that blessed wood whose motion sounds
> With thy sweet fingers when thou gently sway'st
> The wiry concord that my ear confounds.

Whether or not Emilia was Shakespeare's Dark Lady she was also a poet in her own right. In 1611 she wrote the proto-feminist volume entitled *Salve Deus Rex Judaeorum,* which included 'Eve's apologie in defence of Women' and 'The Tears of the Daughters of Jerusalem.' The collection is prefaced by a poem dedicated to the queen, Anne of Denmark:

> Behold, great queen, fair Eve's apology,
> Which I have writ in honour of your sexe,
> And do refer unto your majesty,
> To judge if it agree not with the text.
> And if it do, why are poor women blam'd
> Or by more faulty men defam'd?

She went on to write dedications to 'all virtuous ladies in general' and also to Lucy, Countess of Bedford, who was patron to Ben Jonson. In common with Shakespeare's Silver Street landlady Marie Mountjoy, Emilia was a client of the astrologer Simon Foreman. Her ex-lover Lord Hunsdon would later become the patron of Shakespeare's company in his role as Lord Chamberlain. It is an appealing idea to think that this intelligent and sparky woman was Shakespeare's Dark Lady, two poets and equals.

Emilia's marriage to Alfonso Lanier was not a happy one. He managed to spend all her money before he died in 1613, leaving her heavily in debt. For a short while she managed to live independently by operating a school in St Giles in the Fields, a venture which ended when the lease ran out in 1619. From here her story fades into obscurity.

Just off Clerkenwell Green is the late eighteenth-century church of St James. Its white tower rises above a handsome nave of brown brickwork. It is unmistakably Georgian in style but stands on the site of a much older foundation. Started in the twelfth century as part of the nunnery of St Mary, the present building was designed by the local architect James Carr. Emilia Lanier was buried here in 1645, possibly taking the secrets of Shakespeare's Dark Lady to the grave.

Over the centuries Clerkenwell has been a magnet for radicals, free thinkers and dissidents. In 1381 Wat Tyler gathered the revolting peasants on Clerkenwell Green before attacking the Priory of St John. Groups such as the Lollards, Tolpuddle Martyrs and Chartists also have connections with the area. Today it is very much a genteel, middle-class enclave of architects and designers. If Lucy Negro returned to her old haunt today she would recognise only small patches of it; St John's Gate and perhaps bits of the Charterhouse, but little else. The gentrification of Clerkenwell however has not sterilised it completely. This district has soaked up centuries of pure emotion and drama – the fervently praying nuns and monks of the religious houses, the rioters and rebels, the whores of Lucy Negro's brothel. In later years Charles Dickens would take inspiration from the local slums and rookeries when writing *Oliver Twist*. In Clerkenwell the tension of these human stories seems to hang in the air.

*Visitor Information*

The Clerk's Well on Farringdon Lane was just one of many springs in and around London. Writing in the twelfth century, William Fitzstephen, a clerk in the employment of Thomas a Becket, said the city wells were 'visited more by scholars and youth of the city when they go out for fresh air on summer evenings.' It sounds like the medieval equivalent of kids hanging around in the local park. The Clerk's Well was originally located just outside the nunnery of St Mary's and remained in use until the nineteenth century. It can be seen through the glass at street level from outside numbers 14–16 Farringdon Lane. To get a closer look you can either arrange a free visit via the Islington Local History Centre by calling 0207 527 7988 or join one of the regular guided tours run by the Clerkenwell and Islington Guiding Association. See www.ciga.org.uk for more details or email info@ciga.org.uk.

The Charterhouse monastery, just north of Smithfield Market, was built in the fourteenth century. The site chosen was inauspiciously close to a plague pit and became home to the Carthusians, an order which shunned all tokens of comfort. They wore plain white gowns and they were awoken at intervals throughout the night to pray. Their meagre diet was limited to vegetables. The lack of sleep and food would have been a gruelling test of endurance. Perhaps unsurprisingly, Peter Ackroyd describes the monks as 'particularly prone to weeping', although as he points out, their tears would have been seen as a religious gift rather than a sign of stress. It was among these spartan brothers that Sir Thomas More tested his vocation in the late fifteenth century before deciding he was better suited to the outside world. The monastery was dissolved in 1535 and the prior was executed. The house was given to Lord North and was turned into a comfortable mansion. Elizabeth I stayed here before her coronation. The building has been extensively rebuilt since the time of the monastery but parts of the original fabric remain and it is now an Almshouse. It is possible to visit the Charterhouse by joining one of the guided tours which take place on Tuesdays, Wednesdays, Thursdays and some Saturdays. Tickets cost £10 per person. Please see www.thecharterhouse. org/tours for booking details.

St James's Church, where Emilia Lanier was buried, is much changed since the days when she and Shakespeare walked the streets but is still worth a visit. Inside are several Tudor features which survived James Carr's rebuilding work and which Emilia might recognise if she came back today. Situated over the west door is a wooden statuette of St James which ornamented the church in the sixteenth century. The church is usually open to visitors from Monday to Friday, 9.00–17.00. Call 0207 251 1190 for details.

# Banqueting House and Whitehall

> And we mean well in going to this mask,
> But 'tis no wit to go.
> *Romeo and Juliet*: Romeo, Act I, Scene IV

## Masque of Blackness

The name Whitehall is synonymous with government bureaucracy and officialdom; this is the natural habitat of mandarins, spin doctors and special advisors. Lining the street in a parade stretching from Trafalgar Square to the Palace of Westminster are buildings housing such institutions as the Ministry of Defence, the Cabinet Office and the Foreign and Commonwealth Office. Crowds of tourists can be seen outside the black gates leading to Downing Street. Occasionally the armed police on guard will open the gates to allow an official vehicle to glide through, its black-tinted windows hiding the identity of the official inside. Whitehall is truly the powerhouse of the United Kingdom.

In the middle of the road is the Cenotaph. Designed in 1920 by Edward Lutyens it is the focal point of the annual Remembrance Sunday celebrations when the monarch places a wreath of poppies at its base in a mark of respect for those who died during the Second World War. Opposite Downing Street and a little further along Whitehall is a remarkable building which has stood here since 1619, surviving the late seventeenth-century fire which destroyed its neighbours. Built on the site of its predecessor, the Banqueting House was an integral part of Whitehall Palace, the main residence of British monarchs since 1529. The palace history stretches back to the fourteenth century when a grand house was built on the site for the archbishops of York. It came into the ownership of Cardinal Wolsey in 1514 when he became archbishop and was aptly known as York Place. Wolsey would not enjoy it for long; when he fell from grace in 1529 Henry VIII took it for himself and renamed it Whitehall after the colour of the stones used to build it. For those Londoners who had always known it as York Place, the name change would have taken some getting used to. In the play *Henry VIII*, some gentlemen are having a discussion about the coronation of Anne Boleyn. One of them is in the middle of describing the event to his companions when he makes a classic slip up:

Third Gentleman: At length her grace rose, and with modest paces

Came to the altar; where she kneel'd, and saint-like

Cast her fair eyes to heaven and pray'd devoutly.

Then rose again and bow'd her to the people:

When by the Archbishop of Canterbury

She had all the royal makings of a queen;

As holy oil, Edward Confessor's crown,

The rod, and bird of peace, and all such emblems

Laid nobly on her: which perform'd, the choir,

With all the choicest music of the kingdom,

Together sung 'Te Deum.' So she parted,

And with the same full state paced back again

To York Place, where the feast is held.

First Gentleman: Sir, you must no more call it York Place, that's
    past.

For, since the cardinal fell, that title's lost:

'Tis now the king's, and call'd Whitehall.

Third Gentleman: I know it;

But 'tis so lately alter'd, that the old name

Is fresh about me.

*Henry VIII*: Act IV, Scene I

Henry was an aesthete who recognised the symbolic power of imagery. He quickly embarked on a programme of building work which saw the size of the house increase to a labyrinthine complex of over 2000 rooms on a site covering twenty-three acres. It was lavishly set up for courtly fun; a jousting tilt yard stood on the site of today's Horse Guard's Parade, and there were four tennis courts. The palace was bisected by King Street – the modern road we know as Whitehall – the two sides being connected by a two storied gatehouse said to have been built by Hans Holbein. It provided a private passage for the king to access the tilt yard and the parkland beyond. The gateway itself was a narrow arch through which traffic flowed to and from the Palace of Westminster.

After their marriage, Henry and Anne Boleyn held court at Whitehall, Anne sharing the king's apartments on the first floor. During her short tenure as Queen of England, the palace was still undergoing building work. She would not live to see the completion of the Queen's Apartments which were only finished after her execution in 1536.

Henry VIII was just the first of a long line of monarchs to reside at Whitehall. Elizabeth I spent time here and it was she who built the first known banqueting house on the site. In 1581 her workmen erected a wooden frame draped with canvas painted the colour of stone. It was decorated with flowers and hanging displays of gilded fruit and vegetables. All this was in preparation for the upcoming visit of Elizabeth's suitor the Duc d'Alençon who was on his way to try and win her hand in marriage. Elizabeth enjoyed his visit and the two were said to get along well. Whether or not she ever intended to marry him, the Protestant population was largely opposed to the match so the Catholic *duc* went home, leaving Elizabeth to nurture her image as Gloriana, the Virgin Queen.

Elizabeth's banqueting house was as impermanent as her changeable moods. It was James I who built something more lasting. He did not like Whitehall with its warren like maze of alleyways and dead ends. In 1606 he decided to start afresh and commissioned a new design with clean, logical lines and open spaces. At the same time the Banqueting House was built for the first time in stone. The Venetian Ambassador described it as, 'A large hall is fitted up like a theatre, with well secured boxes all round. The stage is at one end, and his majesty's chair in front under an ample canopy.' It was here that James would enjoy a performance of *The Tempest* by his company of players, the King's Men, on 1 November 1611. The play was performed again two years later to celebrate the marriage of the Lady Elizabeth to Frederick, Elector Palatine of Bohemia. *The Tempest* is a strange, ethereal play full of music and magic. The royal couple would have appreciated the masque scene:

> Juno: How does my bounteous sister? Go with me
> To bless this twain, that they may prosperous be
> And honour'd in their issue.
> *(They sing)*
> Juno: Honour, riches, marriage-blessing,
> Long continuance, and increasing,
> Hourly joys be still upon you!
> Juno sings her blessings upon you.
>
> *The Tempest:* Act IV, Scene I

In this scene, Prospero has called his spirits to perform an entertainment for Miranda and Ferdinand who are newly betrothed. What follows is a classic example of the type of courtly masque performed by, and for, royals and aristocracy. These entertainments were characterised by the liberal use of music, poetry and dance. It was a very visual form of theatre with professionally designed scenery and elaborate costumes. Rich allegory and imagery expressed ideas such as the divine right of kings. An example is Ben Jonson's *Masque of Blackness* which was commissioned by Anne of Denmark and performed at the Banqueting House on Twelfth Night, 1605. This involved Anne and her ladies blacking up to represent daughters of Niger. Anne wanted to express the idea that the king could cleanse them of their blackness. It goes without saying that most people today would find this distasteful but even at the time, the performers' use of black body paint proved controversial, albeit for less enlightened reasons. Dudley Carleton complained in a letter, 'Instead of vizards, their faces, and arms, up to the elbows, were painted black ... and you cannot imagine a more ugly sight.'

The set designer was the architect Inigo Jones. He and Ben Jonson worked together on several other masques but their egos eventually clashed and they fell out. Jones was a multi-talented man; the son of a Welsh cloth worker, he spent the last years of the sixteenth century travelling in Italy picking up ideas about architecture and learning from the masters of the Renaissance. He found inspiration in the work of the Classical architect Andrea Palladio who had been, in turn, influenced by the architecture of Ancient Greece. Jones would bring Palladian architecture to England with the rebuilding of Banqueting House in 1619. England had seen nothing like it before. With its exterior columns and triangular pediments, this was Jones's answer to the Italian Renaissance. In 1636 the ceiling was adorned with a vast painting by Rubens. Its subject was a celebration of the reign of James I and would have reinforced his son, Charles I's, sense of divine right to rule. On 29 January 1649 Charles spent his last night at St James' Palace where he said goodbye to his children. The following morning he was escorted to the Banqueting House where a scaffold had been erected. He was taken inside where he had a last glass of claret and put on an extra shirt against the cold. He then stepped out of the first floor window onto the scaffold. His final words before he was executed were, 'I go from a corruptible to an incorruptible crown, where no disturbance can be.'

Whitehall Palace burned down in 1698. The accident was caused when a pile of linen which had been left to dry by a fire caught light. The blaze destroyed the entire palace except for the Holbein Gate and the Banqueting House. William III decided not to rebuild the palace and moved his court away from the damp river bank and further west to the healthier air of Kensington.

It was the end of a remarkable era. Over a period of 150 years Whitehall had been at the centre of royal power. Walking past Downing Street and the Cabinet Office today, the realisation dawns that nothing has changed except that those wielding the power can no longer claim to do so by divine right.

*Visitor Information*

Banqueting House is located at Whitehall, London SW1A 2ER. Tel: 0844 482 7777.

The Banqueting House is guaranteed to be open Monday to Sunday from 10.00–13.00. If no functions or events are planned the opening hours are extended until 17.00. The venue recommends phoning ahead to check for up-to-date information as they occasionally need to close at short notice. Admission information can be found at http://www.hrp.org.uk/ BanquetingHouse/planyourvisit.

As mentioned previously, Henry VIII's jousting tilt yard was located on what we know as Horse Guard's Parade. Its entrance on Whitehall is not hard to find; located just beyond Downing Street in the direction of Trafalgar Square, the Palladian-style guard house is usually crowded with tourists taking photos of the horses who stand guard in the twin porches. The Guard House was built between 1750 and 1753 based on the designs of the architect William Kent who died before work started. His assistant John Vardy took over as project manager and completed the work leaving us this gorgeous piece of architectural heritage. The building houses the Household Cavalry Museum with its stable of black horses which are used for ceremonial events such as Trooping the Colour on the Queen's official birthday in June.

Exhibits in the museum include vintage ceremonial uniforms and horse tack. For details of opening hours, please call 0207 930 3070. Admission is £7.00 for adults and £5.00 for concessions and children aged between five and sixteen. For details see www. householdcavalrymuseum.co.uk.

# Leicester

> Friends, Romans, countrymen, lend me your ears;
> I come to bury Caesar, not to praise him.
> The evil that men do lives after them;
> The good is often interred with their bones.
>
> *Julius Caesar*: Antony, Act III, Scene II

### The Burial of Two Kings

This section deals with two kings and the city that buried them. These men were the stars of two Shakespeare plays but only one of them existed in real life. Richard III reigned for three years before losing to Henry Tudor at the Battle of Bosworth Field in 1485. King Lear, on the other hand, is a figment of the medieval imagination, a tragic figure whose foolish pride inspired some of Shakespeare's best lines. The legends and folklore surrounding both men have enriched the city of Leicester for centuries.

Not far from Leicester Cathedral, in a traffic-heavy corner of the city, is a huge chunk of Roman wall which looms over a sunken garden. The so called Jewry Wall formed part of the Roman baths which were built here when the Romans arrived in Leicester around AD 47. In the garden below visitors can wander freely around the archaeological remains, enjoying a piece of ancient history in the middle of a modern city. From the gardens the Norman stone tower of the church of St Nicholas adds a dramatic backdrop to the Roman remains. Started in Saxon times around the year 900, the church was built on the site of the Roman forum, or marketplace. Across the road is the Holiday Inn which stands on the site of the Roman Temple of Janus. This brings us to the obscure tale of King Lear.

Ancient tradition says that Lear was buried by his daughter Cordelia in a vault on the banks of the River Soar. The Romans would later build the Temple of Janus on the site of his burial. If legend is to be believed this would mean that Shakespeare's British king lies at rest beneath a Holiday Inn. Unfortunately there is no reason to think that Lear was anything more than a character invented by an imaginative medieval monk. Geoffrey of Monmouth was an eleventh-century Benedictine brother who wrote the chronicle *Historia Regum Britanniae*, or, *History of the Kings of Britain*. The *History* told the story of all the British kings from the Trojans to the early Anglo-Saxons. It was one of the sources for Shakespeare's play *King Lear* which was written around 1606. Shakespeare adapted the story for dramatic purposes, making Lear mad and ending the action with the tragic deaths of Lear and Cordelia.

In the play Lear's downfall begins when he decides to hand over the running of his kingdom to his three daughters. Being a vain, needy type, he asks them to describe how much they love him before getting their share. Having extracted lavish praise from his daughters Goneril and Regan, he hopes for more of the same insincere guff from Cordelia:

> King Lear: ... Now, our joy,
> Although the last, not least; to whose young love
> The vines of France and milk of Burgundy
> Strive to be interess'd, what can you say to draw

A third more opulent than your sisters? Speak.

Cordelia: Nothing, my lord.

*King Lear*: Act I, Scene I

Cordelia is unwilling to play the game so King Lear banishes her, little realising that she is his only true friend.

*King Lear* is one of the only Shakespeare plays to have a British setting. Lear belongs to Britain's pre-Roman, mythical past. He did not exist in history but had he done, he would have been a Celt, a warrior king, whose Corieltavi tribe dominated the East Midlands before the Roman invasion. Leir, as Geoffrey of Monmouth called him, is supposed to have built the city of Leicester. The Saxon name for the city was *Leircestre*, although this probably has less to do with 'Leir' and more to do with the old Celtic name *'Ligore'* and the term for a Roman settlement *'ceaster.'*

During the Middle Ages the city developed into an important market town and the historic centre still bears traces of its commercial heart. Like the City of London, Leicester boasts a Cheapside and Silver Street. The city prospered from the wool trade and in the fourteenth century the townsfolk formed the Guild of Merchants. The pretty half-timbered Guildhall where they met is located near the cathedral. In August 1485 Richard III passed through the town on his way to meet Henry Tudor for what he hoped would be a victorious battle at Bosworth Field. He had travelled from Nottingham, bringing with him his four-poster bed. The party stayed at the Blue Boar Inn on the High Street where Richard enjoyed his last night's sleep in the comfort of a bed before marching onwards towards a tent in a field and death. The site of the Blue Boar is now a Travelodge.

In the nineteenth century the Industrial Revolution brought a manufacturing boom to the city. Boots, shoes and hosiery were the new money spinners. The arrival of the railways brought inspiration for an industry of a more leisurely kind. In 1841 a young man called Thomas Cook conceived the idea of chartering a train to bring the poor to temperance meetings in nearby Loughborough. The idea developed and he was soon arranging affordable trips around the world. For a city made famous by a package holiday pioneer, Leicester seems to have been unfairly overlooked by the tourism industry. Until recent events involving the discovery of a king's bones, Leicester was the city that we whizzed past as we travelled en-route to more exotic locations. Thanks to Richard III however, the city has enjoyed something of a renaissance. Anyone visiting Leicester today will see how proudly the city has embraced him. The short walk from the train station to the cathedral passes a pub on Granby Street called the Last Plantagenet. King Richard's Road is nearby. This is unashamedly Richard III land. Shakespeare can probably take some of the credit for Richard's enduring mystique and subsequent celebrity. If he had painted Richard as a good king, it is doubtful that he would have the fan club he enjoys today. Controversial characters are always the most attractive. For this reason alone, Shakespeare deserves acknowledgement for ensuring that Richard's name has never faded into the obscurity of being just another medieval king.

In 2012 the discovery of his bones beneath a car park off Greyfriars near the Cathedral set off a controversial tug of love for possession of his remains. His intended reburial in Leicester Cathedral was delayed while the Plantagenet Alliance, a group of the king's ancestors, brought a legal challenge with the aim of having his remains reburied in York instead. The gist of their argument was that York had been the king's stronghold; it was friendly territory and the king himself would have wanted to be buried there. Besides, the stunning architecture of York

Minster was more suited to receive him than the more modest surroundings at Leicester. By contrast, the argument for Leicester was simple. The king had lain at peace in Leicester for over 500 years; why move him now? In the end the judges ruled in favour of Leicester. He was buried in the cathedral on 26 March 2015 in a solemn ceremony presided over by the Archbishop of Canterbury, Justin Welby. The actor Benedict Cumberbatch recited a moving poem by the Poet Laureate Carol Anne Duffy. The citizens of Leicester turned out in force to pay their respects, many wearing medieval style fancy dress. They lined the streets in their thousands to watch the funeral cortege pass by; witnesses to the culmination of a drama which had gripped the world. Reportedly, one of the local hairdressing salons started offering Richard III hairstyles.

The king's tomb is an understated and dignified affair. Located near the church sanctuary, it is cut from Swaledale fossil stone, the tiny fossils within it symbolising immortality. The cathedral itself is small and uncrowded; its atmosphere one of peace and tranquillity. Whatever you think about the virtues of York versus Leicester, or the moral qualities of Richard himself, it feels fitting that he has been brought in from the cold.

Outside the cathedral in the gardens is a bronze statue of Richard in full battle cry, sword in hand and waving his crown aloft. One thing he lacks, however, is a horse. In a place where his memory is supposed to be revered, his frenzied cry in Act V, Scene IV of Shakespeare's *Richard III* comes guiltily to mind, 'A horse! A horse! My kingdom for a horse!' The statue was a gift to the city of Leicester from the Richard III Society. Around the corner is a modern sculpture called 'Towards Stillness.' It represents Richard's journey from the horrors of the battlefield and indignity of his final moments, to the discovery of his skeleton under the car park and reburial. Unveiled in 2014, it is a lovely addition to the landscape.

Leicester is a modern city with all the usual shopping malls and multiplexes but its heart is medieval; scraps of its ancient fabric lie dotted about like shipwrecks from another time. For all the changes and regeneration, the old wounds of history are never far from the surface.

## Visitor Information

Leicester Cathedral is formally known as the Cathedral Church of St Martin, Leicester, and is located at St Martin's House, 7 Peacock Lane LE1 5PZ. Tel: 0116 261 5200. There has been a church on this site since Norman times but the present building dates from the thirteenth century with much Victorian restoration. It became a cathedral in 1927.

Opening hours are 8.00–18.00 Monday to Saturday and 8.00–16.00 on Sundays. Richard's tomb can be accessed between the hours of 10.00–17.00 Monday to Saturday. Entry is free but donations are gratefully accepted.

The Richard III Visitor Centre next door tells the fascinating story of the discovery of Richard's bones. Opening hours are 10.00–16.00 Sunday to Friday and 8.00–17.00 on Saturdays and during school holidays. Tours take ninety minutes and cost £7.95 for adults, £4.75 for children aged five to fifteen, £7.00 for seniors and students and £21.50 for a family ticket comprising two adults and two children.

The Jewry Wall Museum is located at St Nicholas Circle, Leicester LE1 4LB. Tel: 0116 225 4971. The Jewry Wall and grounds are cared for by the wonderful English Heritage and are also free to visit. Attached to the grounds is the very good Jewry Wall Museum which showcases Roman and Medieval archaeology including mosaics and painted plaster. The museum is free and is open from 11.00–16.30 February to October. It is closed during the winter months.

After going in search of King Lear in Leicester city centre Shakespeare fans may wish to visit King Lear's Lake in Watermead Country Park. Situated on a platform in the middle of the lake is a group of statues representing the final scene in *King Lear*. Cordelia's dead body lies on its side while Lear kneels down to mourn her. He is watched over by Kent and Albany. Located five miles north of Leicester this 140 hectare nature reserve is a natural haven for wildlife. It boasts a mixed habitat of manmade lakes, woodland and wildflower meadows.

# Wilton House

> We have the man Shakespeare with us ...

## The Countess of Pembroke

How tempting it is to envy the woman who is said to have written these words! Mary Sidney Herbert, the Countess of Pembroke, was an Elizabethan noblewoman who was renowned for her patronage of the arts. At her Wiltshire estate, Wilton House, she hosted a literary salon with a glittering guest list of names such as Edmund Spenser, Ben Jonson and Thomas Nashe. Poetry was in her genes; before his death at the Battle of Zutphen her brother Sir Philip Sidney had been celebrated for his prose romance *Arcadia* which he wrote whilst staying with her at Wilton in 1580. Mary herself was the author of works such as *The Doleful Lay of Clorinda*. It would therefore seem entirely natural for her to have 'the man Shakespeare' at her house.

In the autumn of 1603 the London playhouses had been

forcibly closed after an outbreak of plague. It was a sensible measure; gathering together thousands of people in an enclosed space would allow the contagion to spread with uncontrollable speed. The lack of venues in which to perform was clearly an inconvenience but it also presented the opportunity to tour – and to escape the plague. That autumn Shakespeare's company, the King's Men, left London and did just that. They stopped at Mortlake in Surrey then moved onto Wilton House where they performed for King James on 2 December. A nineteenth-century historian, William Cory, added some colour to this account. He had spent time as a tutor at Wilton and claimed to have seen a letter written by Mary Sidney to her son, bidding him to invite King James and the Queen Anne to her house to see a performance of *As You Like It*. This is when she is supposed to have dangled the playwright as bait: 'We have the man Shakespeare with us.'

Unfortunately the letter is lost, if it ever existed, but the scenario seems plausible enough. If true, then Shakespeare's name and reputation must have been known well enough by his contemporaries for him to be an enticing draw. It is easy to imagine the King's Men performing the pastoral comedy *As You Like It* in such a bucolic setting. The hunting-mad King James would have appreciated the references in the play to his favourite sport:

> Come, shall we and kill us a venison?
> And yet it irks me the poor dappled fools,
> Being native burghers of this desert city,
> Should in their own confines with forked heads
> Have their round haunches gorged.
> > *As You Like It*: Duke Senior, Act II, Scene I

Wilton House is located not far from Salisbury in the lush South

Wiltshire countryside. Its history stretches back to 871 when an abbey was built on the site. After the Dissolution of the Monasteries, Henry VIII gifted the building to William Herbert, the first Earl of Pembroke who set about rebuilding work. It would soon be transformed into a fine Tudor mansion. It is not known who the architect was but an unproven tradition says Hans Holbein had a hand in the design. The house the King's Men would have seen was a rectangular building structured around a central courtyard. At the entrance was a grand tower with a central arch through which visitors would pass into the courtyard. Engraved into the tower are two coats of arms which bear Pembroke's coronet. It is believed the building work was completed by 1561.

In 1630 the southern range of Wilton was demolished to make way for a new design by Inigo Jones. Further redesigning work took place at the beginning of the nineteenth century in the Classical style. Over years of rebuilding the only remaining fabric of the Tudor house is the tower and a Gothic stone porch said to have been designed by Holbein. The porch now stands in the garden as an ornate folly.

Presumably the King's Men performed in the Great Hall, a room which is now sadly missing. It was demolished in the nineteenth century and replaced with what is now a light and airy front hall. In the centre is a statue of Mary Sidney Herbert's most famous visitor, William Shakespeare, who stands leaning rather awkwardly on a pile of books pointing down at a scroll. The statue was designed by Peter Scheemakers in the eighteenth century. Despite what would seem to be a wholesale loss of Wilton's Tudor heritage, the house still retains a collection of artefacts collected and passed down by the Herbert family. In a display cabinet at the end of the Lower East Cloister is a handwritten poem by Philip Sidney and a lock of Elizabeth I's hair. These personal items are a reminder of the humanity behind the stiff portraits and cold historical facts of their lives.

In a pleasing show of continuity Wilton House is still home to the Earls of Pembroke. Like many aristocratic custodians of stately homes, the 18th Earl and his wife have thrown open their home to visitors who come to enjoy a look around this beautiful site. The grounds stretch over 14,500 acres and encompass rolling farmland, rivers and unspoilt woodland. Wilton House and its gardens are a much changed prospect to what the King's Men would have known but this is still the same ground they travelled along on their way to entertain Mary Sidney Herbert and her royal guests. It is easy to imagine a caravan of wagons trundling along the driveway, perhaps escorted by various men on foot playing the tabor and blowing trumpets as they announced their arrival. In the bleakness of a midwinter country estate, they would have been a cheering sight.

*Visitor Information*

Wilton House is located in Wilton, Salisbury SP2 0BJ. Tel: 01772 746714. The House is generally open from 11.30–17.00 but the days are variable so please call or check www.wiltonhouse.co.uk/opening-times for up-to-date information. Admission to the house and grounds is £14.50 for adults, £11.75 for concessions, £7.50 for children and £36.00 for a family comprising two adults and two children.

Private tours are available for groups. The price is £25.20 per person. To arrange a tour, call on the number above or email tourism@wiltonhouse.com.

For a bite to eat, the Palladian Restaurant is open from 11.00–17.30 and is pleasantly situated with views across the parkland.

# Deptford

> When a man's verses cannot be understood, nor a
> Man's good wit seconded with the forward child
> Understanding, it strikes a man more dead than a
> Great reckoning in a little room. Truly, I would
> The gods had made thee poetical.
>
> *As You Like It*: Touchstone, Act III, Scene III

*A Dead Man in Deptford*

A poet's misunderstood lines, a great reckoning in a little room. To audiences at the end of the sixteenth century, Touchstone's words would have been loaded with meaning. *As You Like It* was first performed in 1599, just six years after Christopher Marlowe had been stabbed in the eye in Deptford. The official narrative that he was murdered in a tavern brawl – there had supposedly been an argument over who would pay the bill, or reckoning – has been discredited by historians such as Charles Nichol who investigated the case in his book *A Dead Man in Deptford*. Ingram Frizer, the man who plunged his dagger into the poet's eye was a government agent and Marlowe, too, had been involved in spying for Thomas Walsingham. It was all very fishy.

This brief section is something of a wild card. We shall leave the Bard behind for a moment and pay our respects to Marlowe, whose influence is apparent in his work and must therefore be regarded as an important figure in the Shakespeare story. It was Marlowe who popularised the blank verse style; those rhythmic, unrhymed lines which made the speech patterns of his characters sound natural yet poetic. Shakespeare would employ the same technique in most of his plays.

Marlowe died on 30 May 1593 in a Deptford house owned

by one Eleanor Bull. It is usually accepted by historians that Dame Eleanor's house was not a public tavern but rather a private victualling house, rather like a bed and breakfast. The circumstances of Marlowe's death there have been amply explored by other writers so for the sake of those who would like to follow in his fatal footsteps we shall explore the place of his burial and Deptford itself, a riverside community in south east London. The name Deptford describes its situation on the banks of the creek, a tributary of the River Thames. In its earliest days it was called Depeford, signifying a river crossing. Water runs through Deptford's veins. In 1513 Henry VIII founded a shipyard here in preparation for war with France. It was here that the *Golden Hinde* was brought in 1580 after Sir Francis Drake's piratical circumnavigation of the globe. It was here that Elizabeth I boarded the ship and knighted Drake for his achievement – and for bringing back lots of plundered gold. This heroic galleon remained *in situ*, gradually rotting away and being plundered by curious sightseers until it disintegrated in the mid-seventeenth century. Deptford maintained its importance as a naval dockyard into the nineteenth century when it played its part in the Napoleonic Wars. The town's sense of identity is closely linked with its nautical past and an old ship anchor is proudly displayed on the High Street. The twentieth century saw a period of decline as ships got bigger and moved to deeper waters. An air of cut-price commerce hangs about the High Street today. Heavy industry has been replaced with kebab shops and pound stores while the market is a treasure trove of bric-a-brac – the line of stalls is replete with goods such as suitcases, lighters and antiques.

Marlowe would have known the High Street as Butt Lane. In his day it was a rural lane lined with orchards and gardens. The name was changed to High Street in 1825 after a period of growing commercialisation with shops moving in. The church of St Nicholas lies not far from the High Street, just off McMillan Street. Marlowe was buried here on 1 June 1593 in an unmarked grave. A memorial stone on the churchyard wall reads:

> Near this spot lie the mortal remains of
> Christopher Marlowe
> Who met his untimely death
> In Deptford on May 30th 1593.
> Cut is the branch that might have grown full straight.

The church is a medieval foundation but the present building dates from 1697 when its previous incarnation was pulled down and enlarged. The flint and stone tower is the only surviving remnant of Marlowe's days; he is said to be buried in a spot close to the tower. As you enter the churchyard, look out for the sinister skull and crossbones on the gateposts.

On the other side of Deptford Creek is the royal borough of Greenwich with its spectacular heritage and sense of history and attractions such as the Cutty Sark and the National Maritime Museum. Visitors should also seek out the Queen's House, a classical stone built mansion by Inigo Jones. Legend says that James I gifted it to Anne of Denmark in an extravagant apology to his wife. His crime? Whilst out hunting, Anne had accidentally shot one of his dogs and he swore at her. The building work started in 1616 but was halted in 1618 when Anne fell ill. She died the following year and the work was only completed in 1635. Oliver Cromwell turned part of it into a biscuit factory. Today it houses a fine art collection. It was built near the site of Greenwich Palace, the favourite residence of Elizabeth I.

*Visitor Information*

St Nicholas Church is located at Deptford Green, Deptford, London SE8 3DQ. Tel: 0208 692 2749. As well as having skulls on the churchyard gateposts, the church has a healthy collection of skeletal images inside too. Look out for the Grinling Gibbons wood carving, *The Valley of Dry Bones.*

The Queen's House is located at Romney Road, Greenwich, London SE10 9NF. Opening hours are 10.00–17.00 with last admission at 16.30. Admission is free.

# Statues and Monuments

This figure, that thou here seest put,

It was for gentle Shakespeare cut:

Wherein the graver had a strife

With nature to out do the life

To the Reader: From Ben Jonson's elegy to Shakespeare, 1623

*Images of the Bard*

Ben Jonson was speaking about the famous Droeshout engraving of Shakespeare which appears on the front of the First Folio. It is a strange image, asymmetrical and two-dimensional as if the face was drawn from memory and not from life. His head is balding and his bulbous eyes lack the spark of life that we might wish our national poet to possess. One of the enduring frustrations for those who love Shakespeare is that we do not have a confirmed portrait of him. The 'Chandos' Portrait which hangs in the National Portrait Gallery bears a slight resemblance to the Droeshout image but nobody knows for sure if it is him. It shows a pale, dark-eyed man in a plain black doublet and white collar. He wears a single gold earring which glints brightly against the muted colours. It is a plain, yet strangely powerful image. Painted in the first years of the seventeenth century, Shakespeare would have been a middle-aged man at the time of the sitting. These were his wealthiest years and perhaps he already had his mind on retirement and his legacy. One theory says that the engraver Martin Droeshout used the portrait as the basis for the image he created for the First Folio. Until his likeness is definitively identified, however, it seems we must make do with engravings and statues.

The image of Shakespeare appears in several unexpected London locations. We have already seen that his face is carved in Portland stone outside the Guildhall Art Gallery along with other distinguished men. His bust is the focal point in the gardens at St Mary Aldermanbury around the corner from the Guildhall. This section shall explore two other spots in which Shakespeare or his work has been the source of inspiration for our sculptors and artists.

On Queen Victoria Street in the City of London, not far from the College of Arms, is the rather ugly Baynard House. Built in the Brutalist style in the late 1970s its evocative name is a reminder of the vanished medieval palace on whose site it stands. Until its destruction in the Great Fire of London, Baynard Castle was a royal palace which had existed in various incarnations since the Norman Conquest of 1066. Located on the banks of the River Thames it enjoyed an idyllic situation on the western edges of the City not far from St Paul's and the Blackfriars monastery. Shakespeare sets a scene here in the play *Richard III*. It is at Baynard's Castle that Buckingham helps Gloucester to the crown:

> We heartily solicit
> Your gracious self to take on you the charge

> And kingly government of this your land,
> Not as protector, steward, substitute,
> Or lowly factor for another's gain;
> But as successively from blood to blood
>
> > *Richard III*: Buckingham, Act III, Scene VII

After Richard's short reign, Henry VII transformed it into a royal palace. When Henry's flamboyant heir Henry VIII ascended the throne in 1509 he presented the palace to Catherine of Aragon. In later years it passed into the ownership of the Earls of Pembroke. All that remains of the palace now is the echo of its name in the nearby Castle Baynard Street.

Its successor Baynard House is owned not by royals or aristocrats but by British Telecom. The building was constructed with function, rather than beauty, in mind and it has to be said that this is a rather unlovely stretch of road. It is however worth braving the furious traffic of Queen Victoria Street to view the tall totem pole-type monument in the front courtyard. Unveiled in 1980, the *Seven Ages of Man* was designed by the sculptor Richard Kindersley and makes a striking tribute to one of Shakespeare's most famous speeches. Seven carved aluminium heads form a column seven foot high, each representing one of the stages in the Elizabethan male lifecycle as described by the melancholy Jaques' in Act II, Scene VII of the play *As You Like It*. The following lines from Jaques' speech wrap themselves around the base of the statue:

> At first the infant, mewing and puking in the nurses arms.
> And then the whining schoolboy, with his satchel, and shining morning face, creeping like snail unwillingly to school.
> And then the lover, sighing like furnace, with a woful ballad made to his mistress' eyebrow.

Then a soldier, full of strange oaths, and bearded like the pard, jealous in honour, sudden and quick in quarrel, seeking the bubble reputation even in the cannon's mouth.

And then the justice, in fair round belly, with good capon lin'd with eyes severe, and beard of formal cut, full of wise saus and modern instance; and so he plays his part.

The sixth age shifts into the lean and slipper'd pantaloon, with spectacles on nose and pouch on side, his youthful hose, well saved, a world too wide for his shrunk shank, and his bug manly voice, turning again toward childish treble, pipes and whistles in his sound.

Last scene of all, that ends this strange eventful history, is second childishness and mere oblivion, sans teeth sans eyes sans taste sans everything.

The statue is easily accessible to the public but be sure to take care when crossing Queen Victoria Street.

We move away from the City of London now, and into the frenetic and glamorous West End, where a well-loved marble statue of Shakespeare forms the centrepiece of Leicester Square. The statue, by Giovanni Fontana, was unveiled in 1874 in the middle of the pretty garden at the centre of the square. As one of the forefathers of the English entertainment industry, Shakespeare looks very much at home here. Surrounded on all sides by the neon lights of the cinemas, he has inhabited the square for over a century, watching in approving silence as generations of tourists, pleasure seekers and red carpet celebrities have passed beneath his feet. He stands in what seems to be his usual pose; long cloak flowing behind him, leaning thoughtfully on a pile of books and holding a scroll. The words on the scroll are taken from Act IV, Scene II in *Twelfth Night*, 'There is no darkness but ignorance.' As the inscribed on the plinth tells us, 'this enclosure was laid out and decorated as a garden by Albert Esquire, MP and conveyed by him on 2 July 1874 to the Metropolitan Board of Works to be preserved for ever for the free use and enjoyment of the public.' This Victorian philanthropist may not have reckoned on the ambitions of twenty-first-century developers who do not always have the same care for our cultural heritage as we may wish. When recent plans were in place to redevelop the square in time for the 2012 Olympics, the Shakespeare statue was in danger of being relocated elsewhere but thankfully he remains where he is. The square has since been sensitively revamped, although other historic ornaments in the garden were removed, such as the film star plaques on the pavement and the Charlie Chaplin statue.

Leicester Square was first developed in the late seventeenth century on land belonging to Robert Sidney, 2nd Earl of Leicester, and has evolved into an entertainment district. Today it is surrounded on all sides by cinemas, nightclubs and bars. A stone's throw away is Covent Garden and London's Theatre Land, an area fizzing with creative energy. The West End theatre scene can probably be thought of as Shakespeare's legacy. The actor managers of the Restoration, Georgian and Victorian periods continually staged his work, sometimes with their own eccentric adaptations. In doing so they ensured that his work would never gather dust.

*Visitor Information*
Baynard House is located directly across the road from St Andrew by the Wardrobe and the Church of Scientology. Looking at the building from outside the church, it has the appearance of an impenetrable block of concrete broken up by shadowy staircases and passageways. Do not be intimidated or deterred. Carefully cross Queen Victoria Street and head straight for the concrete

stairs, ignoring the faint tang of urine, and follow them upwards until you reach a concrete platform where the statue awaits.

After your adventure in the Brutalist maze, you will find Leicester Square easy to find. Leicester Square tube station is located two minutes away on Charing Cross Road and is served by the Northern and Piccadilly lines. After viewing the Shakespeare statue you should walk round the corner and pay a visit to the National Portrait Gallery to see the 'Chandos' Portrait, the first painting to be hung in the gallery following its generous donation by Lord Ellesmere. The gallery was founded in 1856 thanks to the efforts of Philip Stanhope, the 5th Earl of Stanhope, who lobbied parliament and Queen Victoria for a publicly funded gallery in which the portraits of British subjects could be displayed. The portrait of Shakespeare's friend Ben Jonson, by Abraham van Blyenberch is also a must-see as well as the excellent collection of Tudor portraiture which features famous images of figures such as Henry VIII, Elizabeth I and their various courtiers. A portrait of Henry Wriothesley, the 3rd Earl of Southampton, dominates Room Two.

The National Portrait Gallery is located at St Martin's Place, London WC2H 0HE. Tel: 0207 306 0055. The gallery is open daily from 10.00–18.00 except on Thursdays and Fridays when it remains open until 21.00. Entry is free.

Look out for the statue of the great Shakespearean actor Henry Irving outside the gallery. One of the seminal Victorian actor managers, Irving worked closely with the actress Ellen Terry with whom he performed in plays such as *Macbeth*, *The Merchant of Venice* and *Hamlet*. Irving, with his aquiline features and quiet authority, provided the inspiration for the title character of Bram Stoker's *Dracula*. The statue outside the National Portrait Gallery was erected in 1910 and funded by his fellows in the acting profession. Each year, on 6 February

– Irving's birthday – members of the Irving Society remember him by laying a wreath at the base of the statue.

## Theatre Land

> Our revels now are ended. These our actors,
> As I foretold you, were all spirits and
> Are melted into air, into thin air.
> And like the baseless fabric of this vision,
> The cloud-capped towers, the gorgeous palaces,
> The solemn temples, the great globe itself –
> Yea, all which it inherit – shall dissolve,
> And like this insubstantial pageant faded,
> Leave not a rack behind. We are such stuff
> As dreams are made on ...
>
> *The Tempest*: Prospero, Act IV, Scene VIII

### All The World's a Stage

Our revels, too, are coming to an end. After a tour encompassing the villages of rural Warwickshire, Leicester, York and the strange delights of Bankside, the Shakespeare Trail finishes amid the bright lights of London's West End where the grand old theatres have continued his legacy since the days of the Restoration. As we shall see, the flame of Shakespeare's genius refused to die in the years after the man himself had faded away at home in Stratford.

When Shakespeare died in 1616 the King's Men lost their principal playwright. He was replaced by John Fletcher who had collaborated with Shakespeare on plays such as *Henry VIII* and the lost *Cardenio*. Fletcher is probably best known for his long partnership with Francis Beaumont which produced a string of amusingly titled plays including *A King and No King* and *Love Lies a-Bleeding*. Between 1616 and 1625, the year of King James's death, the personnel of the company evolved organically as the old faces retired or died and new men joined. In the year 1619 the core body of the King's Men still comprised founding members such as John Heminges, Henry Condell and John Lowin although their star actor Richard Burbage died that year and Heminges and Condell drifted away shortly afterwards. Ben Jonson continued to write up until his death in 1637.

When James I died the company's patronage was transferred to his son, Charles I. This period saw a boom in the building of indoor playhouses to rival the Blackfriars; Richard Gunnell, a veteran of the Admiral's Men, built the indoor Salisbury Court just outside the western boundary of the city walls, not far from the Blackfriars. Further west, on a site near Drury Lane there was the Cockpit. This was to be the first playhouse in what we know as the West End, a pioneer in this new territory. Up until now, the theatre scene had been confined to small patches of land on Bankside, in Shoreditch and at the Blackfriars playhouse. When the fields to the west of the city began to be developed in the seventeenth century, London's entertainment centre gradually followed, shifting to what would become a playground for the rich and the fashionable.

The Puritans closed the theatres in 1642, but far from hanging up their costumes, the King's Men continued to stage the occasional illicit performance. This was a company which had evolved over a period of fifty years, surviving the turbulent political landscape of three different monarchs. Now, the hour glass was running out and it would not be long before a shameful event brought the company's career to a sudden halt. It was 1648 and the ban on theatre had appeared to be easing. The King's Men ventured to present some plays at the

Cockpit, near Drury Lane. Discretion was vital and by limiting the performances to a private audience they managed to remain there for four days. On the final day, they were in the middle of a performance of Fletcher's *Rollo, Duke of Normandy*, when disaster struck:

> A party of foot soldiers beset the house, surprised 'em about the middle of the play, and carried 'em away in their habits, not admitting 'em to shift, to Hatton House then a prison, where having detain'd 'em sometime, they plunder'd them of their cloths and let 'em loose again.

The writer was James Wright, whose *Historia Histrionica* of 1699 was one of the first works of theatre history. Among the players arrested that day was John Lowin who had joined the King's Men in 1603 and was now an elderly man. To be hauled off the stage and locked up, still in his costume, must have been a bitter end to his career. Indeed it was the sad end of a company of players which had been together in some form since the middle of the 1590s.

Not far from the site of the Cockpit, where the King's Men made their ungainly exit from the stage, is the Theatre Royal on Drury Lane. This is the fourth incarnation of a theatre which was built here in 1663 on the site of an old riding school. The first building was constructed by the actor manager Thomas Killigrew. He shared a duopoly on public theatre with William Davenant who operated from Covent Garden in a theatre on the site of the Opera House. Killigrew's theatre burned down a few years later. Sir Christopher Wren designed its successor and it reopened in 1674. Wren's innovative design introduced proscenium doors, an apron stage and perspective scenery. It was a far cry from the bare stages of The Globe or The Rose. In another sign of modernisation, Charles II began to allow actresses to perform on the public stage. Nell Gwyn appeared at Drury Lane having begun her career here as an orange seller. She would later catch the king's eye and become his mistress. Theatre was entering an exciting stage in its evolution. Shakespeare was still popular but his plays were not always treated with much reverence; William Davenant produced a version of *The Tempest* in 1667 which played around with the plot and added extra characters. It is a curious fact that Davenant used to describe himself as Shakespeare's son but he may have been speaking figuratively based on his own playwriting efforts. After Shakespeare's death he wrote a poetic tribute to him called *In Remembrance of Master Shakespeare*. It was in keeping with the florid style of the period:

> Beware (delighted Poets!) when you sing
> To welcome Nature in the early spring;
> Your num'rous Feet not tread
> The banks of Avon; for each flower
> (As it neere knew a Sunne or Showre)
> Hangs there, the pensive head.

A century later, David Garrick staged a hugely successful play called *The Jubilee* at Drury Lane. This was a version of the pageant he had attempted to organise in rain-soaked Stratford the month before. The show enjoyed a run of ninety performances and helped replenish his funds after what had been an expensive wash out in Warwickshire. He must have been relieved at the turnaround in his fortunes.

The present Theatre Royal at Drury Lane has endured since 1812 when it opened with a production of *Hamlet*. On 26 January 1814 the ferociously talented, if troubled, actor Edmund

Kean made his Drury Lane debut playing Shylock in the *Merchant of Venice*. William Hazlitt described his performance:

> His style of acting is, if we may use the expression, more significant, more pregnant with meaning, more varied and alive in every part, than any we have almost ever witnessed. The character never stands still: there is no vacant pause in the action; the eye is ever silent. For depth and force of conception, we have seen actors whom we should prefer to Mr Kean in Shylock; for brilliant and masterly execution, none.

Kean was given a horse by an admiring fan. He called the animal Shylock and apparently indulged in drunken late night gallops up and down the turnpike roads and even into the theatre. He collapsed on stage in 1833 during a performance of *Othello*. He never performed again and died a few months later.

Just off the Strand is the Lyceum Theatre with its classical pediment and columns. Built in 1834 on the site of its previous incarnation, it hosted the Victorian actors Henry Irving and Ellen Terry who performed together in productions such as *Hamlet*, which was staged in 1878. In the same venue Ellen would go on to feature as Portia in *The Merchant of Venice* and as Beatrice in *Much Ado About Nothing*. This remarkable woman's career spanned several decades and she lived to see the advent of the film industry in the 1920s. Her daughter Edith also entered the theatre industry but she decided her talents lay backstage and she became a director and costume designer.

With so many theatres moving into the area around Covent Garden, the neighbourhood was enhanced with a transient population of actors and actresses. The church of St Paul's, located in the piazza is often referred to as the Actors' Church due to the number of theatre folk who have attended over the centuries. Built in 1633 by Inigo Jones, its classical stone façade is topped by an overhanging pediment in the centre of which is a distinctive blue-faced clock. Four classical columns form a sheltered portico beneath which members of the street drinking community can often be found. Entering the hushed interior with its chandeliers and rounded windows, you may wish to browse the memorial plaques which adorn the white washed walls. Each is dedicated to the memories of the great actors and entertainers who worked in the area, including Gracie Fields, Boris Karloff and Noel Coward. The ashes of Ellen Terry lie in a silver urn in the chancel. As well as functioning as a church, St Paul's is also a theatre venue in its own right and hosts productions within the nave and gardens.

In 1662 Samuel Pepys wrote in his diary that he had seen an Italian puppet show outside the church within the shadows of the portico. This was the ancestor of what we know as Punch and Judy. The church still forms the backdrop to local buskers and street performers today; at weekends the piazza at Covent Garden takes on a lively festival atmosphere with fire eaters, living statues and buskers all plying their trade among the throngs of tourists. In Theatre Land, all the world is, indeed, a stage.

Today the West End boasts over thirty theatres offering a repertoire of popular musicals and long-running shows. Off the West End the publicly subsidized houses such as the Old Vic and the National offer high quality drama and new writing. London's theatre scene is the envy of the world and contributes heavily to tourism in the capital. For that we must thank our Elizabethan forebears; pioneers such as James Burbage who built The Theatre, Christopher Marlowe for his innovative blank verse style and of course William Shakespeare for holding up a mirror to nature and tempering it with humour and affection.

His humanity connects with all levels of society and 400 years after he bowed out, he is justly revered.

*Visitor Information*

The Theatre Royal is located at Drury Lane, Catherine Street, London WC2B 5JF. Tel: 0844 412 2955.

For those wishing to take a peek backstage and learn more about this historic venue, the theatre offers a schedule of tours entitled 'Through the Stage Door'. Led by costumed actors you will meet characters such as Nell Gwyn and David Garrick. The hour-long tours cost £10.50 for adults, £8.50 for children and seniors and £20.00 for a family ticket comprising two adults and two children. Groups over ten are offered the lower price of £8.50 per person. Please contact the venue for details of times.

# Afterword

Our journey through Shakespeare's England has now come to an end. It has been a pleasure to guide you along the way and I hope I have been able to illustrate how widely he travelled, both in person and in his mind. Sadly, there has been neither time nor space to include the other locations he dreamt of; France, Burgundy, Elsinore, Verona, Venice, Bohemia, not to mention Scotland. Perhaps these places will form the subject of another book. Meanwhile, it is now over to you. There is only so much a book can do to convey a sense of time and place so if you are able to visit at least some of the locations within these pages I urge you to do so and follow in the footsteps of our greatest playwright.

I am always pleased to hear from fellow Shakespeare fans so please feel free to contact me via my Twitter handle @shakespearewalk as well as my Facebook page www.facebook.com/tudorhistory. As a qualified City of London tour guide I am available to lead guided walks on a private basis. For more details drop me a line at zoella45@hotmail.com.

Alternatively you may wish to join the long-running Shakespeare

City walk run by actor Declan McHugh. Details are available at www.shakespeareguide.com.

For those wishing to explore the history drenched Square Mile with an expert guide, you cannot go wrong in the company of one of the official City of London tour guides. They run regular walks starting from outside the City Information Centre opposite St Paul's Cathedral covering themes such as Charles Dickens, the River, Wren churches and City gardens, there is sure to be something to whet the appetite. For details see www.cityoflondonguides.com.

If you fancy tackling a long distance walk, Shakespeare's Way follows the approximate route Shakespeare took on his journeys to and from Stratford and London. Starting outside the Birthplace in Stratford it winds its way southwards through the Oxfordshire Cotswolds, through Oxford itself and into the Chilterns. The final stretch into London follows the Grand Union Canal and the Thames Towpath before ending at Shakespeare's spiritual home, The Globe Theatre on Bankside. The 146-mile-long route can be done in stages or, for those with time and stamina, all in one go. It takes in some of the most gorgeous scenery in southern England and gives a sense of pilgrimage for those completing it. For details of the route and to share your images of your own trip, see www.shakespearesway.org.

The Shakespeare's Way Association encourages walkers to blend their walk with fundraising on behalf of the Shakespeare Hospice in Stratford-upon-Avon and can provide sponsorship for anyone interested.

# Acknowledgements

For a Shakespeare geek there can be no greater joy than spending the best part of a year buried in research about his world and the places he knew. For this I would like to thank Christian Duck, Eleri Pipien and Clare Owen at Amberley Publishing whose encouragement and enthusiasm helped turn an idea into reality. Lots of amazing people have helped along the way and I'd like to take the opportunity to acknowledge them here: Thanks to Alec Ward and Juliet Barclay at St John's Gate for their fresh insights into the building and its use in the sixteenth century; Suzanne Marie at The Rose for a wonderful tour of the site; Robert Biden and Rose Harding at Southwark Cathedral for their generosity in allowing me to use images in the book; Alan Taylor, the Project Manager at the site of The Theatre for keeping me up to date with developments; Nicola Kalimera at Museum of London Archaeology for her help with The Theatre and The Curtain; Jonathan Drake and Pamela Day at Holy Trinity Stratford for their generosity with images and their enthusiasm about the book; Natasha Kidd and Amy Hulyer at English Heritage for allowing me to use an image of Charlecote and for their kind offer of further help; Robert Noel, the Lancaster Herald at the College of Arms for an interesting telephone chat about Shakespeare's coat of arms; Sue Lampitt, the churchwarden at St Leonard's Charlecote for allowing me to use the image of Sir Thomas Lucy's tomb chest and also for her recommendations on further reading; Sarah King, Assistant to House Manager at Wilton House for her help with the details of the Tudor house; James Mellish, project manager of the Guildhall at Bury St Edmunds for his generous information about its history; Natalie Grueninger and Helen Mears for sharing their knowledge of those mysterious things called 'digital cameras' and coaxing me out of a technophobia-induced panic; Lucy McMurdo and Trevor Jeanes for being inspirational teachers; the members of the City of London Guide Lecturer Association for their boundless enthusiasm about the city; and the Class of 2010 – Rhona, Marilyn, Valeria, Paula, Helene, Jane, Rob et al – for sharing the blood, sweat and tears of the course.

The chapter entitled The Tower of London is based on a piece of writing I did for Pat Reid, the editor of *Shakespeare Magazine*. This is a free online publication packed with theatre news, actor interviews, and articles about Shakespeare's life and times. I'd like to thank Pat for his vision and dedication in creating what has become a 'must read' for all Shakespeare fans. See www.shakespearemagazine.com.

Most of all I want to thank my family for their good-humoured support and for planting the Shakingbeard seed in my heart all those years ago, even I did not realise it at the time. I hope this book manages to convey my passion and respect for the man who was, in Ben Jonson's words, not only the 'soul of the age' but the 'wonder of our stage'.

# Select Bibliography

This book was intended primarily as a visitors' guide rather than a work of historical investigation. I therefore felt that a select bibliography was more appropriate than lengthy footnotes. During the course of my research I have stumbled upon some wonderful resources and publications and am pleased to share them here for those who want to learn more.

## Warwickshire

I found the following books invaluable when researching the Warwickshire section:

*Warwickshire* (from the Buildings of England series) by Nikolaus Pevsner and Alexandra Wedgwood was a mine of detailed information about the architecture of the Shakespeare houses and Warwickshire in general; *The Warwickshire Village Book* written by members of the Warwickshire Federation of Women's Institutes was invaluable for the local knowledge it conveyed. This is a warmly written guidebook with some fascinating snippets of information.

## London

The following titles are a useful resource for anyone researching local London history:

*London 1: The City of London* (from the Buildings of England series) by Simon Bradley and Nikolaus Pevsner was my bible for architectural notes; *The London Compendium* by Ed Glinert was on hand when cross-referencing and triple-checking facts; *A Traveller's History of London* by Richard Tames for its detailed chapters on the major London sites; *A Survey of London* by John Stow is the London historian's best friend. Written in 1598 it is the result of years of painstaking research on Stow's part. In his touchingly conversational style he tells the story of the city streets, churches, livery companies, wards, schools, hospitals, sheriffs and aldermen; *Shakespeare's London (Everyday Life in London 1580–1616)* by Stephen Porter takes the reader right into the heart of the early modern City; *Historic London (An Explorer's Companion)* by Stephen Inwood.

## A Journey into Shakespeare's Imagination

*White Hart, Red Lion* by Nick Asbury was helpful in making sense of the tangled mess that was the Wars of the Roses. Asbury is an actor with the Royal Shakespeare Company and his book is full of insights into the plays.

## General

Here is a selection of books which helped with the biographical details of Shakespeare's life and career as well as members of his family and some of his Tudor contemporaries:

Ackroyd, Peter, *The Life of Thomas More* (Vintage, 1999)

Duncan-Jones, Katherine, *Ungentle Shakespeare: Scenes From His Life* (Arden, 2001)

Holden, Anthony, *William Shakespeare* (Abacus, 2000)

Ives, Eric, *The Life and Death of Anne Boleyn* (Blackwell Publishing, 2005)

Morley, Sheridan, *Theatre's Strangest Act*s (Pavilion Books, 2014)

Pogue, Kate, *Shakespeare's Friends* (Greenwood Publishing Group, 2006)

Randall, Dale B. J., *Winter Fruit: English Drama 1642–1660* (The University Press of Kentucky, 1995)

Salkeld, Duncan, *Shakespeare Among the Courtesans: Prostitution, Literature and Drama, 1500–1650* (Ashgate, 2012)

Trussler, Simon, *British Theatre* (Cambridge University Press, 1994)

Weis, Rene, *William Shakespeare* (John Murray, 2007)

Wells, Stanley, *Shakespeare Survey, Vol 52: Shakespeare and the Globe* (Cambridge University Press, 2007)

# Index